D0787471

*JOYCE and the City*

Sanford Sternlicht, *Series Editor*

OTHER TITLES IN IRISH STUDIES

# JOYCE
## AND CITY
## THE

THE SIGNIFICANCE OF PLACE

*Edited by*

Michael Begnal

SYRACUSE UNIVERSITY PRESS

**Library of Congress Cataloging-in-Publication Data**

Joyce and the city : the significance of place / edited by Michael
Begnal.—1st ed.
p. cm.—(Irish studies)
ISBN 0–8156–2942–7 (cl. : alk. paper)
1. Joyce, James, 1882–1941—Knowledge—Dublin (Ireland) 2. Joyce,
James, 1882–1941—Views on city and town life. 3. Dublin (Ireland)—In
literature. 4. City and town life in literature. 5. Place (Philosophy)
in literature. 6. Cities and towns in literature. I. Begnal, Michael
H., 1939-II. Irish studies (Syracuse, N.Y.)
PR6019.O9 Z6465 2002
823'.912—dc21
2002004736

*This book is dedicated to*
Cathy *and* Clio,
*the girls of Summer.*

# Contents

# Contributors

**Michael Begnal** is professor of English and comparative literature at Pennsylvania State University. He has published widely on Joyce and modern literature, including *Narrator and Character in "Finnegans Wake," A Conceptual Guide to "Finnegans Wake,"* and *Dreamscheme: Narrative and Voice in "Finnegans Wake"* (Syracuse Univ. Press, 1988).

**Martha Fodaski Black** is Professor Emeritus of English and adjunct professor at Brooklyn College, CUNY. She is the author of *George Barker* and *Shaw and Joyce: The Last Word in "Stolentelling,"* as well as many reviews and articles in periodicals and books. Her most recent project is a study of Emma Goldman and Margaret Sanger.

**Heyward Ehrlich** is associate professor of English at Rutgers University in Newark, New Jersey. He organized a centennial conference on the theme of James Joyce and modernism, papers from which appeared as *Light Rays: James Joyce and Modernism*. He is now interested in the historical context of Joyce's use of popular culture and the Irish revival of Orientalism and the occult; he is also working on a hypertext demonstration project, the James Joyce Text Machine.

**Deirdre Flynn** completed her Ph.D. in comparative literature at the University of California, Berkeley. She is currently revising her dissertation for publication while teaching English and women's studies at the University of Toronto.

**Desmond Harding** is a lecturer in advanced writing at the University of Southern California. His publications include interdisciplinary articles on nationality and religion in European and Middle Eastern medieval literatures and cultures as well as articles on the interrelations between architectural theory and contemporary African American urban literature.

**Ignacio López-Vicuña** is pursuing his Ph.D. in Hispanic literature at the University of Pittsburgh. His interests include exile and the public sphere in Latin America, literature and the public use of language, and the influence of James Joyce on the Latin American novel.

**Vivian Valvano Lynch** is an associate professor of English at St. John's University, New York. She is author of *Portraits of Artists: Warriors in the Novels of William Kennedy* as well as several articles on Joyce, William Kennedy, and contemporary Irish literature.

**Christopher Malone** teaches modern and contemporary literature at Northeastern State University in Oklahoma, where he is director of the Living Literature Center. His work on modern Irish poetry and contemporary theory has appeared in *College Literature, ELH,* and *Essays in Literature.*

**Mark Morrisson** is assistant professor of English at Pennsylvania State University, and he is the founder and executive board member of the Modernist Studies Association. He is the author of *The Public Face of Modernism: Little Magazines, Audiences, and Reception, 1905–1920.*

**Michael Murphy,** born in Ireland, now lives in Brooklyn, New York. Primarily a medievalist during his teaching career, he has published articles on medieval literature and editions of Chaucer in print and on the Web. His writings on Joyce have appeared in *English Studies, James Joyce Quarterly,* and *Irish Studies Review.*

**Jean-Michel Rabaté,** professor of English and comparative literature at the University of Pennsylvania, has published fifteen books on Samuel Beckett, Thomas Bernhard, Ezra Pound, James Joyce, and literary theory. His most recent books are *The Ghosts of Modernity, Jacques Lacan: Psychoanalysis and the Subject of Literature,* and *James Joyce and the Politics of Egoism.* He has edited *Writing the Image after Roland Barthes* and *Jacques Lacan in America* and is the editor of the forthcoming *Cambridge Companion to Jacques Lacan.*

**Stanley Sultan** is professor of English at Clark University. His most recent books are *Eliot, Joyce, and Company* and *Joyce's Metamorphosis.* Other publications include "Paradise Outgrown" (on Genesis 3), "Was Modernism Reactionary?" and essays on Elizabeth Bishop and D. H. Lawrence. He is currently working on a book of essays on the literary histories involved in modernism.

**Catherine Whitley** received her Ph.D. from the University of California, Irvine. She is presently completing two books, a critical study of Joyce and a textbook on reading theory.

# Abbreviations

References to Joyce's writings are abbreviated and cited parenthetically. *Ulysses* is cited by chapter and line numbers, while *Finnegans Wake* is cited by page and line number. Standard editions and abbreviations used are as follows:

CW      *The Critical Writings of James Joyce.* 1959. Edited by Ellsworth Mason and Richard Ellmann. New York: Viking.

D       *"Dubliners": Text, Criticism, and Notes.* 1951. Edited by Robert Scholes and A. Walton Litz. New York: Viking.

E       *Exiles.* 1972. New York: Viking.

FW      *Finnegans Wake.* 1967. New York: Viking.

GJ      *Giacomo Joyce.* 1968. Edited by Richard Ellmann. New York: Viking.

Letters  Letters of James Joyce. Vol. 1. 1956. Edited by Stuart Gilbert. New York: Viking.
        Vol. 2. 1966. Edited by Richard Ellmann. New York: Viking.
        Vol. 3. 1966. Edited by Richard Ellmann. New York: Viking.

P       *"A Portrait of the Artist as a Young Man": Text, Criticism, and Notes. 1970.* Edited by Chester G. Anderson. New York: Viking.

SL      *Selected Letters of James Joyce.* 1975. Edited by Richard Ellmann. New York: Viking.

SH      *Stephen Hero.* 1963. Edited by Theodore Spencer. New York: New Directions.

U       *Ulysses.* 1986. Edited by Hans Walter Gabler. New York: Random House.

# Introduction

In the Circe chapter of *Ulysses,* Stephen Dedalus, in drunken fury, swings his ashplant and destroys a lamp shade in Bella Cohen's brothel. Thus he negates time, and he pulverizes what he calls "the ruin of all space." But James Joyce could not get rid of space so easily, nor did he wish to, and his fiction is rooted in the complexities of location. To Joyce, on the one hand space meant urban space—the city—and it was the hustle and bustle of modern life in close quarters that fed his imagination. On the other hand, he was concerned with the spaces of the mind, and this outer-inner tension is central to the convolutions of his work. In the investigations collected here, many of which began in miniature as presentations at the 1999 Joyce's Birthday Conference at the University of Miami, an impressive congregation of Joycean specialists has fleshed out insights into comprehensive and provocative statements.

These essays grow out of our attempts to expand the conceptions of place and space in Joyce's writing. They move from the immediate locales of the city environment to spaces of many different kinds—geographical, textual, gender affiliated, historical, sociological, comparative, and verbal. The final page of *Ulysses* is tagged with the specific location and time of "Trieste-Zurich-Paris, 1914–1921," but this fact, of course, can be misleading. The body of James Joyce may have inhabited these European cities for a discernible number of years, but his mind and artistic consciousness cannot be so easily limited. In this litany of location, where is Dublin? The contributors to this volume move beyond traditional definitions of the city, and they bring contemporary critical and theoretical perspectives to bear on the very idea of space itself. A conventional map can no longer contain Joyce, and a new and different cartography must be employed to chart cultural, linguistic, aesthetic, and psychoanalytic corners that have, until now, remained basically blank.

In many ways, the modern city is shaped by its inhabitants, rather than the reverse. Walter Benjamin and Michel Foucault have engaged this problem, and they are well represented in these essays. Henri Lefebvre (*The Production of Space* 1991) has explored real and perceived spaces as they relate to the body, and Michel de Certeau discusses the individuals who walk the city and who make it their own. "These practitioners make use of spaces that cannot be seen; their knowledge of them is as blind as that of lovers in each other's arms" (de Certeau 1984, 93). The space we focus on can be delineated by metaphors of presence and absence, by the real and the perceived; the commentators in this volume have expanded their critical vocabulary to take us to new and undiscovered places. The paradox of oneness and estrangement bedevils virtually all of Joyce's protagonists as they navigate through the byways of modernity.

In *Pnin,* Vladimir Nabokov writes that "Man exists only insofar as he is separated from his surroundings. The cranium is a space-traveler's helmet. Stay inside or you perish." It is that space inside the helmet that generates the various levels of cityscape in Joyce, and these levels become the subject of this collection. The essays are divided into three sections, titled "Internal Spaces," "Dear Dirty Dublin," and "The Chamber of Words." In the first grouping, contributors discuss metaphors of space and how they affect our reading of Joyce. The second section concentrates on ways in which the city itself is implicated within the short stories that make up *Dubliners,* while the third section is involved with space and Joyce's development of related motifs as subjects in *Ulysses* and *Finnegans Wake.*

Leading off "Internal Spaces," Heyward Ehrlich's "James Joyce's Four-Gated City of Modernisms" locates the relation of modernism to an urban environment. Ehrlich sets Joyce in contrast to T. S. Eliot and Walter Benjamin, and he pursues the intriguing idea that "City men of very different temperaments, Eliot seemed born to command, Joyce to disobey." Ehrlich discusses what Joyce might have learned from centers of Modernist ferment like Trieste, Zurich, and Paris, and how Joyce saw the city as being inextricably linked with the machine. Ehrlich concludes with a structural analysis of the city itself and its function throughout the ages as literary and aesthetic inspiration. Following up on this sort of non-serviam principle, Martha Fodaski Black, in "Joyce on Location: Place Names in Joyce's Fiction," is concerned with Joyce's use of specific place names in the fiction, the fact that these names were not chosen at random, and how they often become veiled indications of Ireland's position in a postcolonial environment. Within her larger argument, she skillfully ferrets out parallel networks of place names drawn from both Homer and George Bernard Shaw to reveal a tightly woven web of allusion.

Catherine Whitley devotes her provocative "Gender and Interiority" to interior and external spaces, especially as these impinge on Joyce's female characters and a narrative technique that is a representation of gender. Whitley contrasts the spatial rhetoric of Gretta Conroy's internal rendering of her youth in Galway with the more objectified, exterior narrative of "The Dead" itself. She describes the ways Joyce transcended the gendered implications of traditional characterization and point of view, and how he "insists on cycles, on ends that are beginnings, on the dissolution of artificial boundaries such as public and domestic, masculine and feminine." From a complementary perspective in "An Uncomfortable Fit: Joyce's Women in Dublin and Trieste," Deirdre Flynn describes the author's progression from stereotyping female characters in *Dubliners* to the development of the more rounded and three-dimensional Molly Bloom. Perhaps in some ways this change was a consequence of Joyce's removal from the stuffy confines of Ireland to the more sophisticated atmosphere of Continental centers like Trieste and Paris, and Flynn discusses both Nora Barnacle's influence on *Exiles* and the fascinating presence of Amalia Popper in *Giacomo Joyce*. For these characters, clothes do make the woman and fashion becomes a significant social determinant.

Christopher Malone examines the relevance of community, and his "The Sense of Place in Joyce and Heaney" provides an overview of the legacy that contemporary Irish poets like Seamus Heaney and Paul Muldoon are still grappling with today. Malone puts Joyce's sense of the Irish country landscape up against Heaney's experience of the farm in Northern Ireland to show how locale can affect the forms and themes of individual works. Contrasting Joyce's more pessimistic view of rural stultification with Heaney's discovery of inspiration in the natural, Malone concludes that in both writers a perception of the land is inextricably tied to culture and to history.

The collection's second section, "Dear Dirty Dublin," gets down to specifics, centering as it does on the stories in *Dubliners*, which continue to intrigue and to demand fresh readings. "Dublin Boy and Man in 'The Sisters,' " by Stanley Sultan, offers a careful explication of phrases in Joyce's opening story that encapsulate in miniature just what it meant to grow up within the confines of a parochial and repressive Dublin. The effect of the church's psychological domination of virtually all of the characters in each of the stories permeates the dark and dank atmospheric spaces of Ireland's capital city. Vivian Valvano Lynch looks at "The Dead" as a single space or structure in relation to the other narratives in "A Pedagogical Note on 'The Dead' of *Dubliners*." She shifts our critical gears to consider the pedagogical ramifications of "The Dead" in the classroom, where the story is often taught simply as a novella, with no tie to the collection as a whole. In regard to presence and absence, how does such a practice affect the ways in which Dublin and Dubliners are presented, when the social and cultural milieu created by the preceding stories is nonexistent?

Extending Martha Black's discussion of place names to encompass Dublin political statues and commemorations in "The Dead," Michael Murphy explores the relevance of these symbols of past history to the story and to the volume as a whole. "Political Memorials in the City of 'The Dead' " traces the ways that such public tributes can be manipulated. Murphy notes that politicians inevitably receive their undeserved due, while truly heroic plebian Irish, like Michael Furey and Lily the caretaker's daughter, are left to disappear into obscurity. Public space thus outlives personal memory, and history itself can be a fluid and misleading concept. Rounding out this section is a third look at the same story, " 'The Dead': Joyce's Epitaph for Dublin," by Desmond Harding. The essay investigates remembrances of the dead and of things past, and ways that geographical locations like Dublin and the West of Ireland were commonly identified as parts of a living present or a dying past. Harding reveals the interrelated otherness of geography, location, history, and culture, and he concludes that " 'The Dead' evokes the historicity of Dublin's past and present in keeping with *Dubliners* as a spiritual autobiography." The capstone story of *Dubliners*, "The Dead" has been recast as theater, dramatic reading, film, and opera, a tribute to the ways its themes and characters continue to tease and tantalize each reader who comes in contact with it.

Part Three, "The Chamber of Words," examines the relevance of space, place, and the city to language and the art of writing and focuses on how words are interlocked with emerging metaphors of space. The section concentrates on *Finnegans Wake,* but first Ignacio López-Vicuña takes on *Ulysses.* In "But on the Other Hand: The Language of Exile and the Exile of Language in *Ulysses,*" Vicuña notes how word choice in Joyce indicates his characters' absence or exile within the modern cities that contain them. Vicuña posits a "language of exile" that gets at truth through denial or undercutting, one statement always countered by its destabilizing opposite without negating the validity or viability of the original assertion. Reading the spaces between words and sentences allows for comedic irony that is also a telling political statement. "Like Wilde, Joyce was serious about not being serious." On a personal note, in the spring of 1998 I was sitting in a Galway pub reading the local newspaper when I came upon a piece about a body discovered in a nearby bog after more than sixty years. (The man in the bog was named Joyce.) This article provided the central impetus for "Hosty's Ballad in *Finnegans Wake:* The Galway Connection," which links Joyce and the *Wake* to Nora's home city through the themes of guilt and betrayal. The Joyce murder and another that followed soon after in 1920 led me to the true identity of Hosty, Joyce's balladeer, and the ramifications of rumor, jealousy, possible infidelity, and the reappearance of Nora's old boyfriend Willy Mulvey. Joyce's awareness of the body that popped up in the bog would almost certainly have reawakened his insecurities and suspicions about the events of Nora Barnacle's girlhood. Like Finnegan at his wake, the corpse in question refused to stay dead.

Mark Morrisson, in *"Tambour,* the 'Revolution of the Word,' and the Parisian Reception of *Finnegans Wake,*" describes the world of little magazines in the Paris of the 1920s and 1930s, and he discusses the journal *Tambour* in the historical context of the critical reception of *Finnegans Wake.* His essay goes a long way toward defining the Parisian modernism of which Joyce's last work was such a central part and explains how *Work in Progress* was crucial to the forms and the themes of the expatriate modernist movement. *Tambour* helped to bring the proto-*Wake* to the attention of experimentalists for whom such an artistic example was crucial, and Morrisson redirects our gaze to the often-overlooked world of the literary journals that shaped the taste of their time. *Tambour* was on the cutting edge. Finally, Jean-Michel Rabaté concludes this volume by bringing a genetic approach to a "City" section of *Finnegans Wake,* "Haveth Childers Everywhere," to elucidate some of Joyce's methods of composition. "Eternest cittas, heil!: A Genetic Approach" analyzes the section as the quintessential fusion of different spatial levels—linguistic, political, and geographical. By examining Joyce's manuscripts in depth and detail, Rabaté discovers that Joyce plundered the *Encyclopedia Britannica* for city, place, and street names, and then punned on these words to extend and universalize their significance. Such a word can be here and everywhere at one and the same time, and space becomes an all-encompassing proposition. Through a process of accretion and compilation, Joyce builds up the geography of his nighttime world to describe the transcendent city that stands at last as the simulacrum of the twentieth century.

Joyce himself was a wanderer in his own lifetime, an exile, moving from Dublin to Trieste to Zurich to Paris, with quite a few stops in between. Carola Giedion-Welcker recalls that her old friend James Joyce "had a deep interest in towns, whether large or small, and in their design and history. They appeared to him as collective individuals, history turned into shape and space, large reservoirs of life" (in Potts 1979, 261). He took in each new locale and established its boundaries, and he transformed constricted areas into limitless space. In his writing, he piles one cityscape upon another to get at the essences of modernity and urbanity. When Anna Livia Plurabelle addresses her husband Earwicker, he becomes a living urban presence, a city, inseparable from the place where he exists. "Soft morning, city! Lsp! I am leafy speafing." She turns a paramour and a husband into an archetype, and her language creates a conception out of an entity.

This essay collection represents a group effort to bring James Joyce's concern with the city and its symbolic environs into the foreground. We hope that these contributions will open up new directions in the charting and defining of Joyce's cultural and artistic mapmaking.

# PART 1

## Internal Spaces

# 1

# James Joyce's Four-Gated City of Modernisms

HEYWARD EHRLICH

Arresting city itineraries appear in the two works that defined high modernism in 1922, T. S. Eliot's *The Waste Land* and James Joyce's *Ulysses*. In *The Waste Land*, Eliot's sequence, "Falling towers / Jerusalem Athens Alexandria / Vienna London / Unreal" (374–77), amplifies his vision of the contemporary "unreal city" (60, 208). At the end of *Ulysses*, Joyce's personal inscription simply notes the cities and years associated with the composition of the work: "Trieste-Zurich-Paris, 1914–1921," just as previously he had signed *A Portrait of the Artist*: "Dublin 1904 / Trieste 1914."

Eliot's footnote traced his distaste for the modern city, the "unreal city," to his reading of Baudelaire's Paris in *Les fleurs du mal:*

Fourmillante cite, cite pleine de reves,
Ou le spectre en plein jour raccroche le passant
[Swarming city, city filled with dreams,
Where the spectre in broad daylight accosts the passerby.]

Later trying to enlist Joyce in his battle, Eliot extended his jeremiad on the debasement of the modern world to his review of *Ulysses*, in which he praises Joyce's "scientific discovery" that the use of a "continuous parallel between contemporaneity and antiquity" could replace linear narrative as an ironic structure to illuminate "the immense panorama of futility and anarchy which is contemporary history" (Deming 1970, 1: 270).

For his part, Joyce intended his inscription, "Trieste-Zurich-Paris, 1914–1921," to be personal, tangible, and neutral, perhaps hinting at the work ahead for future biographers. Although scholars have served Joyce in accounting for much of his life, few literary critics or historians are comfortable considering the remarkable series of metropolitan contexts within which he worked. *A Portrait of the Artist* may be read simply as Joyce's Dublin Bildungsroman, with the central organizing motif being Stephen's embryonic development. But the structures of *Ulysses* and *Finnegans Wake* reflect the more complicated impact of Joyce's continuously changing local creative context through his successive residences in four European cities. All of these cities were outstanding for their distinctive threads of modernism: Dublin, for the neoromanticist Irish Literary Revival; Trieste (and nearby Milan) for futurism; Zurich, for dada; and Paris, for cubism, surrealism, and linguistic experimentation. It is worth exploring the question of whether the paradigm for this unusual set of multiple contexts is best regarded as linear, hierarchical, parallel, organic, or rhizome. The answer may contribute to our understanding of Joyce's unique explorations of complexity in the structures of *Ulysses* and *Finnegans Wake*.

Many monographs have related Joyce to local varieties of modernism, such as the Irish Literary Revival, Italian futurism, Swiss dada, and Paris surrealism and linguistic experimentation. (See, for example, MacCabe 1979, Lobner 1989, Duffy 1994, Hartshorn 1997, and Lawrence 1998.) But Joyce was both a partisan of local modernisms and a pacifist ultimately uncommitted to do battle for any of them, as Frank Budgen reported: "There are hints of all practices in *Ulysses*—cubism, futurism, simultanism, dadaism, and the rest—and this is the clearest proof that he was attached to none of the schools that followed them" (Budgen 1960, 193). Although Joyce explained himself frequently in the early notebooks, in his 1904 "Portrait of the Artist," in his preface to *Exiles*, in his letters, and in his recorded conversations, these hints and explanations remain fragmentary and do not add up to any complete or coherent explanation of his artistic practices. His letters to his brother Stanislaus, to Frank Budgen, and to Harriet Shaw Weaver contain technical discussions of his work but no meaningful stand or commitment to any overall critical or theoretical philosophy. The explanation may be that Joyce responded instinctively rather than programmatically to opportunities he seized in the artistic movements swirling around him, developing his intuitive literary practice without pausing to systematize or explain it. Joyce constructed his own city of modernism not as a fixed, single locus but rather as a flexible, plural assemblage, an ever-changing vision of a four-gated heavenly city, a cosmos of multiple modernisms.

Perhaps no other twentieth-century author was touched by or touched on so many different manifestations of modernism as Joyce. Most other modernist authors of cities of Joyce's era seem embedded in a particular city: Proust in Paris, Kafka in Prague, Dreiser in New York. Yet Joyce's writings both are and are not about Dublin. At first, Dublin is a small town where personal interactions could be studied: "Dublin is such a small city: everyone knows everyone else's business" (*D* 66). But Joyce eventually found in Dublin the quality of all cities: "For myself, I always write about Dublin, because if I can get to the heart of Dublin I can get to the heart of all the cities of the world. In the particular is contained the universal" (Ellmann 1982, 505). On occasion Joyce unabashedly transferred imagery from one city to another when it suited him: Belluomo's "wife's lover's wife," originally located in Trieste in *Giacomo Joyce,* turns up in the Paris scenes in *Ulysses* (*U* 3.211). We should not take too seriously Joyce's famous hyperbole that there was so much of Dublin in *Ulysses* that the city could be rebuilt from the book if it ever were destroyed. He could not have anticipated that portions of Dublin might be made to conform more closely to his pages in order to attract Bloomsday tourists and visitors.

But walking in Dublin to the pages of Joyce serves a serious purpose as well. City life is inherently social and peripatetic, fully appropriate for Aristotelian conversation and classification and leading to the habit of looking at the world as a complex anatomy. City structures seem to be arranged by a combination of chance, necessity, and proximity, not complying to any prior divine order or imposed human hierarchy. For more than a century before Joyce, British fiction had found its narrative center in the voice of the country landowner, magistrate, or neighbor; by contrast, the more recent forms of city fiction seemed organized as collocations of visual icons, ordered spatially. It might be said that oral traditions in the country tended to produce the complete story of a life, whether exemplary or cautionary, while the comparable urban legend remained a fragmentary anecdote in the career of a quasi-anonymous person whose innermost nature remained unknown if not un-knowable. A foreigner in several European cities, Joyce often enjoyed this freedom of the outlaw among neighbors who were unaware and could not possibly guess that he and Nora were not married. As city life was changed more rapidly than country life during the nineteenth century, the city seemed to anticipate the unknown future while the country seemed to continue to re-flect the familiar past. Urban and rural genre painting and literary realism moved in two opposite directions, taking up the new industrial and commer-cial subjects in the city and the old and traditional subjects in the country. Be-fore Joyce, Irish literature, architecture, and art at the start of the twentieth century had scarcely any metropolitan awareness; the very building of Dublin remained oblivious of the revolutionary new style of architecture that used fabricated glass and steel, which had been introduced at the London Crystal Palace exhibition of 1851. The coming of modern information technology to Dublin in 1904 was remarkable and exotic enough for Joyce to wish to cap-ture it in *Ulysses,* his time capsule. Lacking a narrator or intervening character to inform us of it, the typewriter unwittingly clicks out today's date (*U* 10.376). The printing press also assumes a vitality of its own: "The machines clanked in threefour time. Thump, thump, thump" (*U* 7.101). Similarly, the folding apparatus demands to be heard: "Sllt. The nethermost deck of the first machine jogged forward its flyboard with sllt the first batch of quirefolded pa-pers. Sllt. Almost human the way it sllt to call attention. Doing its level best to speak. That door too sllt creaking, asking to be shut. Everything speaks in its own way. Sllt" (*U* 7.174–77).

Joyce breaks with Irish literary tradition by letting Leopold Bloom gaze at the world mechanically, through the eyes of a photographer, the profession of his grandfather, father, and daughter (*U* 8.173, 17.1589). Bloom echoes fu-turist theory in thinking of advertising posters that convey "the velocity of modern life" (*U* 17.1773). He wonders about the production techniques used by the mutoscope, an early cinematic device (*U* 13.794); he envisions how a story he has in mind might be costumed as a pantomime production (*U* 4.534–36); and he even thinks about the mesial details of the representational realism of statues (*U* 9.615). Similarly, Stephen's memories of Paris include the production details of scenes of sexual exhibitions (*U* 15.3882–94). As Donald Theall has shown in two recent studies (1995, 1997), Joyce also included remarkably extensive details of the new technologies of broadcasting, television, and electronic communications in *Finnegans Wake*. The typographic oddities of *Ulysses* make readers aware that they are reading printed matter that records how people see, feel, think, and speak. Bloom's worn hatband reads "high grade ha" (*U* 5.26); Molly unexpectedly uses the Arabic numeric forms 1, 2, and 2nd—when we expect her to use the words one, two, and second. Beginning in about 1720 the city had played a vital role as the center of printing technology; previously, much literature had been performed or sung (Homer and Shakespeare did not write for print). As long as the act of performance brought together the audience and the artwork, the latter could still seem a direct representation of nature. But closet dramas introduced a second level of representation, and printing thereafter imitated not nature but a performance in front of an actual audience. The new ordering of time and space in city life led to the further distancing of representation from nature; when the earliest magazines appeared, the very names of Addison and Steele's *Spectator* and Samuel Johnson's *Rambler* (the latter uncannily suggesting today's Web browser) indicated the further drawing back of representation in literature to a third remove from nature (performance, book, magazine), no longer demanding either the physical presence or even the extended attention of the audience.

Previously the exact length of a work of literature depended on internal features, but in periodicals and newspapers the writing process was mechanized to make writing conform to a fixed production schedule that soon dictated exactly how much was to be written, as well as when and where. In the oral tale the passage of time is represented in the narrative or intonation of the speaker, but in periodicals real time passes according to the date of each issue—day, week, month, quarter, or year—a circumstance entirely separated from narrative, itself further fragmented by the introduction of serialization. One periodical issue may contain a dozen unrelated speaking voices that exist simultaneously, compiled not for reasons of similarity and unity but for their discontinuity and variety. In transforming literature into an increasingly visual arrangement, a composite of separate discourses, the periodical press had interrupted the unified narrative coherence of old oral traditions. In "Aeolus"

Joyce toys with a fourth remove of representation from nature: clever newspaper headlines, introduced in the late nineteenth century, divert the inattentive reader into finding unexpected associations that are often quite unrelated to the text of the articles. These headlines, as has often been noticed, take on an unexpected life of their own, all but breaking the limits of narrative form.

Joyce usually found Mediterranean and Continental cites more attractive than those in Ireland or Britain. Nineteenth-century archaeological excavations of ancient cities were overturning eighteenth-century social-compact theories, which had placed the origin of ancient civilizations in the primeval forests, a view that extended to the pastoral evocations of James Frazer's *Golden Bough*. In 1876, Heinrich Schliemann excavated a site believed to be Homer's Troy; in 1900, Sir Arthur Evans discovered artifacts of the Minoan civilization of Crete with its association to Dedalus; in 1922, Lord Carnarvon and Howard Carter unearthed King Tutankhamen's tomb at Helopolis. Nevertheless, the Irish Literary Revival built itself on a pastoral amalgam of Celticism, Orientalism, and Theosophy. We should not forget that Joyce's guide to the Irish Literary Revival was the mystic George Russell, who wrote as Æ; nor that the Celtic twilight of William Butler Yeats was built in part on his years of apprenticeship with Madame Blavatsky and his three decades as head of the Dublin Lodge of the Temple of Golden Dawn, promoting occult compendia by S. L. MacGregor Mathers and A. L. Waite (Cope 1981, 74–75).

To make it appear that he possessed an encyclopedic knowledge of old Dublin, Joyce incorporated responses to query letters from the Continent and facts from *Thom's Directory* for 1904 into the composition of *Ulysses*. Ironically, at the very moment that ancient cities were being rediscovered and ancient philosophies were being revived, the old neighborhoods of modern cities were being threatened with demolition to make way for large construction projects, mass transportation systems, and new applications for steel and electricity. In opposition, preservation movements arose to spare the artifacts of urban archaeology, to preserve or at least to document them before the whole preindustrial, precommercial past vanished forever. Perhaps the most memorable documentary project of the early twentieth century was that of the Paris photographer Eugène Atget, who recorded the Paris neighborhoods, storefronts, and petty trades threatened with extinction. Although there is no known evidence that Joyce knew of Atget's project when he lived in Paris in 1902–03 or later, during the years of composition of *Ulysses,* Joyce had ample opportunity to hear of Atget's work when afterwards he sat to be photographed by Berenice Abbott, Atget's former darkroom assistant and later the executor of his photographic estate. There is an inspiring parallel between Atget's attempt to preserve a visual record of vanishing Paris street life and Joyce's project to preserve the indigenous patterns and expressions of traditional Dublin speech, many of which Joyce took from the personal observation of his father.

For many British authors, the rise of the city in the late eighteenth and nineteenth centuries spurred a deep sense of moral and cultural aversion. Wordsworth, in Book 7 of *The Prelude,* addresses the city as the source of detested turbulence and trade, "thou monstrous anti-hill on the plain," which destroyed human character: " 'The face of every one / That passes by me is a mystery.' " Similarly, in Edgar Allan Poe's "Man of the Crowd," the narrator follows an old man who compulsively wanders the city streets, displaying the new characterless urban character: *"er lasst sich nicht lesen*—it does not permit itself to be read" (Mabbott 1978, 2: 506, 515). But a different response to the rising of the city emerged in Europe after the failed revolutions of 1848 in the form of the new stance of the urban *Symbolistes*— self-conscious, intellectual, radical, dissenting, alienated. In Baudelaire's Paris (as opposed to Eliot's version of Baudelaire's Paris), the same anonymity that had distressed Wordsworth also made possible a new personal, erotic, voyeuristic subculture. Meanwhile, in Whitman's New York the heterogeneity of egalitarian crowds made possible a transparent new self speaking an entirely new language in literature, "the blab of the pave" ("Song of Myself," section 8).

Walter Benjamin has extensively studied two new literary character types that emerged in Baudelaire's Paris, the *flâneur* (idler), whose identity is concentrated by the presence of crowds, and the *badaud* (rubbernecker), who diffuses himself in the crowd (Barta 1996, 10). It is interesting to note in this connection that Joyce's first impression of Nora describes her as a female *flâneur,* sauntering down a Dublin street. In "The Return of the Flâneur," Benjamin distinguished between two types of travel literature: one written by outsiders, who selected exotic and picturesque scenes, and the other written by native inhabitants, who inevitably journey into the past. Benjamin saw the iconic features of Paris as a "mnemonic for the lonely walker," especially for the *flâneur,* who "memorizes lists like a child, insisting like an old man of the truth of what he knows," the entire city becoming "an Egyptian dream book for those who are awake" (Bullock and Jennings 1996, 262, 266). For Benjamin, contemporary Paris was "the promised land of *flâneurs,*" its continuous visual background serving as "a landscape made of living people" (Bullock and Jennings 1996, 262–63).

In speaking of an "immense *panorama*" Eliot had used the word figuratively, but Benjamin carefully considered the literal panoramas of nineteenth-century cities and regarded them as central to understanding modern material culture. The panoramas had appeared late in the eighteenth century as large theatrical sceneries, often mounted as huge mechanical moving scrolls, all background without human actors or other features in the foreground. (The first panorama in Paris was built in 1799 by Robert Fulton, inventor of the steamboat.) Sometimes reaching mammoth dimensions, the panoramas were the first realistic popular entertainments, offering to city audiences the technological marvel of an apparently literal and semi-animated representation of their everyday world, a striking alternative to the fixed, heroic, and symbolic historical paintings that decorated official buildings. One recurring subject of the panoramas was the city itself, capturing all the aleatory diversity of modern life. In diverting the focus from the foreground to background the panoramas were, so to speak, texts made entirely of context. Their remarkable popularity stimulated literary imitations in the form of the *roman feuilleton* or serialized newspaper novel. Eugène Sue's kaleidoscopic *Mysteries of Paris* (1842–43), perhaps the best-known example, was a radical social exposé that contributed to the uprisings of the revolutions of 1848, challenging the values of the established order and marshaling sympathy for the downtrodden and excluded classes. While the novel of society depicted the traditional landed culture as an integrated structure, the protocinematic panorama and newspaper novel—and the hastily contrived theatrical adaptations of them—presented the emergent culture of the contemporary city in the form of a fragmented anatomy. Benjamin saw connections among the new media, the new subjects, and the new forms, which required the proliferation of multiple plots and semirelated characters: "Literature is subject to montage in the *feuilleton*" (Bullock and Jennings 1996, 261).

Between 1927 and 1940, while Joyce was working on *Finnegans Wake,*

Benjamin was working on his unfinished master work, the massive *Arcades Project,* to collect and analyze the material culture of nineteenth-century Paris. His methods of preparation, described by John McCole, were quite Joycean; in classifying his notes, Benjamin's markings consisted of thirty-two different colors or shapes: "He assembled his copious notes in bundles whose headings range from the material culture of the nineteenth century (arcades, fashion, iron construction, interiors, railroads, panoramas, photography, world exposition halls) to forms of experience (boredom, collecting, *flânerie,* prostitution, gambling), individual writers and artists (Baudelaire, Grandville, Fourier, Marx, Blanqui, Saint-Simon), and constructive principles (epistemological notes, critiques of historicism and the idea of progress, observations on dreaming and awakening)" (McCole 1993, 280–81). For Benjamin, Paris was the archetypal city of nineteenth-century European materialism, just as Paris later became the archetypal city of twentieth-century modernism. For Benjamin, Paris was not defined by the acts of great men but rather through its detritus, making it possible to drill down to its *Urgeschichte* or ultimate level of primal history by means of the massive collection of documentary sources, which had the power to speak directly for themselves, requiring no authorial commentary. Benjamin organized his materials into several bundles, rendered into English as "convolutes." (The entire text, newly translated into English, uses different typefaces to distinguish Benjamin's primary passages in German from his secondary passages in French.) Against the city as landscape, the empathetic *flâneur* might play a variety of alternate roles as detective, journalist, sandwich man in the street, and careful observer of storefronts (Benjamin 1999, 446–51). Interestingly, Atget's photographic documentation of store window displays, done by natural light during off hours when neither store owners nor pedestrians were present, often captured an overlay of reflected ambient street scenes upon already ambiguous base images of clothing manikins, anticipating surrealist art. But Benjamin's method in the *Arcades Project* was the opposite of surrealism, the unexpressed dreams of nineteenth-century Parisians in building their material culture serving as a schematic for contemporary historical consciousness. Benjamin saw the panorama and its close relative, the translucent diorama, as the paradigms for Balzac's *Comédie Humaine* in that as many as 500 nonce characters had been unintegrated into the main plots (Benjamin 1999, 536). The unique quality of city life was so important for Dickens, Benjamin observes, that he was unable to write whenever he went on country retreats that took him away from the stimulation of London crowds (438). Although Benjamin's work is not known to have come to the attention of Joyce, it shows a remarkable similarity of interests to the Dublin that Joyce depicted in *Ulysses.* For these reasons Benjamin's theories of the cultural significance of the material city can be used as an incisive tool for the critical analysis of Joyce.

Although it is tempting to think of Joyce's several cities—Dublin, Pola, Trieste, Rome, Zurich, Paris—as structured stations in Joyce's pilgrimage to reach an ordered goal, it is difficult to find any single theory, principle, or rule to account for Joyce's remarkable changes and growth. Even in Paris, Joyce remained nomadic, as though still in a state of exile. He and Nora spent nineteen years in Paris, and Louis Gillet's address book contained nineteen known domiciles there for the Joyces. Joyce's letters often express his intention to quit Paris for Dublin, Zurich, or London, and he moved ceaselessly if not compulsively from residence to residence within Paris as he had from city to city. Joyce once admitted that he lacked at times a certain sympathy with his Dublin characters (*Letters* 2: 231). What interested him most deeply about Dublin was its most famous work of art, the *Book of Kells,* with its distinctive "workmanship" (*Letters* 2: 545), immediately identifiable from any page. Perhaps the presence of the *Book of Kells* in the Trinity College library, a short walk from Joyce's own University College, made him more aware of the significance of recent archaeological discoveries of ancient Celtic art. The form's remarkable craftsmanship, ornament, and abstract design were widely imitated in popular Irish jewelry of the late nineteenth century; in "The Dead," the Irish nationalist Miss Ivors wears a brooch ornamented with such a "Celtic device." These recent discoveries should have reminded Joyce that the treasures of ancient Celtic art were the personal possession of warriors, priests, and bards in a mobile culture very different from that being unearthed in the more durable and massive ancient cites of the Middle East. Surely there was something potentially disturbing to any person of Irish birth in the fact that the most important ancient Celtic archeological finds of the *La Tène* era were made in a zone reaching from present-day France, Switzerland, and Germany to Eastern Europe, not in the westernmost reaches of Europe where the Celtic languages survived. If ancient Celtic art did not belong in Ireland, then it belonged everywhere and nowhere as highly portable craftsmanship. Joyce felt comfortable in just this sense working on *Ulysses* not within a tradition and context but rather independently and "technically," he told Harriet Weaver, "writing a book from eighteen different points of view and in as many styles, all apparently unknown or undiscovered by my fellow tradesmen" (*SL* 512). In referring to *Ulysses* as "this chaffering allincluding most farraginous chronicle" (*U* 14.1412), Joyce poses as an itinerant urban vendor of mixed wares.

Joyce confessed to Pound while composing *Ulysses,* "I am doing it, as Aristotle would say, by different means in different parts" (*SL* 225). Philosophically, Joyce was suspicious of Platonistic abstract forms or ideas: "What makes most peoples' lives unhappy is some disappointed romanticism, some unrealizable misconceived ideal," Joyce remarked. "In *Ulysses* I tried to keep close to fact" (Power 1974, 98). It seems especially significant that young Joyce, arriving in Paris in 1902, made it his priority to study Aristotle in the library. Joyce's early Pola essays show his attempts to apply Aristotelian methods to defining his future literary practice. This discipline for Joyce led to results that are recorded in Stephen's discussions of neo-Aristotelian rules of unity, particularly Lessing's formulations, scattered throughout *Stephen Hero, Portrait,* and the Circe chapter of *Ulysses.* Literature, accordingly, was the art of time, its events perceived *nacheinander* by the ear, while painting and sculpture were the arts of space apprehended *nebeneinander* by the eye. But the city panoramas had inverted the traditional representations of time and space; foreground and background were confounded, and human figures were eliminated in the new aesthetic of the cityscape. Lessing's principles were further challenged by two developments that were still recent in Joyce's day: first, iconographic or spatial organization was brought to literature by *Symboliste* poetry, soon followed by the imagists' use of schemes of representation borrowed in part from cubist painting; second, a hitherto forbidden temporal organization was brought to visual art through the illusion of moving images in the panorama, the diorama, and finally the motion picture. The subvarieties of modernism that most interested Joyce were often those that had introduced time into the visual arts, as one contemporary reviewer noted in describing Joyce's method in *Ulysses* as "jerky and elliptical" (Deming 1970, 1: 198), as though it occupied the middle ground between cinema and still photography. Of the many postmodernist and multimedia artists who have used Joyce's city imagery in *Finnegans Wake* as a point of departure, few are as interesting as John Cage; his *Roaratorio* selects vertical acrostics based on midline random mesostics from Joyce's text as the basis for spatial-acoustical expansion. Cage, believing that there were 2,462 place names in *Finnegans Wake,* half of them in Ireland, and half again of these in Dublin, used 626 volunteers (one for each page) to make or collect locally recorded audiotapes, which he then synthesized into a new work, said to exploit the dematerialized space of Dublin as an "informational city" distinguished by its "Dublinicity."

In *Portrait,* Stephen's visit to the "diorama in Rotunda" leads to troubled dreams of a "curving gallery . . . peopled by the images of fabulous kings, set in stone" (*P* 249). In *Finnegans Wake* the ordinarily visual and kinetic panorama becomes olfactory and acoustical by synesthesia in "the panaroma of all flores of speech" in the "sooty," the latter a collapsed variant on "dear Dirty Dublin," the entire puzzle paragraph concluding in the solution, a "collideorscape!" (*FW* 143.28). In *Ulysses* Joyce follows the form of the panorama in presenting a background that rivals the importance of the figures before it. In the *roman feuilleton,* with its serialized and semiconnected episodes, the principle of external structural discontinuity applied; Joyce pursued the principle of fragmentation one step further, coming as close as possible to the direct radical presentation of the surface disorder of the mental processes of ordinary men and women in the city. (One cannot imagine Stephen, Bloom, and Molly living in the countryside.) *Ulysses* was not intended to follow the novelist's usual inspiration from "a conceived idea or a temporary emotion" (Power 1974, 36) but rather to track the continuous rendering of experience. Joyce urged the modern writer to avoid the dramatic or sensational, which appeal to the journalist: "We prefer to search in the corners for what has been hidden; and moods, atmospheres, and intimate relationships are the modern writers' theme" (Power 1974, 52–53). Joyce insisted that writing create "an endlessly changing surface" (Power 1974, 95)—a description that recalls the salient feature of the panoramas. The writer must be "an adventurer above all, willing to take every risk" in order to "write dangerously" if he wishes to capture the sense of change and "flux" of modern life: "In *Ulysses* I tried to express the multiple variations which make up the social life of a city—its degradations and its exultations" (Power 1974, 95). *Ulysses* and *Finnegans Wake* as literary performances are distinguished by a method of writing that makes a primary layer out of the record of their own composition: "A book, in my opinion, should not be planned out beforehand, but as one writes it will form itself, subject, as I say, to the constant emotional promptings of one's personality" (Power 1974, 95).

Joyce projected something of himself into Bloom's combination of Baudelaire's *flâneur* and Whitman's all-absorbing self, the wanderer who sees all but remains or hopes to remain unseen. Joyce himself never could have become "part of English life, or even have worked there, for somehow I would have felt that in that atmosphere of politics, power, and money, writing was not sufficiently important" (Power 1974, 64). This stifling authority Joyce found in all of England, where everyone appeared to him to be a censor or a volunteer for self-censorship; only in cities like Dublin and Paris did Joyce find personal freedom. "In the Dublin of my day there was a kind of desperate freedom which comes from a lack of responsibility, for the English were in governance then, so everyone said what he liked" (Power 1974, 65).

Eliot and Joyce, looking at the modern city in very different ways, also had polar views of the nature of the English language. Eliot, the midwestern American from St. Louis, Missouri, a city on the river of Mark Twin and Huckleberry Finn, transformed himself into an adult Londoner who out-Englished the English in his defense of British-centered literary tradition and culture. By contrast, Joyce the Irishman indicted Dublin in *Dubliners* and then fled from it in *Portrait*, returning in *Ulysses* and *Finnegans Wake*. While Eliot fixed literary London as the public center of Western civilization in the first half of the twentieth century, Joyce removed civilization from any particular city, relocating it to his idea of an abstract city located wherever an English-speaking reader might be found. Eliot the American made the English language more English than ever before, while Joyce the Irishman took English out of England. Joyce rejected Eliot's pessimistic view of *Ulysses* as an indication that modern life was an "immense panorama" of "futility and anarchy," hoping that Eliot would abandon his cultural theory of the degraded present and thereafter describe *Ulysses* as "two plane," a simple phrase that Eliot had used in conversation (*Letters* 3: 83). City men of very different temperaments, Eliot posed as one born to command while Joyce was ready to disobey. Joyce, grouped with Ezra Pound, John Quinn, and Ford Madox Ford in a famous Paris snapshot, stands back, while Pound and Quinn are vying to display control by playing up to the camera and Ford keeps talking even as the shutter clicks. Only Joyce remains reticent, timid, orphic, his body reluctantly present, his mind on the threshold of dissolving into the background. The same preference for backgrounds emerges in the only painting present in Joyce's Paris flat, the *Portrait of Delft* by Vermeer, which he admired simply as "the portrait of a city" (Power 1974, 103). In this well-known cityscape, based on camera obscura studies, the dock and wharves of Delft are arranged in a single plane like a riverside panorama, all background and no significant foreground.

For Joyce, the continual human flux of the city became, paradoxically, the matrix of its unexpected durability: "Cityful passing away, other cityful coming, passing away too: other coming on, passing on. Houses, lines of houses, streets, miles of pavements, piledup bricks, stones. Changing hands. This owner, that. Landlord never dies they say. Other steps into his shoes when he gets his notice to quit" (*U* 8.484–87).

In his essay on Blake, Joyce compared two views of eternity, St. Augustine's heavenly city and Swedenborg's source of his "immense system" of correspondences in the "likeness of a heavenly man, animated in all his limbs by a fluid angelic life that forever leaves and re-enters" *(CW* 221–22). Joyce parodies the connection in Bloom's speech in "Circe:" "My beloved subjects, a new era is about to dawn. . . . ye shall ere long enter into the golden city which is to be, the new Bloomusalem in the Nova Hibernia of the future" (*U* 15.1542–54). The structural principle of *Ulysses* that replaces temporal narrative is the visual connection of the iconography of the city to the anatomy of the organs of the human body, each component possessing simultaneous and equal presence. Any instant of time in the city, as Pound captured in his "In a Station of the Metro," could demonstrate its fields of force.

In "Proteus," Stephen's deep vision of the correspondences or signatures of all things leads him to pun on retrograde evolution: "God becomes man becomes fish becomes barnacle goose becomes featherbed mountain" (*U* 3.377–79). Stuart Gilbert calls this trope a "variant on 'the kabalistic axiom of metempsychosis' " (Gilbert 1952, 128). Joyce claimed that he was more deeply moved by the imagery of the "mystery of animal life" he found in Egyptian and Assyrian art in Paris museums than by the excessive Christian emphasis on "man made in the image of God" (Power 1974, 48). By means of metamorphosis and metempsychosis, all people, all things, and all cities were conjoined. Stephen envisions a dazzling telephone call: "Hello! Kinch here. Put me on to Edenville. Aleph, alpha: nought, nought, one. Spouse and help-mate of Adam Kadmon: Heva, naked Eve. She had no navel" (*U* 3.36–54). Gilbert remarks: "The umbilical telephone extends back to Eden, to Eve the navelless and her spouse, Adam Kadmon (the kabalistic first man)" (Gilbert 52). Gilbert glosses Stephen's idea of the city of Edenville by quoting the mystic Thomas Traherne: "I thought it had stood from everlasting to everlasting. The dust and stones of the street were as precious as gold: the gates were at first the end of the world. . . . The city seemed to stand in Eden, or to be built in heaven" (Gilbert 52–53).

Stephen's *Aleph, alpha* identifies the first letters of the Hebrew and Greek alphabets with each other, both of them once expressing the same numerical value of 1; his nought, nought, one is an incantation to create unity from nothingness. The entire combination, Englished as AA001 or 11001, is a primal telephone number. In conflating four levels—the arcane myth of Adam Kadmon and Lilith, the familiar myth of Adam and Eve, embryonic biology, and communications technology—Joyce gives Stephen an umbilical telephone line that, starting from the secular city of Dublin on June 16, 1904, reaches back to the paradise city of Edenville before human time began.

# 2

## Joyce on Location
### Place Names in Joyce's Fiction

MARTHA FODASKI BLACK

Like other Irish literature, from *The Tain* to Yeats's "Fiddler of Dooney" and poems about Coole Park and Thor Ballylea to Shaw's *John Bull's Other Island* and Flann O'Brien's *At Swim-Two-Birds,* James Joyce's fictions often emphasize locations. However, like other effective realists, in *Dubliners, Portrait,* and *Ulysses,* Joyce selected place names that work overtime and his portmanteaus in *Finnegans Wake* tantalize the reader with allusions to place. As his obituary in the *Irish Times* noted, "If Dublin were destroyed, [Joyce's] words could rebuild the city." In locality names that establish the geography of Joyce's hometown in *Dubliners,* that map the geography and archetypal analogues of *A Portrait of the Artist as a Young Man* and *Ulysses,* or that provide deconstructed clues to the double acrostic of *Finnegans Wake,* Joyce not only grounds his work in the reality of the city but also chooses locations whose implications and ironies deepen his depiction of Irish life and his Irish characters.

For example, in the first story of *Dubliners* the home of the priest and his spiritually impoverished "Sisters" is in Great Britain Street—a street named for one of the two masters that, according to Joyce, kept the Irish in thrall. The story is about the power of one of the masters, the Pope, whose representative, a failed priest, had tried to sell his office to a boy. That the indigent sisters live on Great Britain Street among Dublin's poorest poor is ironically appropriate, for Great Britain had betrayed Ireland by reducing many of its Irish subjects to penury. That the sisters and their dead brother were born in Irishtown underscores their roots in poverty, for, whereas Great Britain Street is ironic, Irishtown is appropriate—a poor, working-class, Roman Catholic slum near the Liffey Quays.

In his fictions about Dubliners, Joyce associated the Liffey Quays with the desire for escape. The Pigeon House, which the boys in "An Encounter" set out to visit, is an ironic terminus foreshadowing the movement of the story. Because they long to escape, it is an appropriate goal for the day's adventure, for some pigeons carry messages to far-off destinations, but pigeons often live on the crumbs (as the Irish did in the time of *Dubliners*) of others, like the English Jesuit teachers who are indoctrinating their students—victims of colonialism—in the glories of Roman imperialism, which was the model for the empire building of the British. The pigeons are probably homing pigeons, like the boys in the story and Joyce himself, who flew away only to return repeatedly to Dublin in his imagination. The Ringsend setting at the mouth of the Liffey underscores the fact that the trip to the quays will be circular. In its circuitous ending, the boys encounter a pervert who tries to impose alien literary preferences on the sensitive boy whose point of view limits the story. The meeting is part of a vicious circle that began in the classroom, where the priest imposed an alien history upon his pupils. Just as the boy in "The Sisters" dreams of exotic Persia and the boys in "An Encounter" read escape literature about America's Wild West, the boy in "Araby" is lured by the name of a distant place that represents exotic romance to him, even though the allusion to the *Arabian Nights* directs the reader to fictions of sexual adventure. Ironically, Joyce's young narrator is frustrated when he arrives on location, for the bazaar is a tawdry affair whose Café Chantant suggests French vulgarity that affronts and frustrates the romantic adolescent.

In "Eveline" the man who destroyed the natural environment of Eveline's family is from Belfast. His urban renewal is really a form of English usurpation and exploitation of Dublin's poor, whereas Melbourne locates the escape of the priest who had been Eveline's father's friend—an escape forbidden to Eveline by her gender socialization. To Eveline, Buenos Ayres is a dream of freedom from servitude to family and church, but the Hill of Howth, always in Joyce's imagination associated with romance, provides Eveline with her only memory of a pleasant day with her father, who had lately begun to court her with a ghost story and toast. At the quays, which offer the possibility of freedom, Eveline's attempt to leave Ireland and find happiness ends in pathetic failure.

The Continent represents sophisticated cosmopolitanism to Jimmy in "After the Race." His sojourn at Cambridge put him in contact with the fast set that will outstrip the provincial Irishman. The American's yacht, *Belle of Newport,* establishes the perimeters of Jimmy's frustrated desires for life in the fast lane, for, of course, Newport, Rhode Island, symbolizes the lifestyle of America's wealthy yachting set, but the Dubliner loses out to fellows from more liberated and liberating locations. In "Two Gallants" two Dublin losers representing a different class, impoverished male street walkers, wander through the streets of fashionable Dublin in an area populated by wealthy Anglo-Irish who live in Georgian townhouses forbidden to Lenehan and Corley. The self-centered Corley's lust and ego are satisfied by a pathetic slavey quartered, suitably, downstairs in Baggot Street. That the vulgar couple meet on the corner of Merrion Square is ironic, for the square was the heartland of well-to-do Anglo-Irish like Oscar Wilde's parents and, at one point Æ and the great romantic lover Yeats, who sublimated sexual desire in verse—unlike the brazen Corley, who gets more than a brown penny for his efforts.

Joyce persists in using place names ironically in "The Boarding House." The butcher shop near Spring Gardens advertises the contrast between Polly's reality and her aspirations. Although her estranged father is a butcher and her mother deals with moral issues like a meat cleaver, the park near the shop evokes the season when love is supposed to bloom. Mrs. Mooney's clientele from places like Liverpool and the Isle of Man reflects the real social level of the rowdy denizens of the boardinghouse. No wonder Polly and her mother fix on the meekly conventional Bob Doran in their marriage plot. In "A Little Cloud," Chandler, already trapped in a proper marriage, longs for the glamour of London and Paris. He envies the fast life suggested by Gallaher's braggadocio about the music halls of the Moulin Rouge, but Chandler's own world is limited to a glimpse of the flashy bar in Corless's Hotel and the reality of the tamely correct Bewley's Grafton Street coffee shop, where he forgot to stop off to get coffee for his wife. His walk from Capel Street north of the Liffey over the Grattan Bridge—named for the Anglo-Irish statesman—reinforces the fact that Anglo-Irish influences often dominate Dubliners. Unaware of his betrayal of real Celts, Chandler dreams of writing poetry reflecting *"The Celtic note"* (*D* 74) in the Anglo-Irish mode of Yeats's literary revival. In Joyce's fiction the Liffey is often the dividing line between chic Georgian (hence Anglo-Irish) Dublin south of the river and lower-middle-class life north of it. Clearly Chandler aspires to identify with the Anglo-Irish set south of the Liffey.

In "Counterparts" Farrington's subservience to Great Britain is established early on: his boss, a solicitor, is from the North of Ireland. Having shirked his menial duties, in a pub on fashionable Duke Street, Farrington suggests going to the Scotch House, whose alien, supposedly smart name foreshadows Farrington's fate. There he meets artistes from London who, later in the after-hours joint, Mulligan's (with its Irish name), humiliate the macho Irishman, threatening his manhood doubly: the female artiste rejects his sexual advances, the male defeats him at arm-wrestling. London scores one more victory over the Irishman, whose strength has been drained by alcoholism. Predictably, Farrington's feelings of inferiority are underlined by the fact that he lives on the southern outskirts of the city. The demon drink condemns him to a life on the fringes of power—and his son to a life of abuse.

The location of Duffy in "A Painful Case" is also significant. He lives in Chapelizod, the Chapel of Isolde. That the reclusive fellow should be living in the place where Tristram and Isolde fell deeply, irrevocably, and illicitly in love is ironic, for, unlike Tristram, the repressed Duffy is not, like his urban Isolde, destined to die for love. His dining in George Street (as in King George) implies his English preferences, as does his reading a unionist paper. That Mrs. Sinico was run down by a slow train from Kingstown intimates the repressive dominance of colonialism, for the port at which boats left for Holyhead and hence England was the King's town (the name has been changed to Dun Laoghaire because of Irish awareness of this usurping place name). In "A Painful Case," Kingstown alludes to the political master complicit with stern Jansenist Catholicism to thwart the illicit affair. Whereas the female victim might have been a willing adulteress, her pusillanimous suitor and thus her betrayer has absorbed the repressive morality that helped to keep Ireland a subject nation. While walking on the lonely road from Parkgate to Chapelizod, Duffy discovers the newspaper article about Mrs. Sinico's pathetic death and later realizes that he will never commit the Edenic sin (at least the one Milton emphasizes) that occurred in the first park of humankind. Nor will he be re-born through the fire of passion, even though the entry to Phoenix Park calls up the myth of rebirth on the bed of one's own ashes. The reference in the ac-count of Mrs. Sinico's death to her broken ribs may be a slyly ironic allusion to Eden, for, unlike Eve, Joyce's sinner will never be flesh of Duffy's flesh. The place name in the title of "Ivy Day in the Committee Room," Joyceans know, refers to the room in the House of Parliament in London in which Parnell's sympathizers wore ivy leaves, whereas in the same room his detractors de-posed him. The allusion dominates the story, in which supposed patriots sell out the fallen leader, wearing ivy leaves in his memory as they betray him. Henchy's references to Dublin Castle, in whose pay he thinks Hillsiders and Fenians may be, underwrites the real dominance of Britain and the treachery of the Irish. The politicos are, ironically, soliciting votes in the Royal Ex-change Ward, near Dublin Castle and City Hall, from whence the British ruled Dublin. In reality, the inept Parnellites have accepted British rule.

"A Mother" also uses place names to point up its ironies. Mrs. Kearney's reliance on her husband is comparable to her faith in the solidity of the G.P.O. In a story about a woman with nationalist sympathies, the location is ironic, for the General Post Office—replete with the Ionic columns of imperial power— symbolized British rule in Ireland. It is one of the early nineteenth-century classical structures built by the British to display the glories of empire (in 1916 it would be the focus of the abortive Easter Rising). In Joyce's story the scene of the tawdry nationalist concert in the Antient Concert Rooms is an immediate, derisive reminder of the notoriously successful nationalist plays performed in Yeats's Abbey Theatre. Second-rate London singer Madam Glynn sings "Killarney," a maudlin evocation of a romantic setting in Ireland. However, when Miss Healy reminds the baritone that another performer from London is on stage in Dublin, the discrepancy between genuine artistry and the bogus concert is clear. In Dublin in 1905, at the time Joyce assigned to his story, Stella Campbell had come from London to perform opposite Sarah Bernhardt; Campbell's performances would no doubt have kept dis-cerning Dubliners away from the bathetic nationalist concert.

In "Grace," made ecumenical by drink, topers gather in Dublin's stylish Grafton Street. The name of Dublin's Fifth Avenue has its roots in British domination of Ireland; it was named after Charles II of England's illegitimate son, who seceded to William of Orange and died in the Protestant's service at the siege of Cork, thus representing Ireland's master in England. Mr. Power, a member of the Royal Irish Constabulary who comes from Dublin Castle— seat of British rule—is friendly with the seemingly apolitical Kernan, who works for a London firm. Both apathetic Irishmen have, by implication, sold out to unionism. To get absolution for drunkenness the expedient sots go to the Jesuit Church in Gardiner Street, to which Joyce's own alcoholic father had applied for forgiveness. As early as the time of Louis XIV, Jesuits were, of course, known for their easy absolution. Place names like Grafton Street and the Jesuit Church in Gardiner Street imply once again the hegemony of the two masters of Ireland, Great Britain and Roman Catholicism.

"The Dead," a ricorso of the themes of *Dubliners,* also refers to locations to evoke its basic tensions and conflicts. The site of the Morkan sisters' house on Usher's Island on the south side of the Quays suggests their ironic entrapment in Dublin, despite the proximity of the Quays—portals of escape of which the old women seem unaware. Gabriel and Gretta are not going back to Monkstown, whose name hints at a sheltered and ascetic love life, but are going to the Gresham Hotel, associated with middle-class Irish who can afford it (just as the Shelburne on Stephen's Green was associated with the Anglo-Irish). Freddy Malins's mother says he is going down to Mount Melleray "in a week or so" (*D* 200). The Cistercian Monks at Melleray provided refuge for alcoholics who were drying out. Whereas Mrs. Malins's remark reminds us of the collusion between the church and the drunks of Dublin, Gabriel's story about the old gentleman whose horse went mechanically around the statue of King Billy is an oblique commentary on the whole of "The Dead" and of *Dubliners,* for Joyce's characters seem always to be blindly circling the rule of the British, represented by William of Orange, whose statue fronted College Green outside of Trinity College. The Protestant monarch symbolized the defeat of Irish Catholic aspirations for independence, crushed in 1690 at the Battle of the Boyne. That William's statue is near the O'Connell Bridge, over which the cab takes Gabriel and Gretta, is in itself an ironic juxtaposition, for Daniel O'Connell famously agitated for Catholic Emancipation, if not for Irish independence from British rule. Although Gabriel jokes about the great liberator, he himself will discover that he is in no way liberated and that he is alienated from Ireland and the Irish wife who represents her.

When Miss Ivors accuses Gabriel of being a West Briton she is, of course, allying him with those who have sold out to unionism—those who consider Ireland simply as a western bastion of Britain. Ironically Gabriel's wife is from Connacht, to which Oliver Cromwell drove Irish Catholics in the seventeenth century. (Bent on ethnic cleansing, Cromwell swore to send Irish Catholics to hell or Connacht.) Gretta's origins in the West also subscript the inner conflict with which the events of the evening confront Gabriel. Nationalists romanticized the West, even though in reality its climate and geography, if not its striking scenery, are harshly unromantic. Implicit in his choice of European vacations is Gabriel's desire to flee from Ireland, but Miss Ivors chides him for not going to the Aran Islands, symbol of the old Ireland, the Irish language movement, and romantic nationalism. Gabriel's final vision of Ireland as a snow-covered wasteland dominated by the Shannon, which has not led him to freedom, and the Bog of Allen, which figures the degraded state of the country, is almost as ironic as his decision to begin his journey westward—west being a direction that has long puzzled Joyceans, for Gabriel had rejected the journey to the west coast of Ireland, even though he yearns to make a journey to a more archetypal West in which sunset promises a new dawn and a new life.

At the end of "The Dead," Joyce was already turning away from the naturalism that informs the earlier stories. In *A Portrait of the Artist as a Young Man,* Joyce combines the specifics of place with symbolic locations such as Eden, Hell, Calvary, and the labyrinth of Crete. The novel is set in the seemingly Edenic little green place which is Ireland, where Stephen, the wild rose, will grow, but not before experiencing the hell of guilt and the agony of persecution for his unorthodox belief in art as salvation. In contrast to symbolic sites, locations on the map of Ireland reveal Stephen's position in society. Whereas Clongowes Wood implies the social pretensions of Stephen's father, addresses in Bray and Blackrock exemplify the gradual decline of the family's social status. The place name of the setting for Stephen's epiphany is, however, appropriately pagan and archetypal. On Bull Island Stephen recognizes that he is the son of a mythic father, Daedalus, who built the labyrinth to contain the bull-man, the Minotaur. North Bull Island is near the Bull Lighthouse, which protects travelers such as Stephen is about to become. Stephen will escape the imprisoning maze of Dublin, which Joyce already had created in *Dubliners*. Significantly, the bull is a symbol for Ireland (as *The Cattle Raid of Cooley* and *The Tain* established centuries before Joyce elected the location for Stephen's conversion). After wandering the streets near Stephen's Green, the little green microcosm with which the ephebic artist identifies, Stephen, as Icarus, will fly from Ireland with Bull Island as the symbolic site of liftoff.

Whereas in *Portrait* the movement from Christian to pagan locations underscores the movement of the novel, in *Ulysses* Joyce uses real place names and, admittedly, Odyssean parallels to inform his novel. The Martello Tower, setting of the Telemachus episode, evokes several of Joyce's themes, among them usurpation and betrayal. The Martello Towers were built by the British to protect John Bull's Other Island from possible invasion by the French during the Napoleonic Wars, one hundred years before Bloom's Day. Whereas the English were defending their colonial property, the Irish would have welcomed their coreligionists, the French. The towers are thus symbols of militant British hegemony in Ireland, but in *Ulysses* two Irishmen have rented the tower, by then superfluous, hence themselves usurping a run-down bastion of empire. Mulligan and Haines are, to Stephen, obstreperous intruders like the suitors of Penelope in Homer, but the comparison becomes ironic when the only female who appears at the tower is the old milk woman, a debased Shan van Vocht and hence Mother Ireland. Like Telemachus, Stephen resents the intrusion of trespassers—the Englishman who patronizingly admires Mother Ireland and Mulligan who invited in the outsider. When he thinks of Elsinore, Stephen/Telemachus melds with Shakespeare's moody Dane, another young man troubled by his mother.

Later in Bloom's Day, Joyce challenges us to consider Barney Kiernan's pub as Cyclop's cave, but the comparison is rife with reversals of implication. The citizen patriot is a brute like the single-visioned Cyclops, but Bloom does not, like Odysseus, enter private property and steal provisions. Unlike the Greek, Bloom is not an expedient opportunist. It is Odysseus who is prejudiced in Homer's Cyclops episode, whereas Bloom is an exemplar of tolerance. A pragmatic expansionist with a colonialist mentality, Odysseus deems the Cyclops inferior because his one-eyed countrymen do not have the institutions and community life that the proud Greek left behind in Ithaca. Like an Englishman first viewing Ireland, he says, "This isle —seagoing folk would have annexed it and built their homestead" (*U* 9.137–38). In musing over how he would improve and civilize the Cyclops's land, Odysseus differs little from the British regarding the Irish. And the citizen as Cyclops almost confirms the self-exculpatory, British view of the Irish as savages.

Bloom shares little with Odysseus except his shrewd instincts for survival. The bigoted Greek reserves manipulative good manners for utopian Phaiacia and aristocrats like Princess Nausicaa and her parents, whom he thinks of as equals from whom he needs hospitality. Bloom, who does get something from Gerty as Nausicaa, takes nothing from the Citizen Cyclops. Whereas the sneaky Greek handily violates all rules of hospitality in the cave of his supposed inferior, the prudent Bloom enters a public house and, until anti-Semitism rears its ugly head, is polite, even though he defends pacifist politics totally unlike those of the militant Greek. Although from the point of view of the thirsty Irish drunks, Bloom violates the rules of Irish hospitality by not buying a round of drinks, he distinguishes himself from Odysseus, who gets the Cyclops drunk in order to facilitate escape from the cave. Joyce's Guinness patriot needs no one to help him get fluthered. In his heart of hearts Bloom, disgusted with the Citizen, might have sympathized with the misused Cyclops in Homer, who was, like himself, abused by a prejudiced male who rationalized his superiority. Even while he is in the pub the sensitive Bloom is thinking of how the rules of hospitality are being violated, like Molly, in his own home. Although like the Greek, Bloom damages the Cyclops's single vision, his rabid nationalism, Bloom is at bottom more like the Other—the Cyclops—than like the Greek. Even the location of the pub on Little Britain Street resonates with ironies, for, whereas Odysseus muses on colonization, the street on which the pub is located betokens the fact that the occupation has already occurred in Dublin. Joyce's Cyclops—all talk and ineffectual action—takes on Great Britain only in his drunken political rhetoric. When he attacks Bloom, who has not actually damaged him, his biscuit tin is an absurdly ineffective missile, unlike the boulders that the Cyclops throws at the escaping Greek. The besotted and inept Citizen is indeed a representative of the Ireland that is a Little Britain.

The events in the whorehouse in Joyce's Circe episode are another great stretch of Homer, ironic indeed. In her domain, the ugly, bellicose madam, an unlikely femme fatale, turns Bloom into a grunting, snuffling pig. Unlike

Odysseus, master mariner and soldier who had the moly from the gods and thus entered Circe's flawless bed of love fully in control, Bloom's only talisman is the "pomme de terre," hardly a symbol for masculine sexuality. After forcing Circe to change his men back into human beings, the Greek, a macho sexist, accepts her invitation to stay in her palace: "As we were men we could not help consenting" (10.503). She then proves to be a generous hostess—as the whores in Joyce's palace of lies only pretend to be. Meanwhile, Joyce's impotent hero is throughout the day reminded of Blazes Boylan, the real sexual imperialist of *Ulysses*. Like Odysseus, however, Bloom is eager to get home to his wife on Eccles Street.

Homer's Circe warns Odysseus that he must go through Hades before he can get home. In Joyce's novel, Bloom went to Hades (Glasnevin Cemetery) in the morning for Paddy Dignam's funeral. The bordello itself is, however, a hades to Bloom, a dark night of soul in which he must, like Odysseus, confront the dead—his mother and the ghosts of other women. Bloom's hallucinatory nightmare is, however, underscored by meeting his father, whereas in Homer, Odysseus's father Laertes is back in Ithaca. In Hades, the Greek tactician obtains advice and warnings of what is to come. He learns that insolent men have been courting his wife and that he will make these men "atone in blood" (11.126). In Joyce, however, there is only one suitor back in Ithaca on Eccles Street and Bloom will not butcher him. In Hades, Odysseus is reassured that his Penelope is faithful, but Bloom's anxieties about his faithless wife are not assuaged. Like that of Odysseus, however, Bloom's trip through hell is essential preparation for his homecoming.

Joyce dubbed his penultimate episode "Ithaca" in order to exploit the parallels between the meetings in *Ulysses* and those in *The Odyssey* of the Telemachus figure and the father. Once more Joyce's scene, set in the protagonist's home, is satiric, for Bloom and Stephen do not join forces to destroy the suitor; instead, Bloom almost invites Stephen to become one. When the two enter the house by a stratagem, Bloom finds that the furniture has been moved. But there is no one there to throw it at him. True, Telemachus goes off on an errand after the carnage in Homer, but he does not go off permanently, as Stephen does. Ithaca in Joyce is a catechism instead of a series of ruses in preparation for a blood bath. Near the end of the episode, Bloom distinguishes himself from the Greek sexual athlete and warrior by thinking of "the unsympathetic indifference of previously amiable females, the contempt of muscular males" while simultaneously referring to "the acceptance of fragments of bread" (*U* 17.1949–50) such as those the hero, disguised as a beggar, accepted in the palace of Homer's Ithaca.

Whereas the final scenes of *The Odyssey* establish the hero's return to power and to his faithful wife, in Joyce's Ithaca Bloom considers leaving Molly. He contemplates visiting Ireland's beauty spots—"the cliffs of Moher, the windy fields of Connemara, lough Neagh . . . the Giant's Causeway" (*U* 17.1974–6)—and traveling to places abroad of which Odysseus would never have dreamed. Unheroically and humorously, Bloom wants a 5-pound reward to be posted regarding his disappearance (*U* 17.2001), even though he identifies himself with "Everyman or Noman" (*U* 17.2008), two famous pilgrims, the latter being Odysseus's alias in hoodwinking the Cyclops. In his declaration that "Ever he would wander" (*U* 17.2012), Bloom identifies with the Ulysses of Dante and Tennyson, a quester outside of the range of Homer's nostos. In search of adventure, he imagines going off, however, unheroically, not by sea, but from "the terminus of the Great Northern Railway, Amiens Street" (*U* 17.2085).

The bed is, of course, the terminus of both Odysseus and Bloom, but Penelope finally welcomes Odysseus because he knows the secret of their marital bed. Bloom, however, recognizes "the imprint of a human form, male not his" (*U* 17.2124). He does not think the illicit sexual act is as "calamitous" as other crimes. At the end of a long list Bloom names the violations that he eschews—crimes that the Greek committed—"impersonation . . . manslaughter, willful and premeditated murder" (*U* 17.2189–90). In contemplating his final location, the marriage bed, Bloom disassociates himself even further from Odysseus: "assassination, never, as two wrongs did not make one right" (*U* 17.2201). When Molly asks what he did during the day he covers up his own sins by naming the locations for supposedly harmless entertainments: the Gaiety Theatre followed by supper at Wynn's Hotel in Lower Abbey Street (*U* 17.2257–59). Throughout the day Bloom had associated his Gea-Tellus with her faraway birthplace, Gibraltar. In her monologue Molly's exotic origins bob up in her stream of consciousness. She links herself with flowers (unwittingly relating herself to her husband's alias) in the Alameda gardens and remembers being kissed under the Moorish wall. Thus Joyce persists in using place names to amplify character through associations. Molly's girlish dreams of romantic fulfillment are linked with Gibraltar and her blossoming romance with Bloom with Howth.

In *Finnegans Wake* place names continue to surface in the murky stream of consciousness of the narrator. Dublin's River Liffey is a central locale, associated as we all know with Anna Livia Plurabelle, the beautiful female Life Force. One corridor of Joyce's "nightmaze" (*FW* 411.8) leads to locations associated with George Bernard Shaw. That the Liffey goes past Eve and Adam's suggests a major leit motif in Joyce's "meandertale"—the story of the fall in Genesis and of Shaw's reinterpretation of Genesis in part one of *Back to Methuselah*—"In The Beginning." Like Shaw, Joyce makes the female first in creation. Joyce's coded "new book of Morses" (*FW* 123.35) also locates itself in Phoenix Park, whose name connotes rebirth from one's own ashes. Much has been made of the dreamer's exposing himself in the park. Such exposure is, in part, the aim of the *Wake;* the distorted dream fixates on the sin of which Shaw had accused *Ulysses*—incontinence and exposing forbidden sexual behavior. Joyce wrote that H.C.E.'s encounter in the park with the Cad (perhaps an adumbration of Joyce as the cad who stole two Shaw plays and produced them illegally in Zurich) was "the basis of my book" (*Letters* 1: 396). John Gordon avers that the major scene of the action is Chapelizod, appropriate in Joyce's ruminations on "an eatupus complex" (*FW* 128.36) because its meanderings often concern a painful triangle, oedipal as such triangles are in medieval romance in which a younger man competes for a woman with an older, father figure like King Mark in Tristram and Isolde's tale. But Joyce's other central theme is sibling rivalry in the "house of Atreox" (*FW* 55.3)—the house of Atreus in which one brother betrayed another by bedding down his wife and was repaid by having his children served up for supper.

Everyone who has attempted to read *Finnegans Wake* knows that it concerns the rivalry of brothers, Shaun and Shem. The narrator dubs the scene of the action "the house of O'Shea or O'Shame" (*FW* 182.30). In studying Gaelic, Joyce found out that the names O'Shea, Shaw, and Joyce are the same in that language. Joyce had a complicated "notion of 'coincidence' as convergence" (Sandelescu 1987, 12). He must have been struck by the fact that he and Shaw were "in fact namesakes. Shaw is the Scottish translation of the Gaelic Seogh (Joyce)" (Ussher 1952, 9). And the writer who set his novel in the house of Shame had plenty to be ashamed of regarding the Irish playwright: he pirated *Mrs. Warren's Profession* and *The Dark Lady of the Sonnets* and badmouthed the old dramatist for not sending money in support of the publication of *Ulysses*. Although there is evidence that Shaw was innocent of the charge, Joyce blamed the playwright for the failure of *Exiles* to get produced in London. He also condemned him for not protecting *Ulysses* against pornography charges. Over aperitifs in Paris he reportedly often talked with Robert McAlmon about his "namesick" (*FW* 489.20). Despite Joyce's meager income, while in Trieste he amassed a large collection of Shaw plays, novels, prefaces, and socialist tracts; and the newspapers and periodicals that Joyce read or had read to him often published Shaw's letters and ostentatiously reported the world-famed writer's opinions, antics, and travels. In the *Wake* Shaun the post, Shem's "doblinganger [is] much about your own medium with a sandy whiskers" (*FW* 490.17–18)—a Dublin doppelganger (whose medium, like Joyce's, was language) with red whiskers.

As Vincent Cheng has observed, one setting for Joyce's night book is the stage (1991). "[T]his drury world" (*FW* 600.2) calls up the Drury Lane Theatre—not an Irish but an English theater. Although the obscurities of the novel argue for its indeterminacy, its stage references often allude to the "Red theatrocrat" hailed by "pinkprophets" (*FW* 29.15–16), who must be Shaw; Adeline Glasheen avers that allusions to most if not all of his plays are present in the *Wake* (1977, 236). The program of Mick, Nick, and the Maggies takes place in the "Feenichts Playhouse" (*FW* 219.2), perhaps in Phoenix Park, admittance to which is free. The "performance of problem passion play of the millentury" (*FW* 32.32) may refer to *Back to Methuselah*. Its author is probably "our worldstage's practical jokepiece" (*FW* 33.2–3).

Because Shaw had written that all great literature begins in a joke, one setting of the novel is "the hoose that joax pilled" (*FW* 369.15) and "the hoax that joke bilked" (*FW* 511.34). It is the house that Jack built, one created by an audacious Jack of beanstalk fame; "by the jerk of a beamstark [he took us] back in paladys last" (*FW* 615.24–25), Eden—the last paradise about to be lost and the setting of the first play of Shaw's *Back to Methuselah*, "In the Beginning." In the fairy tale, hungry Jack, like Joyce's "note snatcher" (*FW* 125.21–22), successfully enters the giant's domain and steals from him, appropriating his wealth and power to create, it seems, his own "Mousoumeselles buckwould's look" (*FW* 339.16). Settings like "eldorado or ultimate thole" (*FW* 134.1) compact Voltaire's *Candide* with the utopian limits of the last play of *Back to Methuselah*, "As Far as Thought Can Reach." Shaun accuses Shem of using a "pelagiarist pen" (*FW* 182.3), for "Every dimmed letter of it is a copy and not a few of the silbils and wholly words I can show you in my Kingdom of heaven" (*FW* 424.32–35), which is in Shaw's penultimate play, *The Tragedy of an Elderly Gentleman,* in the West of Ireland to which supplicants come to hear the holy ("wholly") words of a Sybil. Noting that the old dreamer resembles Shaw's ancient mariner, Captain Shotover, Matthew Hodgart avers that "Shem's house is Shaw's *Heartbreak House*" (1978, 150). Old H.C.E. is at one point at "his windower's house with the blushmantle upon him from earend to earsend" (*FW* 24.9–10)—an allusion to Shaw's play *Widowers' Houses* and to his red "blushmantle" beard covering his face from ear to ear. While Shaw was living in the Vicar's Rectory at Ayot St. Lawrence in Herefordshire, Shem wonders whether his "altar's ego" is "at the Rectory? Vicarage Road?" (*FW* 291.18).

But "the insufficiently malestimated notesnatcher" (*FW* 125.21–22) also holds forth "in the Salmon House" (*FW* 25.14–15), which seems to be the name for the abode of Cuchulain's mystical salmon of wisdom and for Shaw, whom Joyce relates to fish by spelling the word in Shaw's phonetic system and then writing, "That's U" (*FW* 299n3). Throughout the *Wake* fish are associated with old "Parr" Shaw; a parr is a young salmon as well as a name for Methuselah. In the finale of Shaw's *Methuselah*, a brash adolescent named Strephon tells the Ancient, "You old fish! I believe you don't know the difference between a man and woman" (Shaw 1987, 152). The avowed subject of Joyce's "nightynovel" (*FW* 54.21) is "parricombating" (*FW* 597.17) with a parent figure, and the Butt of Shem's jokes is a "frother"—both father and brother. Shem's "samesake sibsubstitute" is a "hooky Salmon" (*FW* 28.34) and a "sainted salmon" (*FW* 141.2–3); "the salmon he was coming up in him all life long" (*FW* 132.35–36). Since the action is in the Salmon house, the book is "Finny. Vary vary finny!" (*FW* 622.36), because it superimposes Finn McCool on Tim Finnegan, and on the "queer fish" (*FW* 463.12) "forever cracking quips on himself" (*FW* 463.8), who is clearly Shavian. When the four gospelers congratulate themselves in the "Old Man's House, Millenium Road" (*FW* 397.14), they are probably referring to Shaw, whose gospels recycle history to the millennium and beyond. This might also refer to Shaw's home in Dalkey on the Vico Road, which simultaneously calls up philosopher Giambattista Vico, whose "historical cycles," according to Mary and Padraic Colum, Joyce somehow associated "with the Vico Road" of Dalkey (Colum and Colum 1958, 221).

However, in his "Collideorscape" (*FW* 143.28), Shem calls his "hoary frother" (*FW* 310.35) the "First liar in Londsend" (*FW* 535.15)—London, Shaw's location. "Daniel in Leonden" (*FW* 541.16) is a fractured reference to Daniel, like Shaw's Androcles, in the Lion's den; Shaw as Daniel when he wrote *Common Sense about the* [First World] *War,* becoming a pariah who seemed to survive in London by a special grace; and Elder Daniel, the "good" brother in *The Shewing up of Blanco Posnet,* a Shaw play about battling brothers, which Joyce had reviewed for *Il Piccolo della Sera* in Trieste. At one point Joyce's dreamer dubs Ireland the "Green Patch" (*FW* 17.4.27), which was Shaw's term for it.

One route through the "Allmaziful" (*FW* 397.5) tale leads Shem's rival to Russia—not surprisingly, for Shaw, a supporter of the Soviet Union, went on a notorious visit to Russia in 1931 while Joyce was writing his "Work in Progress." Place names suggest the world-famous playwright's vast connections. Shaun was "making friends with everybody red in Rossya, white in Alba and touching every distinguished Ourishman" (*FW* 463.23–25). The Shaun character says, "I went on to sankt piotersburg that they gave my devil his dues" (*FW* 549.24–25). When Shaw went to Russia he went to St. Petersburg, where the Russians applauded the devil's disciple. At one point Shaun threatens to send his rival to "Tiberia" (*FW* 424.9), where the Cad can atone. Earlier, on the Tiber in Rome, Caseous and Burrus betray "The older sisars" [Caesars] (*FW* 162.1), plotting "risicide" (*FW* 161.17)—regicide and killing laughter; in "shamebred music" (*FW* 164.16) the Joycean "arrivaliste" is "zealous" of Brutus (*FW* 161.17). For assassinating the older, more powerful Roman—an adumbration of H.C.E. and Shaw's Caesar of *Caesar and Cleopatra*—both Cassius and Brutus, like Shaw and Joyce, will go into exile, on location in foreign places.

Another setting is the "Willingdone Museyroom" (*FW* 8.10), through which "the janitrix, the mistress Kathe" (*FW* 8.8) leads the reader. Kathe may be a spoof on Shaw's eponymous Great Catherine, considering that, after

Shaw condemned the "dirt" in *Ulysses*, everyone cleaning up dirt in *Finnegans Wake* seems to be Shavian. The empress envies "the scullerymaids" when she has "earaches and colics." The business of her day is to go to the museum (Shaw 1987, 809). The museum tour vaguely contrasts the Duke of Wellington, an Anglo-Irishman who became an English war hero, with French Napoleon. The contrast between the "Wounderworker" (*FW* 8.35) and "the petty lipoleum boy" (*FW* 8.26) underscores Joyce's basic conflict between mockheroic Shaun, who often seems to be in England, and the "skillfilled felon" (*FW* 355.27) in Paris.

The West of Ireland is another locale that keeps bobbing up in Joyce's stream of consciousness. "Tear-nan-ogre, my little grey home in the west, in or about Mayo" (*FW* 479.2–3) was a Shavian locale; he vacationed in both Counties Mayo and Kerry with his wife, an Irish heiress. To the "westerness" of "Wouman's Land" (*FW* 22.8) the Prankquean carries off Joyce's twins, avatars of the jokester Shaun and his cunning rival, "jiminy Tristopher," related to a sad Tristram Shandy. "Washed," for Adeline Glasheen believes that "wash" is always an anagram for Shaw in Joyce's novel (1977, 261), by the Prankquean, jiminy became a "luderman" (*FW* 21.27–28, 30) like Shaw, but his hilarious twin "became a tristian" (*FW* 22.17) as Shaw had seemed to become when he wrote *The Shewing up of Blanco Posnet*. The queen of the pranksters subverts patriarchal authority by taking "Tristopher and Hilary" (*FW* 21.12) to the woman's land of woe in the West of Ireland, from which the wives of both Shaw and Joyce came. Subsequently the brothers become "piractical jukersmen" (*FW* 337.23–24).

But Dublin and environs are the main setting of Joyce's "traumscript" (*FW* 623.36). "Allkey Dalkey" (*FW* 317.5) intimates that there is a key to the labyrinth. Dalkey, a seaside village south of Dublin, was Shaw's home as a boy. He is probably "Diaeblen Balkley" (*FW* 326.25), a Dublin/Dalkey/diabolonian, superimposed upon Irish philosopher George Berkeley, whose initials (like Shaw's) are G. B. and perhaps even the Buckley who shot the Russian general. In Dalkey, Shaw lived on "The Vico Road" (*FW* 452.21), which has sent Joyceans off to study Vico's philosophy of history, but the "evangelion . . . from Saint Joan's wood" (*FW* 223.19–20)—author of *St. Joan,* who lived in London—also had lived on "The Vico road [which] goes round and round to meet where terms begin" (*FW* 452.21–22). The "dream monologue" (*FW* 474.4) also alludes to "Platonic garlens" (*FW* 622.36), like the gardens of the enlightened Ancients in the conclusion of *Back to Methuselah,* but "Dublin country" (*FW* 446.35) is the central location of the Protestant who stood in for "orange peelers" and the Catholic who represented "greengoaters" (*FW* 522.16–17). In the end/beginning the double ends that Shaw and Joyce shared in *Methuselah* and the *Wake* "reamalgemerge" (*FW* 49.36); their "Doublends [double aims, Dublins, double ends] jined" (*FW* 20.16).

Whether Joyce wrote as a naturalist, a pioneer of the stream of consciousness, or the inventor of a new language for fiction, he was fascinated with the geography of his imagination and shared with other Irish writers what Yeats found in Shaw's *John Bull's Other Island*—the "geographical conscience" that evokes locations by using place names, whether from *Thom's Directory,* from the archetypal place names of Greek and Biblical literature, or from sly portmanteaus compressing the sources and setting of Joyce's deconstructions of locale and language in the "Work in Progress" about "Shaun or Shem" (*FW* 215.35). Whatever scenario Joyce's pen described, directed, or covered with "quashed quotatoes" (*FW* 183.22) in "piously forged palimpsests" (*FW* 182.2), he was "on location." His oeuvre resonates with the sense of place, even when the stage directions are confusing and the "corrosive sublimation" (*FW* 185.36) almost drowns us in the "new Irish stew" (*FW* 190.9), which purports paradoxically to be an "IMAGINABLE ITINERARY/ THROUGH/ THE / PARTICULAR /UNIVERSAL" (*FW* 260R3). What the dreamer in Joyce's "crossroads puzzler" (*FW* 475.3) reveals of his "liffeyside people" (*FW* 42.25) might be said for all of the Irish genius' major works: in creating his Irish characters Joyce makes Ireland the geographical center and the microcosmic omphalos of the world—"Oh Kosmos! Ah Ireland!" (*FW* 456.7).

# 3

# Gender and Interiority

CATHERINE WHITLEY

## Introducing the Interior

J ames Joyce abhorred institutions, and over the course of his career his fiction explored and undermined the institutions of colonialism, nationalism, gender politics, and narrativity, among others. He realized that power relations inform traditional narrative modes, and that male privilege and the male gaze are implicated in masculine-identified narratives.[1] Joyce experimented with various ways to interrogate these power relations by playing with the concepts of interiority, both of people and places. Specifically, in his fiction Joyce connects women to interior spaces and to the "interior monologue" in his efforts to craft a prose less intrinsically oppressive—one that challenges the institutions of representation and fiction from within. Initially men are associated with the external spaces of the city while women are impli-

---

1. Joyce obviously would not have thought in these late-twentieth-century terms, but he challenged gender relations both in themselves and as they are implicated in narrativity. Richard Pearce discusses the ways in which traditional narrative is male-identified: "In traditional realistic fiction . . . the male gaze is inscribed in the controlling and unifying point of view, in the education of writers, in the publishing industry, in advertising and the modes of distribution, and in the way people are taught to read" (Pearce 1994, 43–44). Over the course of his career Joyce subverts this paradigm, usually offering no "controlling and unifying point of view" tending to teach his readers how to read his works.

cated with the internal, domestic spaces of the home. Over the course of his first three books, Joyce gradually moved from the naturalism of *Dubliners* to the free indirect discourse of *Portrait* to *Ulysses'* mixture of styles while using his female characters to explore the connections between interior spaces, "interiority," and the interior monologue. Molly Bloom's soliloquy represents the end point of this particular stylistic odyssey and the jumping-off point for the new formal and linguistic journey that is *Finnegans Wake*. Thus if modernism attempted to "shift attention from externally rendered reality to the realm of the interior," as Joseph Boone has recently argued (1998, 4), then Joyce's own particular stylistic evolution mirrored that of modernism itself. Many critics have noted the multiple ways in which the characters and text of *Ulysses* and *Finnegans Wake* challenge and subvert gender stereotypes and thus the phallogocentrism of an early twentieth-century capitalist society based on binaries.[2] Joyce's play with ideas of interior space and the interior monologue is part of his project of dismantling and reconstituting the social order and its modes of representation. Thus after a short discussion of the ways Joyce connects space, gender, and narrative, this essay will briefly focus on the four most important female characters in his work, one from each of the four books, Gretta from "The Dead," Mrs. Dedalus from *Portrait*, Molly from *Ulysses*, and ALP from *Finnegans Wake*, in order to consider the development of Joyce's thinking about interiority and style. In his stylistic journey Joyce found a means of expression that allowed him to go beyond categories of referentiality and gender.

### The City as a Woman's Place

For men and women Joyce's Dublin always serves as a sort of litmus test, because the city allows us to read the characters as consumers and judge their financial abilities by their actions, noting whether they are they harried and in search of provisions or leisured and in search of pleasure. However, Joyce's thinking about women's relationships to the city evolved over the course of

2. See, for instance, two very different recent full-length studies that both demonstrate Joyce's subversion of the status quo: Christine Froula, *Modernism's Body: Sex, Culture, and Joyce* (1996), and Margot Norris, *Joyce's Web: The Social Unraveling of Modernism* (1992).

his career, as his depictions of specific female characters demonstrate. In his career Joyce at first seems to be replicating the stereotypical social arrangements that prescribed for women a domestic space, while giving men free run to inhabit all spaces but especially permitting them access to those spaces coded as "public." As a corollary in the early works, women are frequently described as finding the city to be alien and perilous, but by the time of *Ulysses* the obvious necessity of women's presence in public spaces has affected their descriptions, which mostly become less charged (the appearance of the prostitutes in the "Circe" chapter being an obvious exception). In *Dubliners* the appearance of women in the "masculine" domain of public spaces usually signals that there is something wrong with the situation. Thus Maria in "Clay" works surrounded by Protestant former prostitutes in a commercial establishment, and then is flustered on the streetcar because she has no real home of her own. The slavey in "Two Gallants" returns to her household from an evening out with Corley, who presumably then encourages her to steal money from her employers. These women, like others later in *Ulysses*, are depicted as working outside the home because of economic necessity; as Shari Benstock has noted, "the women who negotiate [the city's] terrain do so because the husbands, brothers, and fathers in whose steps they walk have failed their tasks" (S. Benstock 1988, 296), the first and foremost of which would be to provide materially for the family. There is a dearth of men who can and do act as sober, financially responsible civic mediators for their womenfolk; Leopold Bloom serves as Joyce's best example of a prudent male member of society.

The narrative frequently depicts being outdoors, in the "masculine" domain of public spaces, as a situation that is fraught with peril for women and children in *Dubliners*, a fact that is in contrast to *Ulysses*.[3] For instance, when the boy in "Araby" accompanies his aunt on Saturday evenings to the market, they are described as "walk[ing] through the flaring streets, jostled by drunken men and bargaining women, amid the curses of labourers, the shrill litanies of shop-boys" and "the nasal chanting of the street-singers" (*D* 31). This swirling chaotic scene contrasts sharply with the idealized domestic order

---

3. Of course it is problematic to imply (as I do here) that there is a singular narrative voice in *Dubliners*, in which the narrative viewpoint shifts with each story, or in *Ulysses*, with its myriad narrative viewpoints; the essay will more closely consider point of view later on.

of the boy's aunt's home, and he fantasizes about the dangers inherent in this outside world, a world alien to his preadolescent sensibilities, one in which he can romanticize himself as a questing hero, "imagin[ing] that [he] bore [his] chalice safely through a throng of foes" (*D* 31). Similarly, when Eveline manages to wheedle from her abusive, alcoholic father part of her *own* wages, which she earns as a salesclerk, she must "elbow" through crowds, "holding her black leather purse tightly in her hand" in order to buy provisions for her younger siblings, on a tense, rushed shopping trip (*D* 38). The two young boys playing hooky from school in "An Encounter" run into a "queer old josser" with "bottle-green eyes" (*D* 26, 27) who is sexually excited by thoughts of flagellating boys and who thus does not represent the precise sort of wild adventure they were looking for. For women and young boys in *Dubliners,* the commercial city can be an uncomfortable, threatening space to be in.

However, in *Ulysses* women and children traverse the city and appear in public spaces without quite the same sense of danger or displacement as was present in Joyce's earlier work. Like the aforementioned characters in *Dubliners* (or the flower girl or prostitutes in *Portrait*), they are mostly in the city due to economic necessity, not having a man on whom they can really depend. But when the servant girl from next door to the Blooms is out buying meat, the narrative treats it as a commonplace occurrence ("She tendered a coin, smiling boldly, holding her thick wrist out. . . . She stood outside the shop in sunlight and sauntered lazily to the right" [*U* 4.168, 173–74]) rather than a perilous pilgrimage. In *Ulysses* the text seems to be more relaxed in its treatment of women in public spaces, as if admitting that the public/private distinctions upon which the modern family are founded are artificial and unrealistic, especially in a nation marred and marked by colonial subjugation. In a nation with high unemployment, large families, and few high-paying jobs, men are preordained to fail in the public sphere, necessitating that women, in order to survive and provide for their children, will have to leave the sacred hearth in search of wages and will have to transgress the public/private distinctions. That this important binary is not absolute foreshadows the demolition of other absolutes yet to come in chapters such as "Circe" and "Penelope," wherein the binary masculine/feminine, among others, is interrogated. No longer, as in *Dubliners,* are women outside the home imagined as being imperiled by the city; the reader of *Ulysses* is given instead such monstrosities as Simon Dedalus, a real imperiler of women and children.

## Gretta: Pretty as a Picture

Joyce attempts to derail the power relations inherent in masculine-identified narratives in several ways in *Dubliners*. First, instead of relying solely on male narrators, Joyce uses a third-person limited-omniscient narrator who is linked to female characters in four stories. Second, although most of *Dubliners*—and all of *Portrait*—can be considered masculine-identified since they portray the thoughts and feelings of male protagonists, yet as always Joyce encourages his reader to read against the grain of the dominant narrative voice, even if doing so proves counter to one's training or instinct. Judith Fetterley describes the way in which the traditional literary canon and (many) teachers of literature produce readers who, even if biologically female, are encouraged to "identify with a male point of view, and . . . accept as normal and legitimate a male system of values, one of whose central principles is misogyny" (Fetterley 1997, 569). However, Joyce's texts constantly erupt as the repressed member of society returns with a vengeance to disrupt the seemingly smooth narrative functioning; lacunae and that which usually goes unsaid act to dismantle the smooth, bourgeois narrative voice. *Dubliners'* coda, "The Dead," especially invites this sort of resistant reading; Margot Norris ably argues that "Joyce dramatizes in 'The Dead' the politics of art's determination to conceal its own politically oppressive functions by raveling a primary narrative text, Gabriel's story told in what we might call the audible or 'loud' text, with a largely silent but disruptive feminist countertext" (Norris 1992, 98). Thus if one is what Fetterley would term a "resisting reader," one who in this case attends to the countertext as well as the primary text of Joyce's stories, then one is encouraged to read "like a woman" and read with an eye to the oppression of both society and narrative constructions. Third, in "The Dead" Joyce plays with ideas of interiority and gender in order to expose Gabriel's objectification of his wife while showing Gabriel to be an utter stranger to Gretta's inner life.

The first three stories in *Dubliners* all have first-person, male narrators; all subsequent stories have third-person narratives, whether the main characters are male or female. In "Eveline," "The Boarding House," "Clay," and "A

Mother," all of which have female protagonists, Joyce's third-person narrative depicts the thoughts of female characters in the same manner as those of male characters are depicted in the other third-person stories in *Dubliners*—in a sort of modified naturalism that is tending towards free indirect discourse. Thus when Eveline ponders the wisdom of her decision ("She looked round the room. . . . She had consented to go away. Was that wise?" [*D* 37]), the narrative technique is similar to that used in a story such as "Two Gallants," in which Lenehan worries about Corley's assignation ("All at once the idea struck him that perhaps Corley had seen her home by another way and given him the slip. His eyes searched the street: there was no sign of them. . . . Would Corley do a thing like that?" [*D* 59]). In both stories Joyce alternates between "objective" descriptions of the characters' actions ("She looked round the room," and "His eyes searched the street") and an omniscient knowledge of the characters' thoughts ("Was that wise?" and "Would Corley do a thing like that?"). At this point in his career, in these particular stories, Joyce does not distinguish when representing male or female interiority; rather, the narrative presents female and male characters in a similar fashion, slipping readily in and out of the characters' minds. In contrast to his depiction of male characters, Joyce's female characters are generally portrayed as physically occupying interior spaces, yet these spaces serve as deadly traps for both women and men. Home for Eveline represents a lifetime of abuse; her decision to stay instead of fleeing for a potentially better life elsewhere is an act of self-immolation. Adult men, as if sensing the degree to which these homes are stifling to women, both desire and fear domestic spaces and matrimony since home as a "stultifying domestic space" is "also death to the male, another womb/tomb" (Garvey 1995, 111). Because of attendant socioeconomic conditions, women in domestic spaces often serve as sirens on rocks for the men of Dublin.

In "The Dead" Joyce portrays a seemingly happy marriage both by bifurcating the narrative, as discussed above, and by thematizing Gabriel's objectification of Gretta. In doing the latter Joyce calls into question a woman's "exterior" (or physical appearance) versus her "interior" (or mind), showing males to be objectifiers of the former and bad readers of the latter. As a narrative "The Dead" is masculine-identified. It exclusively follows the male protagonist, Gabriel Conroy, while its dominant narrative invites the reader to consider the main female character, Gretta Conroy, through her husband's eyes, as he treats her as a "female *objet d'art*" at the party by aestheticizing her (Norris 1992, 102); however, the counter-narrative unveils to the resisting reader the oppressive power relations involved in adopting such a stance. In the last scene of "The Dead," Gretta Conroy proves resistant to Gabriel's attempts to objectify and possess her, but the narrative offers the reader no direct entry into Gretta's mind, into her "interiority." Because in *Dubliners* Joyce does offer such insights into Eveline, Maria, and several other women through a third-person limited omniscient narrator, the fact that we have no access to Gretta's thoughts is very much a choice and not an indication that in his early career Joyce hesitated to adapt his narrative methods to represent the inner workings of a woman's mind. Instead, the reader is put in the same position as Gabriel when he asks his wife of many years "what are you thinking about?" (*D* 218) and who insists, when he gets no answer, "Tell me what it is, Gretta. I think I know what is the matter. Do I know?" (*D* 218) when he most emphatically does not. Gabriel's arrogant assumption is that his control over his wife's person (Norris points out that Gabriel enjoys "petty paternal tyrannies" such as forcing his wife to wear galoshes [1992, 104]) equates to control over her inner thoughts. Gabriel is assuming that his wife is overcome with sudden desire for him, in accordance with his own amorous mood of the moment, and that he is somehow able silently to influence the direction of her thoughts and emotions: "Perhaps her thoughts had been running with his. Perhaps she had felt the impetuous desire that was in him and then the yielding mood had come upon her" (*D* 217–18). In fact, Gretta has been thinking for some time of her first, lost lover, the dead Michael Furey; Gabriel has proven to be a bad reader of his wife's inner thoughts and moods, as based on her outer appearance, and after hearing the story of the dead boy's love, he watches his wife, "overcome by emotion, [fling] herself face downward on the bed, sobbing in the quilt" (*D* 221). Gretta, within the very domestic space of a bedroom, lying on a bed, proves an opaque surface to her husband and the reader; we—and he—are treated only to her exterior. The masculine-identified narrative affords neither Gabriel nor the reader an experience of Gretta's interiority; instead, the complacent reader's complicity in Gabriel's casual objectification of his wife is exposed, or the resisting reader is invited to condemn such masculine objectification of women.

## Mrs. Dedalus: Dear Diary

After his initial forays into representing female consciousnesses in *Dubliners*, Joyce sidesteps the issue in *Portrait*—the only consciousness the narrative has access to is Stephen's. The limited-omniscient narrator follows Stephen's thoughts and mirrors Stephen's intellectual development in a type of free indirect discourse. Because the narrator's omniscience is limited to Stephen's thoughts, the reader has no direct access to the female characters in the novel and must instead get the narrator's version of Stephen's interpretation of these characters. The most prominent women in the novel, Mrs. Dedalus and E. C., are both presented in "exterior" views and only as they relate to Stephen. The reader learns, for instance, that the narrator claims that a very young Stephen thinks that "His mother had a nicer smell than his father" (*P* 7), but the reader does not find out what she thinks of Stephen's smell, or if she is exasperated by his habit of wetting the bed. As a young man Stephen is clearly threatened by the composure of E. C., a young lady to whom he is attracted who walks freely around the city and invades the university, that masculine space; his fearful jealousy paints all other nearby men as her lovers, including his friend Cranly and a priest who teaches her Gaelic (*P* 232, 221). However, although the reader has no access to the interior thoughts of these two women, the narrative's portrayal of Stephen's views of them reveals much about Stephen's own interiority and his shortcomings. For ten years Stephen weaves a fantastic relationship between himself and E. C. based on a very few encounters (like the early one at the children's party), although he never talks to her about her feelings or his concerning a possible relationship.[4] The reader

4. Stephen finally confesses certain feelings to Emma Clery in *Stephen Hero;* he proposes to spend a night with her, then say goodbye and never see her again (*SH* 198). Her response, not surprisingly, is to tell him "You are mad" (*SH* 199). In *Portrait*, although the reader gets no access to E. C.'s thoughts concerning Stephen, she is obviously very significant to him. Michael H. Begnal argues the importance of both Eileen Vance and Emma Clery to Stephen's own interiority, demonstrating that Stephen serially uses the girls as artistic muses and masturbatory fetishes (1999). A real-life counterpart to Eileen/Emma is a matter of speculation, but as a grown man Joyce had several well-documented unsuccessful flirtations, even writing poems about and letters to the women involved before he was rebuffed (*Letters* 2: 342–49; 418–19). According to Ellmann (1982), Joyce recognized the absurdity of these affairs but was stirred by them nonetheless.

is provided with absolutely no access to E. C.'s thoughts and thus cannot judge the young woman apart from Stephen's appraisal of her. Whether she is the femme fatale that Stephen would like to believe, or merely a young woman trying to get an education who is slightly bemused at the attentions devoted to her by a very intense young man, is a matter of conjecture. In depicting Stephen as a shy, scornful romantic, Joyce suggests his emotional immaturity and highlights the need for better interpersonal relationships between men and women, just as he had in his portrayal of the domineering Gabriel.

Yet further shortcomings are suggested by Stephen's callous relationship with his loving mother. When Cranly argues with Stephen over the latter's failure to do his Easter duty, he urges his nonbelieving friend to placate his mother by going through the motions, noting that "Whatever else is unsure in this stinking dunghill of a world, a mother's love is not" (*P* 241–42), Stephen answers by primly asserting that Pascal "would not suffer his mother to kiss him" (*P* 242). Stephen seems to have scant compassion for his mother, who struggles to feed her brood on bread fried in dripping, who washes his face and neck for him, and who tries to keep peace in the house by helping Stephen to avoid Simon Dedalus's wrath by hiding the fact that he is late to university (*P* 174–75). Although the narrative offers no direct reportage of Mrs. Dedalus's interiority, the reader can interpolate some of her thoughts from her dialogue, which is supposedly directly reported, especially as she gets the last word at the end of the novel. In his diary Stephen reproduces the following comments supposedly made by his mother: "Said I have a queer mind and have read too much. Not true. Have read little and understood less" (*P* 248) and "She prays now, she says, that I may learn in my own life and away from home and friends what the heart is and what it feels" (*P* 252). To the perceptive reader Mrs. Dedalus seems to have a penetrating understanding of her son's personality; she realizes that he is young and arrogant in his superior mind and education, but woefully immature emotionally. Together these two comments offer an unlearned but humane woman's judgment on her book-learned but inhuman son. Mrs. Dedalus's second remark especially seems a clear criticism of her self-centered son, while his answering comment of "Amen. So be it" (*P* 252) shows that he does not recognize the inherent critique or feel its sting. Stephen thus shows that, like when he was six years old, he has no clue about his mother's interiority (or, for that matter, any woman's), but the reported dialogue shows that his mother has keen insight into his. Stephen and Gabriel are therefore linked by their inability to successfully read the women in their lives. Gabriel is more aware of his personal failings than Stephen is; after hearing Gretta's revelation, "He saw himself as a ludicrous figure, . . .the pitiable fatuous fellow he had caught a glimpse of in the mirror" (D 220). Stephen, on the other hand, remains blissfully unaware of the fact that his mother, an uneducated woman, has taken his measure and found it wanting, an irony the reader finds it hard to miss. Thus in Joyce's first two books the distance between a male's interpretation of a woman's opaque exterior and her actual thoughts, as expressed in her dialogue, proves to be a crucial one, a distance that allows for an ironic assessment of the man and of the expectations aroused by the narrative.

### Molly: Joyce's Inner Woman

In *Dubliners* Joyce represents a female consciousness in some of the earlier stories but chooses not to do so in "The Dead" in order to interrogate male objectification of women. Within *Portrait* this exposure of masculine privilege continues, as the narrative shows how Stephen objectifies E. C. and patronizes his mother. In *Ulysses*, however, after being objectified for seventeen chapters Molly Bloom suddenly is granted a voice in the eighteenth chapter in what purports to be a female monologue, an instance of pure "interiority." Within the action of *Ulysses*, Molly might be and has been considered to fulfill a stereotypical role, in part because the glimpses of Molly that the reader gets during the day are all three external "views" that share in the narrative's masculine perspective. However, Molly ultimately eludes this narrative perspective since the method Joyce uses with Molly is the inverse of that he used in depicting Gretta. Whereas the reader does not participate in Gretta's interiority except through her answers to her husband's questions, in "Penelope" the reader is denied any external point of view at all; the narrative voice seems to disappear, and we are left with Molly's monologue. Thus of these two female characters, both of whom lie in a bed in a bedroom (that most domestic of spaces), of one we get no inner access at all while of the other we get no exterior view but only what purports to be sheer interiority. Moreover, Molly not only escapes objectification by the male gaze in this chapter (unlike Gretta) but she also denies male agency with "a gaze that is independent, indifferent, [and] all-embracing" (Pearce 1994, 47). If Stephen's earlier monologue on the strand in "Proteus" could be considered to be an attempt to exclude the body in its philosophical ruminations on the senses and eternity, then Molly's bedroom monologue seems to insist emphatically on that body, in all of its disturbing fleshy splendor. Thus the two balanced monologues, one male and one female, would seem to reify binary oppositions of gender definitions. However, the net effect of Molly's monologue is to unsettle any such certainties; her use of polysemous words and puns disallows definite coincidence of words and meaning, opening up a textual space for polysemous play that foreshadows the radical prose of *Finnegans Wake*.

Joyce forces the reader into an acknowledgment that, in Molly's monologue, the textual *is* the sexual; Molly's textual body is just that—text. A reader who has participated in the male narrative perspective on the novel's women, with its objectifying gaze and implicit judgment, now must contend with the text's insistence on its own textuality, which effectively disrupts any voyeuristic tendencies in the reader. For instance, the lack of apostrophes that would demarcate the word "were," clarifying it as a contraction rather than as a past tense of "to be" (as in "were not to ask any questions but they want to know where were you" [*U* 18.299]), causes the reader to read such passages twice in an attempt to sort their linguistic sense.[5] Such passages insist on their surfaces, refusing to be taken as a transparent window into the character's "inner thoughts." Thus when we get what purports to be an interior monologue by Mrs. Marion Bloom and that monologue contains many descriptions of Molly's body and her sexuality, supposedly from her point of view rather than that of the narrator or a male character, the textual ambivalence caused by typography and punctuation forces the reader to realize that, when dealing with fictional characters, any attribution of interiority or opaqueness is a textual effect. What's more, the idea of interiority itself is revealed to be a fictional construct, since as Joseph Boone discusses, "assumptions of 'interiority' . . . are the *effects* of the sexual and gender ideologies whose power lies in their

---

5. For an account of the agency of the apostrophe in *Finnegans Wake*, see Shari Benstock's "Apostrophizing the Feminine in *Finnegans Wake*" (1989).

ability to posit as 'natural' or 'innate' social constructions that are in fact en-
acted upon the body. From this 'surface,' their performance is then intro-
jected by the subject as originating *cause,* as essence or truth of being" (Boone
1998, 8). Given the reconsiderations of Molly's soliloquy by Cheryl Herr
(1994) and Kimberly Devlin (1994), in which both suggest that it functions
as a gender performance piece, the chapter's textual resistance to being read as
the inner thoughts of a woman highlights the degree to which the categories
of inner/outer, hidden/seen, and feminine/masculine are being challenged.
Thus when "Penelope" causes us to question the binaries of inner and outer,
or those of gender, it destabilizes the foundations of logocentrism that permit
the existence of "fictions of centered truth" and "coherent identity" (Boone
1998, 8). As Boone notes, "what promises to be a privileged glimpse into
Molly's feminine 'essence' or 'core' turns out instead to reveal a series of
masks, of performative *surfaces,* upon which are inscribed those gender pre-
scriptions the culture produces, while it pretends they originate in some 'interior fixity' " (1998, 168).

Several other critics also reject "Penelope" as a naturalistic monologue
connecting it instead to a "masquerade," although they are divided as to
whether the chapter's obvious artifice is a measure of its success or its failure.
For instance, Karen Lawrence has claimed that "Molly represents *the problem
of woman represented by the male pen,* a staging of alterity that reveals itself as
masquerade" (Lawrence 1990, 253). Lawrence seems to feel that Molly, as a
"problem," represents a type of failure for Joyce, that he tried but did not succeed in concealing himself as the male author of a female character. In contrast, I—like Patrick McGee, Cheryl Herr, and Kimberly Devlin—find instead
that Joyce purposely frames the last chapter of *Ulysses* as a masquerade of femininity. McGee emphatically states that "With Molly's soliloquy Joyce does
not aim at writing the feminine, at least not the feminine as essence. Molly's
word has no essence. It is a masquerade, a play of conventions, and not a representation of the eternal-feminine, the absolute other, Mother, and so on"
(McGee 1988, 172). Cheryl Herr takes the concept of Molly's monologue as
"masquerade" even farther; in her essay " 'Penelope' as Period Piece," she
connects the last chapter of *Ulysses* to a stage performance, arguing that
Molly's soliloquy is not meant to be naturalistic, but is instead akin to a "star
turn" or "bill 'topper' " performed not by "a woman but [by] a male or gen-

der-indeterminate actor" (Herr 1994, 71). Devlin notes that "Molly is interesting to examine as an engendered character, insofar as Joyce represents her not as the feminine but as cultural femininities—constructed, labile, assumable, rejectable" (Devlin 1994, 83). In "Penelope" Joyce unmasks the concepts of both "gender" and "interiority" as being nonessential, potentially oppressive categories in a prose that itself destabilizes binary distinctions and referentiality.

Although some critics have seen "Penelope" as a retreat back into naturalism and away from the experimentation of the chapters immediately preceding it, I instead see it as a continuation of these experiments and as a bridge to the language of the *Wake*. Because "Penelope's" lack of punctuation and its typography seem to enhance the chapter's flow while they simultaneously serve as an impediment to the narrative's movement, the reader must frequently stop and reread phrases to sort their sense, in a manner analogous to that called for by the *Wake*'s portmanteau words. Thus I would agree with Frances Restuccia that "Molly claims the most playful, nonrepresentational language in *Ulysses*" (Restuccia 1985, 111), language that insists upon its textual, constructed nature. Joyce uses his female interior monologue, that of a woman talking in a bedroom late at night, to strip away the last vestiges of naturalism as he interrogates interiority as an effect of another social construct: gender. His explorations of the power relations implicit in narrative modes ends with a dissection of the text as a purveyor of socially constructed points of view.

### A.L.P.: Flow Away Home

In his last great prose work, Joyce moves beyond the gendered implications of narrative point of view, of traditional characterization, and of mimesis with his radical formal experiments. The very form of Wakean language, specifically the portmanteau word, itself challenges an acceptance of binaries since, as Suzette Henke has noted, "We are always of 'twosome twinminds' about any particular linguistic unit because we have been denied the logocentric closure of direct statement" (Henke 1989, 39). Traditional characterization and plot have also mutated, leaving behind indeterminate action and shape-shifting characters. Thus A.L.P., as chicken and river, is far from being a realistic, traditional female character. But to the degree that Joyce has his characters act in recognizably socialized ways, he still trades on received ideas of gender; A.L.P., for instance, is not only a river but is also a mother and housewife. The final section of *Finnegans Wake* disrupts notions of gender and/or interiority in two ways. First, in a book that portrays, parodies, and subverts the act of authorship (especially in section 1.7, "Shem," with its pungent ink recipe and its acerbic references to Joyce's own career), the last depiction of writing refuses to be connected to an authorial masculinity since it relies on "feminized" activities for its operative vocabulary. In this act of domestication, the narrative translates A.L.P./Biddy's act of creation into terms of cookery; the machinery for producing text, or the historical "vicociclometer," is described as a mill for grinding wheat into wholemeal and the time frame hinges on the serving of a meal "piping hot":

> Our wholemole millwheeling vicociclometer, a tetradomational gaze-bocroticon . . . receives through a portal vein the dialytically separated elements of precedent decomposition for the verypetpurpose of subsequent recombination so that the heroticisms, catastrophes and eccentricities transmitted by the ancient legacy of the past, type by tope, letter from litter, word at ward . . . when cup, platter and pot come piping hot, as sure as herself pits hen to paper and there's scribings scrawled on eggs. (*FW* 614.27–615.10)

A.L.P. is here the "ancient legacy of the past" responsible for recombining elements in order to transmit H.C.E. as "heroticisms, catastrophes and eccentricities"; to do so she must serve up the letter/history, "herself pits hen to paper," and scrawl on eggs, food symbolic of new beginnings. A masculine history based on heroes and catastrophic events (like the history of Ireland itself) undergoes gender reassignment and is served up in a much more palatable new form.

This is A.L.P.'s own version of historical materialism; in this passage she insists that an historical, religious, and/or mythological production is a cyclical, homely, nourishing event—like breakfast—instead of being some sort of transcendent meta-narrative. In this passage form, particularly Joyce's specific use of portmanteau words, helps deny the possibility that history or religion could be a transcendent meta-narrative. A.L.P.'s domesticated version neatly materializes the spiritual, transforming the Father, Son, and the Holy Ghost into "the farmer, his son, and their homely codes, known as eggburst, egg-blend, eggburial, and hatch-as-hatch can" (*FW* 614.31–33). They may be homemade and handy, but ultimately all narratives and codes are just as his-torically determined and arbitrary as gender.

A skeptical reader could argue that this translation of (masculine) author-ship and creation into (feminine) housekeeping terms, although it mocks and unsettles gender categories, merely inverts the masculine/feminine binary while keeping its (oppressive) structure intact. However, this criticism is laid to rest by the end of the book, which provides the chapter's second method of disrupting notions of gender and interiority by exteriorizing the end of gen-der in a type of death. The very end of *Finnegans Wake* participates in Joyce's critique of the categories of inside and outside, masculine and feminine, in a narrative that, of all the *Wake,* most closely approximates an "interior mono-logue" in its feel. The long, long paragraph that ends the book, which begins "Soft morning, city! Lsp! I am leafy speafing" (*FW* 619.20), echoes *Ulysses'* "Penelope" chapter both in its stream-of-consciousness mode and in its the-matic concerns. A.L.P. has left the house and her sleeping husband; outdoors she greets the city and the nature all around her. Unlike Gretta, Mrs. Dedalus, and Molly in the last scenes of Joyce's previous works, A.L.P. is not associated with an interior here but with an exterior; she is a feature of the landscape. In her guise as the river, A.L.P. is flowing out to sea, as she (like Molly in "Pene-lope") reminisces about her life and loves, her children and her husband. A.L.P., as a fluid river described in a flowing prose, has been taken as a symbol of the eternal feminine. Richard Lehan, for instance, claims, "The city for Joyce embodied a masculine, the river a feminine principle" and "The femi-nine vision seems to win at the end of *Finnegans Wake*" since "the river flows to the sea, where it will return to the city as life-giving rain" (Lehan 1982, 259). To accept these two claims uncritically would be re-essentializing gen-der in the *Wake* by accepting stereotypical gender attributes and attaching them to the socialized bodies of a female and a city.

Joyce in fact does the opposite; symbolically he destroys gender in the last image of his last book, canceling out entirely feminine and masculine, female and male. In the first chapter of *Ulysses,* the ocean is "our great sweet mother" (*U* 1.80), "Our mighty mother!" (*U* 1.85), but A.L.P. flows "back to you, my cold father, my cold mad father, my cold mad feary father" (*FW* 628.1–2). Water is thus not associated only with women; "fluidity" can be achieved by both "masculine" and "feminine." In merging with a "male" body of water A.L.P. would be losing herself, dissolving any individuality and likewise, one would believe, any gender, in a sort of post-androgynous death. As the text then circles back, "riverrun" (*FW* 3.1) to the city, Joyce insists on cycles, on ends that are beginnings, on the dissolution of artificial boundaries such as public and domestic, masculine and feminine, because all are constructions that flow along in society's wake.

# 4

# An Uncomfortable Fit
## Joyce's Women in Dublin and Trieste

DEIRDRE FLYNN

Wrapped tightly in a confusion of cheap Sunday garments, the young woman in James Joyce's "Two Gallants" waits at a street corner for Corley. She stands like a wind-up doll on display, hardly moving except to make carefully "executed" gestures of seduction ("swinging a shade in one hand") and feminine modesty (laughing and bending her head "when he spoke to her at close quarters" [*D* 55]). She says nothing. Nor does she move freely, "taking quick short steps, while Corley kept beside her with his long stride" (*D* 59). Thus dehumanized, this woman functions not as a character in her own right but as an object of desire around which Corley and his friend, Lenehan, unite. She is a "fine decent tart" that (*D* 54), as Garry Leonard contends in *Reading "Dubliners" Again,* is "picked by Corley with the same sort of discerning eye any shopper might employ in selecting pastry in a bakery" (1993, 123). As such, Leonard adds, she "becomes an object of exchange that validates a (spurious) phallic economy" (1993, 123). In this context, she appears to become the prized asset in what Luce Irigaray (1985) argues is a "ho(m)mo-sexual monopoly" based on the "exclusive valorization of men's needs/desires, of exchanges among men." In the process she is "disinvested from [her] body and reclothed in a form that makes [her body] suitable for exchange among men."[1]

The "Two Gallants" slavey is quite literally "reclothed" to appear suitable for such exchange; in effect, her clothes are carefully ordered (and disordered) to appeal to a wide range of men. Dressed in her "Sunday finery" (D 55), she seems clad for religious men. However, upon closer inspection the dissonant parts of her outfit evoke other potential male targets who might pass her on the corner: "Her blue serge skirt was held at the waist by a belt of black leather. The great silver buckle of her belt seemed to depress the centre of her body, catching the light stuff of her white blouse like a clip. She wore a short black jacket with mother-of-pearl buttons and a ragged black boa. The ends of her tulle collarette had been carefully disordered and a big bunch of red flowers was pinned in her bosom stems upwards" (D 55). Here, cheap evening wear ("ragged black boa" and "big bunch of red flowers") contrasts with day wear ("blue serge skirt" and "white blouse"), creating a "look" that does not quite fit in either day or night, church or street. Nor do the disparate pieces of her outfit come together around her body in any formal coherence. Rather, the pieces "depress," "catch," and "clip" distinct body parts.

Neither formally coherent (as a desirable whole) nor generically legible (as a streetwalker or churchgoer), this woman is impossible to price as an "object of exchange among men" (Irigaray 1985, 171). Nor is she contrasted with other women in ways that might emphasize her relative value in such an exchange market. Instead, she is aligned with an awkward doll, a farm animal (with her "broad nostrils," "straggling mouth," and "two projecting front teeth" [D 56]), and a slave (or "slavey" [D 50]). In this light, she seems more like a useful object than a desirable woman.[2] In fact, it is precisely such use

1. Leonard here quotes from Luce Irigaray, stating that "a commodity—a woman—is divided into two irreconcilable bodies: her 'natural' body and her socially valued, exchangeable body, which is a particularly mimetic expression of masculine values. . . . At the most, the commodities—or rather the relationship among them—are the material alibi for the desire of relations among men. To this end, the commodity is disinvested of its body and reclothed in a form that makes it suitable for exchange among men" (Irigaray 1985, 179–80).

2. Irigaray distinguishes between exchange value, relative value, and use value. The last is the raw material that "must be abstracted from all natural qualities . . . [via] a process of generalization and of universalization [that] imposes itself in the operation of social exchanges" (Irigaray

value that Corley and Lenehan appraise when they aim *not* to get the girl (as the reader initially assumes) but to get a gold coin through her. Both the slavey and the men are stripped of humanness by this hidden motive, engaging in interdependent pimping and prostitution in ways that reduce everyone involved to hard, heartless objects.

Although Lenehan and Corley here seem to assume a position of mastery vis-à-vis the woman they use, in fact, neither of these men is actually portrayed as powerful. Lenehan, for instance, reveals his weakness as he whimpers to Corley, "are you sure you can bring it off all right? You know it's a ticklish job. They're damn close on that point. Eh? . . . What?" (*D* 53). After Corley frowns at Lenehan's concerns, the latter appears all the more impotent as he "morosely" wanders Dublin while Corley gets the coin from the girl (*D* 60). In a similar state of demoralized dis-ease, Corley stares "grimly before him" when he reveals the coin to Lenehan (*D* 60). Both these men suffer from the alienation they experience as a result of their procuratorial actions. In this respect, they resemble the slavey they use. Like her, they are trapped in the lower echelons of a capitalist, patriarchal society, forced to go on "knocking about," "pulling the devil by the tail," and making up "shifts and intrigues" (*D* 57). Such men and women thus appear to be radically interimbricated with one another; Irish gallants use Irish slaveys and Irish slaveys allow themselves to be used. Both thus reinforce the economic and psychosocial enslavement of their people.

In *Joyce, Race, and Empire,* Vincent Cheng elaborates upon the imperialist underpinnings of such mutual enslavement (1995). He argues that British imperialism strips Irish men and women of individual agency, making them anonymous coins in an oppressive economy. He notes, "the currency of exchange in this story of exploitation, prostitution, and sexual conquest is a gold coin whose very name suggests the power of Empire—that Empire whose . . . sovereignty over its Irish subjects prostitutes them to its coin, and robs them of their own sovereignty, of their own self-determining role as sovereign subjects in their own right" (Cheng 1995, 116). Trapped in the confines of an ex-

---

1985, 183). A woman's use value would be that which is still attached to her natural body, for instance, labor, reproduction, child care, sex.

ploited, impoverished Ireland, neither women nor men invest in their own power or feel a sense of self-worth that would enable them to form potentially liberating interpersonal alliances with one another.

Chandler and Annie in "A Little Cloud" are a case in point. Robbed "of their own sovereignty" in the home and in the marketplace (Cheng 1995, 116), they are stuck in a debilitating antagonistic rapport with one another:

> A little lamp with a white china shade stood upon the table and its light fell over a photograph which was enclosed in a frame of crumpled horn. It was Annie's photograph. Little Chandler looked at it, pausing at the thin tight lips. She wore the pale blue summer blouse which he had brought her home as a present one Saturday. It had cost him ten and elevenpence; but what an agony of nervousness it had cost him! How he had suffered that day, waiting at the shop door until the shop was empty, standing at the counter and trying to appear at his ease while the girl piled ladies' blouses before him, paying at the desk and forgetting to take up the odd penny of his change, being called back by the cashier, and, finally, striving to hide his blushes as he left the shop by examining the parcel to see if it was securely tied. When he brought the blouse home Annie kissed him and said it was very pretty and stylish; but when she heard the price she threw the blouse on the table and said it was a regular swindle to charge ten and elevenpence for that. At first she wanted to take it back but when she tried it on she was delighted with it, especially with the make of the sleeves, and kissed him and said he was very good to think of her.
>
> Hm! (*D* 82)

The cost of this blouse is much greater than ten and elevenpence; it is also the emasculating embarrassment of being unable to act the part of a gallant man at the counter, where Chandler fumbles in an "agony of nervousness," as well as that of being rejected by a wife who berates him for being swindled. The only payoff, it seems, is a meager acceptance kiss from "thin tight lips." But Chandler is not the only one who pays dearly for this blouse. His wife also undergoes an agonizing series of emotional responses: first, she enjoys the pleasure of receiving the gift; then, she feels outraged and swindled at the price; next, she angrily rejects both gift and giver; and, finally, overcome by delight, she accepts the garment.

What gives this little blouse the power to plunge both wife and husband into such turmoil? As a "stylish" product of commodity culture, this blouse would appear to make Annie and Chandler acutely aware that they do not belong; lacking the means and social bravado of fashionable, consumer society, they teeter between desire and resentment. They are locked in an oppressed state, socioeconomically and culturally disenfranchised subjects who constantly run the risk of being swindled. The blouse in the photo, then, serves as a reminder to Chandler that both he and his wife are captive, like caged animals "enclosed in a frame of crumpled horn."

Not surprisingly, Chandler wants to escape from this demoralizing cage, with its tight kisses and cold looks ("he looked coldly into the eyes of the photograph and they answered coldly" [*D* 83]). He does so by fantasizing about an exotic Other's eyes so "full . . . of passion" they would release him from the harsh realities of his marriage: "He thought of what Gallaher had said about rich Jewesses. Those dark Oriental eyes, he thought, how full they are of passion, of voluptuous longing! . . . Why had he married the eyes in the photograph?" (*D* 83). Chandler's fantasy eyes are windows to much more than a vague, ahistorical, subjective desire, here. In fact, as Leonard notes in *Advertising and Commodity Culture in Joyce*, these eyes shed light on a desire mediated and even created by specific "technological, sociohistorical, and psychological" factors (Leonard 1998, 75). Focusing in particular on the proliferation and popularity of erotic postcards in early twentieth-century Dublin, Leonard contends that, given Chandler's limited travels and experience, the most likely source for his vision of "dark Oriental eyes" is "the nude pictures of primitive beauties who populated the colonies, portrayed on postcards using the excuse of anthopological documentation" (Leonard 1998, 94). Given this source, "eyes like Annie Chandler's are, it seems, disparaged in contrast to a mass-produced 'erotic organization of visibility', configured by the eyes of women on erotic postcards" (Leonard 1998, 95).

When examined from this perspective, Chandler's route of escape into Orientalist fantasy appears to be anything but liberating. For, in struggling to get away from the oppressive dynamics of imperial colonization, Chandler actually implicates himself deeper than ever in its carefully produced and marketed "semerotic pleasure machine" (Leonard 1998, 72). In other words, he fantasizes escaping into "erotic scenarios" that imperial Britain disseminates en masse (Leonard 1998, 97), scenarios that enslave not only the postcard girls but actually the Irish consumers themselves.

In this respect, Chandler replicates the very power paradigm he would need to subvert if he wanted real freedom. According to Cheng, by re-inscribing cliché fantasies of "masculine rapaciousness" toward his exoticized object of desire (Cheng 1995, 119), Chandler simply occupies a different side in the same old system of binaries without challenging the structure itself. This is a system of binaries that situates the Irish as a victimized/feminized/Orientalized Other vis-à-vis the victimizing/masculine/British Same. Notably in this case, Chandler does not really even switch positions in the binary. After all, the fantasy woman is quite active, with her wide eyes "full . . . of passion and voluptuous longing." Chandler, on the other hand, seems passive as one who is seen and desired, colonized yet again by a foreign force who has, itself, already been colonized by the imperialist photographer's gaze.

While Joyce ostensibly critiques the complex power structure that paralyzes Chandler and other Dubliners in debilitating passivity, he also paradoxically implicates himself in this very net of abusive relationships. Indeed, at one level Joyce objectifies and uses the women he portrays much as do Chandler and the two gallants. Presenting the women in these stories as identity-less pawns of a society that paralyzes them, Joyce uses the women to convey his moral message. Far from entering their thoughts in consistent moments of identificatory alignment, as he does with Lenehan and Chandler, Joyce distances himself from the women characters, whom he portrays from the outside. As the puppeteer of these doll-like figures, Joyce fixes himself in the masterful role of a man who exposes the truth through an object he controls. Joyce thus implicitly establishes a conventional oppositional gender dynamic; he situates himself as the righteous, male observer/subject vis-à-vis a dumb, female observed/object. He is, in this light, just another Dublin man using another Dublin woman. In this light, he inadvertently aligns himself with the very imperialist Author-ities he explicitly critiques.

Toward the end of *Dubliners,* however, Joyce presents a potential alternative to this colonizing, masculine stance. He also portrays a man and woman who begin to claim their own identities as sovereign subjects. Though somewhat warmer toward one another than Chandler and Annie, Gabriel and Gretta Conroy in "The Dead" are also stuck in a dynamic of frosty miscommunication. After a festive party, Gabriel follows his wife, Gretta, to their hotel room. Watching her mount "the stairs behind the porter, her head bowed in the ascent, her frail shoulders curved as with a burden, her skirt girt tightly about her" (D 215), Gabriel feels the urge to fling "his arms about her hips and [hold] her still" (D 215). He only restrains his "wild impulse" by digging his nails "against the palms of his hands" (D 215). Struggling between desire and "diffidence," Gabriel then attempts to open dialogue with Gretta, who distractedly takes off "her hat and cloak" then unhooks "her waist" (D 216). Lust wanes as Gretta tells Gabriel the story of her lost love, Michael Furey. After experiencing the roller coaster of feelings evoked by this story— from "terror," to shyness, to curiosity, and finally to "a strange friendly pity" (D 221–22)—Gabriel watches Gretta sleep: "His eyes moved to the chair over which she had thrown some of her clothes. A petticoat string dangled to the floor. One boot stood upright, its limp upper fallen down: the fellow of it lay upon its side. He wondered at his riot of emotions of an hour before. From what had it proceeded?" (D 222). Having forgotten his initial surge of desire for Gretta, Gabriel finds himself in a post-coital heap of dangling petticoats and limp boots, all of which offer signs of the "riot of emotions" that culminated, not in sexual climax, but in an oddly anticlimactic "friendly pity."

Like Chandler, Gabriel experiences an urge to escape from such an incapacitating state. As he lies "down beside his wife" and hears the snow "falling faintly . . . faintly falling," he notes that "the time had come for him to set out on his journey westward" (D 223). However, unlike Chandler, Gabriel does not seem to want to leave his wife for some abstract embodiment of otherness. Rather, after hearing the story of his wife's past, he sees a certain otherness within her: "he thought of how she who lay beside him had locked in her heart for so many years that image of her lover's eyes when he had told her that he did not wish to live" (D 223). At this, "generous tears [fill] Gabriel's eyes" and he realizes "he [has] never felt like that himself toward any woman" (D 223). Although such a realization compels him to think of going west toward his own adventure, it does not seem to make him want to go there without his wife. Nor does it make him objectify and distance himself from her. On the contrary, Gabriel identifies with his wife intimately, even as he realizes he can neither master nor possess her.

Gabriel sheds light on a shift Joyce himself appears to have experienced at some point between *Dubliners* and *Ulysses*. During this time, Joyce ceases to stereotype women as paper-doll embodiments of his country's sociopolitical impotence. Instead, he lets more complex, self-conscious female characters come to life and people Dublin's cityscape. In the process, he develops women who are not merely hollow objects "reclothed in a form that makes them suitable for exchange among [and/or use by] men" (Irigaray 1985, 171), but full-bodied subjects who *clothe themselves* in a way that expresses their own psychosocial history, desires, aesthetic sensibilities, and performative self-reflexivity. At the same time, he envisions a complex multicultural and Irish identity, such as that of Molly Bloom, the "Spanish/Moorish-Irish product of poly-cultural Gibralter" (Cheng 1995, 174).

How does Joyce get from the gallants' two-dimensional, Irish slavey to more three-dimensional, "poly-cultural" women like Molly Bloom? How, first, does he stop viewing women as soulless objects in an imperialist, masculine monopoly and begin perceiving them as human beings with complex interior narratives and desires? In so doing, how does he not only shift his "center of sexual sympathy" (Brown 1990, 34)[3] but also envision a powerful offensive tactic to colonizing forces in Ireland? Ultimately, in what ways does this political and sexual re-vision manifest itself in Joyce's changing views of authorship and language?

### Giacomo Joyce

Joyce's prose poem *Giacomo Joyce* offers crucial insights into the process by which he reconsiders his relationship to women, language, and authorship. Written just before he published *A Portrait of the Artist as a Young Man* (1914), *Giacomo Joyce* reveals a stunning moment at which Joyce steps inside

---

3. In making this shift, I will here contend, Joyce renounces the Ibsenian moral high ground of an author who critiques his country's social and religious paralysis. He also relinquishes the omnipotent mastery of an artist who forges in the smithy of his soul the uncreated conscience of his race. In this way, he ceases to struggle to define his role as a writer among male masters in a society of men and begins to align himself more fully with the female and male characters in his story. For another interesting reading of Joyce's identificatory evolution, see Jean-Michel Rabaté's *James Joyce* (1993).

the mind and body of a young woman whom he admires. The object of Joyce's admiration is a pupil, most likely Amalia Popper, whom he tutored in Trieste from 1907 to 1908. Wealthy and Jewish/Italian, this student embodies Joyce's sexual, economic, ethnic, and cultural other. As such, she is not easy to know, even from afar. But Joyce performs literary acrobatics to get closer to her. He finds a distinctly nonintrusive way to be in this woman's body by elaborately describing the details of her "boots laced in deft crisscross," "short skirt," "great bows on her slim bronze shoes," "underskirt," "web of stocking," "green-broidered gown," "hem of her rustleback dusty skirt," "hat, red-flowered, and umbrella," and so forth (*GJ* 1–16).

In these descriptions, Joyce situates himself less on the outside, as a man who observes or critiques the girl, and more on the inside, as one who experiences how her clothes feel. For instance, noting "a green fillet upon her hair and about her body a green-broidered gown" (*GJ* 12), Joyce uses prepositions, "upon" and "about," in a way that subtly highlights the relation between the girl's clothes and her body, rather than elaborating the way a male character perceives her clothes. By thus situating himself at the intersection of this girl's clothes and body, Joyce moves very close to the object of his desire.

The girl's shoes get Joyce even closer. In fact, the sound of her shoes temporarily transports the poet to the woman's vantage, letting him walk along "winding turret stairs" in her stead: "High heels clack hollow on the resonant stone stairs. Wintry air in the castle, gibbeted coats of mail, rude iron sconces over the windings of the winding turret stairs. Tapping clacking heels, a high and hollow noise. There is one below would speak with your ladyship" (*GJ* 1). Mobilized by this woman's heels, Joyce's poet here crosses gender lines with remarkable fluidity; hearing the clacking heels above, he seems to be the waiting man below, but, hearing the attendant's message, he seems to be the girl above. Slipping from body to body, he both waits (as the man) and walks (as the woman).

By thus temporarily inhabiting a woman's body, Joyce assumes a mobile site of one who identifies across corporeal limits, seeing and hearing from inside the bodies of both women and men. In the process, Joyce not only expands his identificatory flexibility but also begins to humanize women. He presents a woman who actively engages in her own battles, with her "gibbeted coats of mail" and "iron sconces over the windings of the winding turret stairs." This warrior battles like a man, arming herself with heels and other such vestimentary weapons: "a woman's hat, red-flowered, and umbrella, furled. Her arms: a casque, gules, and blunt spear on a field, sable" (*GJ* 16). These weapons convey a powerful presence but keep it contained under a veneer of dormant decorum. They operate indirectly, making visual and/or acoustic impressions that have lasting, though imperceptible, power.

Notably, Joyce here uses words the way the woman uses clothes: to make acoustic and/or visual impressions. Throughout *Giacomo Joyce,* an ornate network of such impressions draws attention to the linguistic material with which Joyce makes his statements. For example, in the high-heel fragment cited, a screen of alliteration (repeated "h," "s," and "w") and shadowy war images calls attention to itself. Such overworked sounds and images take precedence over the poem's narrative integrity. In fact, the poem's fifty-one stanzas, interrupted by blank spaces of varying lengths, are held together less by a clear thematic or narrative thread than by a loosely woven network of recurrent visual and acoustic effects. It is as if, using language like clothing, Joyce cuts and pastes an ensemble of sounds and images much as the woman cuts and assembles her clothes in coherent outfits. Joyce's language, like "your ladyship" 's dress, thus functions as translucent material brought together in a suggestive combination that speaks at multiple, often subliminal, levels.

Through such acoustic interplay, Joyce introduces a compelling way of activating political change, whether through words or through clothes. It is by embroidering language with new threads—be they sounds, resonances, meanings—that, he suggests, an Irish writer can alter the very fabric of English language. In this way, the writer can take a strong weapon of imperialist Britain—its language—and re-weave it to fit his own, distinct national body. If, as Vicki Mahaffey suggests in *Reauthorizing Joyce,* "clothing is the language of flesh and language is the clothing of thought" (Mahaffey 1998, 19), then Joyce here imagines a way to re-dress thought by reconfiguring the weave of ill-fitting linguistic material.

While Joyce details the interplay between clothing and women's bodies in *Giacomo Joyce,* he appears to arrive at a heightened appreciation of this political imperative not only to re-weave the English language but also to reconsider the fabrics that construct Irish femininity. He does the latter throughout the poem, drawing attention to the various dresses and materials that adorn the women he admires. In this way, Joyce seems to expand his ability to perceive the profound mystery of women who might otherwise be reduced to bland familiarity.

Joyce's narrative perspective on women seems to shift dramatically as a result of this insistent observation; he begins to wonder at the details of each layer of clothing. While helping his domestic partner with her dress, for instance, the narrator of *Giacomo Joyce* revels in a heightened appreciation of its many layers:

> She raises her arms in an effort to hook at the nape of her neck a gown of black veiling. She cannot: no, she cannot. She moves backwards towards me mutely. I raise my arms to help her: her arms fall. I hold the websoft edges of her gown and drawing them out to hook them I see through the opening of the black veil her lithe body sheathed in an orange shift. It slips its ribbons of moorings at her shoulders and falls slowly: a lithe smooth naked body shimmering with silvery scales. It slips slowly over the slender buttocks of smooth polished silver and over their furrows, a tarnished silver shadow. . . . Fingers, cold and calm and moving. . . . A touch, a touch. (*GJ* 7)

By paying attention to the "websoft edges," the "opening of the black veil," the "orange shift," the "ribbons," and the silvery skin itself, the narrator engages in a dynamic interplay with the woman and her clothes. The woman of this scene is both familiar and exotic. She engages in a common activity of hooking a dress and gesturing for help, but at the same time she has the exotic underside of an "orange shift" and "silvery scales." Appearing almost like a surreal snake/fish figure, she complicates reductive molds of Irish femininity.

What is at issue here is the poet/Joyce's ability to perceive with wonder that which might easily be overlooked if one were blinded by preconditioned ideals and views. In other words, it is the poet's mode of active receptivity that lets him see what is exotic in the everyday—without reducing it to old, ready-made parameters. The poet remarks upon such an affirming state of receptive "unreadiness" in the penultimate stanza of *Giacomo Joyce:* "Unreadiness. A bare apartment. Torbid daylight. A long black piano: coffin of music. Poised on its edge a woman's hat, red-flowered, and umbrella, furled. Her arms: a casque, gules, and blunt spear on a field, sable" (16). The war imagery imposed upon the clothing is significant. It tells of a battle that never ceases, one that consists of a complex movement between perceiving what is present in a state of "unreadiness" and appropriating what one sees by imposing one's own metaphors and stories upon it (i.e., the battle metaphor). Active engagement in this movement would appear to enable the poet to appreciate multiple narratives, textures, cloths, and/or perspectives without pigeonholing them according to given ideological, sociopolitical, or linguistic structures. Such appreciation, it seems, enables Joyce to open up linguistic, cultural, and gender constraints.

## Exiles

In *Exiles,* Joyce further challenges such constraints while expanding his views of language, women, and Irish identity. He also identifies with a female figure even more intimately than in *Giacomo Joyce*. He does so by following the free associations of his life-partner, Nora Barnacle. Beginning with the word "blister," he notes her train of thought: "amber—silver—oranges—apples—sugarstick—hair—spongecake—ivy—roses—ribbon" (*E* 168). He then glosses this list:

> The blister reminds her of the burning of her hand as a girl. She sees her own amber hair and her mother's silver hair. This silver is the crown of age but also the stigma of care and grief which she and her lover have laid upon it. This avenue of thought is shunned completely; and the other aspect, amber turned to silver by the years, her mother a prophecy of what she may one day be is hardly glanced at. Oranges, apples, sugarstick—these take the place of the shunned thoughts and are herself as she was, being her girlish joys. Hair: the mind turning again to this without adverting to its colour, adverting only to a distinctive sexual mark and to its growth and mystery. . . . The softly growing symbol of her girlhood. Spongecake; a weak flash again of joyous which now begin to seem more those of a child than those of a girl. Ivy and rose: she gathered ivy often when out in the evening with girls. Roses grew then a sudden scarlet note in the memory which may be a dim suggestion of the roses of the body. The ivy and roses carry on and up, out of the idea of growth, through a creeping vegetable life into ardent perfumed flower life the symbol

of mysteriously growing girlhood, her hair. Ribbon for her hair. Its fitting ornament for the eyes of others and lastly for his eyes. Girlhood becomes virginity and puts on 'the snood that is the sign of maidenhood'. A proud and
shy instinct turns her mind away from the loosening of her bound-up hair—
however sweet or longed for or inevitable—and she embraces that which is
hers alone and not hers and his also—happy distant dancing days, distant,
gone forever, dead, or killed? (*E* 168–69)

Food, articles of clothing, hair, and other "girlish joys" here bring the interior
world of Nora's memories and past sensations into Joyce's field of perception.
"Ribbon," for instance, evokes a series of repressed desires, loves, and losses
that, Joyce sees, are all part of Nora's present identity. By here analyzing
Nora's associations vis-à-vis various objects, Joyce perceives Nora as an evolv-
ing individual with a rich interiority. He also situates himself in her body and
mind, noting her responses as if he were experiencing them: "a weak flash
again of joys," "a sudden scarlet note in the memory," "a proud and shy instinct [that] turns her mind away."

Simultaneously inhabiting Nora's body/mind and examining Nora's
stream of associations, Joyce occupies an in-between site of a male-identified
analyst and a female-identified analysand. From this site, he comes not only to
know Nora more intimately, but also to see a rich new potential for language.
Words, like Nora's ribbon, interface a linguistic exteriority and a less accessible, psychic interiority. Ribbon, amber, and other fragments, for instance,
trigger memories for this woman. These memories provoke a plenitude of
emotions but do not come together in a clear, coherent narrative until Joyce
assembles the fragments according to some linear logic. Words function like
symptoms, in this respect; they call forth a loosely woven network of repressed
desires and sensations.[4] In so doing, they actually disrupt narrative movement
by taking the text into itself, or onto a fluid level of endless internal associations, as is the case with *Finnegans Wake*. This view of words is central to

4. In his seminar on Joyce, *"Joyce le symptome," Joyce avec Lacan* (1987), Jacques Lacan
bridges the apparent distance between the Real, Imaginary, and Symbolic registers via what he
calls the symptom. The symptom, according to Lacan, becomes a crucial link in the barromean
knot of *Finnegans Wake*.

Joyce's most celebrated stylistic play in *Ulysses* and *Finnegans Wake*. Marking a radical departure from conventional narrative uses of language, it reveals an important way in which Joyce begins to reconfigure old forms and patterns of thought so as to "forge in the smithy of [his] soul the uncreated conscience of [his] race" (*P* 253).

# 5

# The Sense of Place in Joyce and Heaney

CHRISTOPHER MALONE

W hile critics more readily trace his influences back through Montague, Kavanagh, and Yeats, Seamus Heaney has also persistently reckoned with the legacy of James Joyce, a figure who has challenged a generation of contemporary Irish poets to avoid easy solutions when posing questions about Irish identity and national community.[1] No other contemporary Irish poet has more openly embraced Stephen Dedalus's imperative that the artist "forge in the smithy of his soul the uncreated conscience of his race." At the same time no other has more acutely expressed his reservations about this sort of pronouncement, or conveyed more sharply Joycean irony over the kind of arrogance Stephen displays; reticence and caution inflect Heaney's poetic voice in ways that repeatedly compromise the authority required to act as spokesperson that Stephen tacitly assumes. Certainly Heaney has been capable of Stephen's optimism, if not arrogance, when making claims for poetry's purpose. Writing as cultural critic early in his career, Heaney argues earnestly for understanding poetry "as divination" and "poetry as revelation of the self to the self, as restoration of the culture to itself; poems as elements of continuity, with the aura and authenticity of archaeological finds, where the buried

---

1. Certainly others have embraced Joyce's example even in the generation succeeding him, such as Patrick Kavanagh and Louis MacNeice. See Dillon Johnston's study, *Irish Poetry After Joyce* (1997).

shard has an importance that is not diminished by the importance of the buried city; poetry as a dig for finds that end up being plants" ("Feeling into Words" 1980, 41). The extent to which Heaney's recent criticism and poetry would call into question this intuitive vocabulary both atavistic and romantically nationalist in implication—in the metaphor of the land, or the promise of a culture "restored"—comments on the continuing impact Joyce might be said to have on Heaney.[2]

Nowhere is Joyce's influence more evident than in Heaney's "Station Island" (1984), a portion of which was first published separately as a commemorative poem for the James Joyce centenary. Joyce's ghost, blinded, "his voice eddying with the sound of all rivers," confronts Heaney's disbelieving penitent just after he has made his way halfheartedly through the stations of the cross at St. Patrick's Purgatory, Lough Derg.[3] This encounter serves as an occasion to reflect on the poet's relation to place, cultural identity, and the tension-filled relationship Heaney maintains with his Catholic heritage. Like Yeats's ghost to whom Eliot must answer in "Little Gidding," Joyce helps Heaney understand the proper function of poetry and the nature of the poet's responsibility to place—a lingering preoccupation for Heaney and a Northern Irish poetics more generally that his verse has come to represent.

Heaney's Joyce steps out of the world of modernism and into postmodernism, where he has something to say about the fraught relation between art and history. For the contemporary Northern Irish poet, it is a question of poetry's potential to address social crisis, particularly over Ireland's border in the North. For a generation of recent Irish cultural critics addressing this issue, Joyce's sense of place has proven much more satisfactory than that of Yeats. As Terence Brown summarizes a recent turn in this critical debate, Joyce typifies how "Irish identity can be reformulated not in nationalistic fashion but in European and indeed universal modes, which can liberate from myth conceived of in absolute terms, and from provincial stereotyping"

2. Reviewers of Heaney's *The Spirit Level* have commented on his "walking on air," which is different from his early poetry seeking identification with the land. See David Lloyd's discussion of the trope of the land in Heaney's verse, in *Anomalous States: Irish Writing and the Post-Colonial Moment* (1993).

3. See Michael Dames's discussion of Lough Derg in *Mythic Ireland* (1992), 22–42.

(Brown 1996, 286). The extent to which this contrast remains true is arguable, now that recent studies have given us the postmodern Yeats to go with the poststructuralist Joyce.[4] But Joyce helps Heaney formulate an important problematic along the lines that Brown suggests. Dillon Johnston has argued that Heaney's artistic development through "Station Island" reflects that of Stephen Dedalus in moving "from the lyrical toward the epical and the dramatic," culminating in the "dispersal of narrative authority among various speakers" (Brown 1996, 166).[5] One might add that Joyce's influence at the level of voice also applies to other Northern Irish poets such as Paul Muldoon and Ciaran Carson. This essay will extend the comparison between Joyce and Heaney to shed light on the dialogue that one contemporary poet has constructed with his modernist predecessors. The poem "Station Island" raises concerns that are reflected in the example of Stephen Dedalus's life, his development as an artist, and by extension Joyce's own concerns about language, the artist's exiled relation to place, and the creative act in modernism—an act that Heaney revises to respond to the demands and contingencies of postmodernism as they bear on questions of national identity.

One recurrent figure that both Joyce and Heaney used to dramatize their conception of place is that of Hamlet. In *North* (1975) Heaney evokes the comparison to comment on his sense of helplessness in the face of social as well as personal crisis:

> I am Hamlet the Dane,
> skull-handler, parablist,
> smeller of rot
> in the state, infused
> with its poisons,
> pinioned by ghosts

4. See Seamus Deane's discussion in *Nationalism, Colonialism, Literature* (1990) of the dangers of reading modernism through the lens of poststructuralism. For an example of postmodern treatments of Yeats, see *Yeats and Postmodernism* (1991) and in particular Leonard Orr's introduction, "Yeats and Poststructuralist Criticism."

5. Johnston's version of Heaney's development, as well as that of others (like Michael Molino), implies that Heaney eventually abandons lyrical properties, a suggestion which discounts the way he also undermines the autonomy of voice within the tradition of lyric poetry.

and affections,
murders and pieties
coming to consciousness
by jumping in graves
dithering, blathering.

With no clear poetic vision or sense of purpose, the poet may only reflect hap-
lessly on the events of the past. In Yeatsian fashion Heaney struggles with the
ineffectual nature of poetic pronouncement: he may only record the actions of
history, helpless to intervene, unable to embrace popular opinion because of a
reflective, critical self-consciousness. In *Ulysses* Stephen similarly casts himself
in the role of Hamlet—an identification he displaces into his famous theory
about the play—to convey his feelings of dislocatedness and exile, having rejected the call of his mother's religion and his father's nationalism. Memories
of his mother's ghostly visitations in dreams haunt him on the Martello
Tower, and Buck Mulligan's ribbing does not help matters. In fact Mulligan
typifies all that Stephen has reacted against, as suggested in their conversation
with Haines, who has plans to assemble a collection of Irish "sayings" (which
Stephen, like Oscar Wilde, is full of):

> Buck Mulligan kicked Stephen's foot under the table and said with warmth
> of tone:
> —Wait till you hear him on Hamlet, Haines.
> —Well, I mean it, Haines said, still speaking to Stephen. I was just think-
> ing of it when that poor old creature came in.
> —Would I make any money by it? Stephen asked.
> Haines laughed and, as he took his soft grey hat from the holdfast of the
> hammock, said:
> —I don't know, I'm sure.
> He strolled out to the doorway. Buck Mulligan bent across to Stephen
> and said with coarse vigour:
> —You put your hoof in it now. What did you say that for?
> —Well? Stephen said. The problem is to get money. From whom? From
> the milkwoman or from him. It's a toss up, I think. . . . I see little hope . : .
> from her or from him. ( *U* 1.14)

If Mulligan recognizes the opportunity for acclaim or connection in Haines, Stephen holds to a higher purpose, one that nonetheless forces him to admit his need for people like Haines. It is a tension that haunts him throughout the novel; he is caught between the desire to remove himself from history as it unfolds, as Hamlet does through endless contemplation, and the unavoidable needs that come with living in the world.

Hamlet's questioning intellect is integral to Stephen's creed, insofar as he still adheres to the artistic commitment announced in *Portrait* that he will "no longer serve" that in which he no longer believes: "whether it call itself my home, my fatherland or my church" (*P* 247). Once upon a time he might have taken seriously the advice of his father, who admonished him to "raise up [Ireland's] fallen language and tradition," to breath new life into "his father's fallen state by his labours." Stephen chooses instead to "halt irresolutely in the pursuit of phantoms" (*P* 84). At the same time he admits the inescapable impact of circumstance, growing up in Ireland his father's son, as he tells Michael Davin, "This race and this country and this life produced me. . . . I shall express myself as I am" (*P* 203). It is a connection the artist necessarily struggles with—his ties to place or location in culture—and one he invariably expresses, just as Stephen records in a journal before he leaves his "struggle all through the night" (*P* 252) with the dream of an old man who embodies the romantic "west of Ireland." Stephen may "mean him no harm," but Stephen's struggle represents a healthy distrust all the same, an attempt to distance himself from political and national ties. Artistic expression to Stephen's mind always risks sterility in such allegiance; it must always remain capable of re-evaluating and reconstructing allegiance to the world just as the artist "encounter[s] for the millionth time the reality of experience."

But guilt consumes Stephen all the same, nowhere more strongly than in the Circe episode of *Ulysses*. When the ghost of his mother appears and prays to the "Divine Sacred Heart" to "Save him from hell" (*U* 15.475), Stephen's resolve stiffens all the more to pursue the "intellectual imagination" without compromise. He raises his ashplant in defiance and bursts asunder "Time's livid final flame" (*U* 15.475), and at that moment Stephen's unconscious takes material form and surges with images that embody various threats posed to his artistic integrity: the likes of Kevin Egan, the Citizen, and the Croppy

Boy—figures who signify allegiance to Ireland appropriately at the very moment when Stephen is accosted by two English soldiers. In defiance he taps his brow and announces to Bloom that he is the one who "in here . . . must kill the priest and the king." Even old Gummy Granny, "the deathflower of the potato blight on her breast" (*U* 15.485), appears as mother Ireland herself, admonishing Stephen to "remove" the two soldiers and he "will be in heaven and Ireland will be free." And in that moment of recognition Stephen associates his condition with Hamlet's own moment of truth:

> "Aha! I know you, gammer! Hamlet, revenge!":
>
> OLD GUMMY GRANNY
>
> (*rocking to and fro*) Ireland's sweetheart, the king of Spain's daughter, alanna. Strangers in my house, bad manners to them! (*she keens with banshee woe*) Ochone! Ochone! Silk of the kine! (*she wails*) You met with poor old Ireland and how does she stand?
>
> STEPHEN
>
> How do I stand you? (*U* 15.486)

Joyce's Gummy Granny is an image of Kathleen Ni Houlihan turned on her head; Yeats's portrayal of her in the play by that name is echoed, in particular in the line "Strangers in my house." Stephen is prompted to act, but only to counter her call, and he finds himself inadvertently sharing a side with Private Carr, who will not abide a word against his "fucking king." But she is "the sow that eats her farrow," that image of Ireland as self-destructive, stifling any creative impulse; nationalist concerns such as those she embodies fail to produce anything consequential, being caught up in disabling contradictions, just as those forces in Stephen's mind take shape and rage against one another.

Prompted by these conflicting impulses, Stephen in *Ulysses* contemplates his place in the world; like Hamlet he wonders about the nature of existence and examines human reason and apprehension. At one point, having drank too much and among the company of prostitutes, Stephen boldly affirms man's potential—as Hamlet begins to do in the "What is man?" soliloquy— proclaiming himself a "most finished artist." Having pondered the "reduplication of personality" figured in musical patterns and octaves, Stephen imagines through this image of formal perfection the possibility for escape from the cycle of regeneration that binds him to the world and to the past: "What went forth to the ends of the world to traverse not itself, God, the sun, Shakespeare, a commercial traveller, having itself traversed in reality itself becomes that self. Wait a moment. Wait a moment. Wait a second. Damn that fellow's noise in the street. Self which it itself was ineluctably preconditioned to become. *Ecco!*" (*U* 15.412). In a passage that anticipates the intrusions experienced by Nabokov's insane literary biographer in the preface to *Pale Fire,* Joyce suggests that such aesthetic resolutions to real, material dilemmas are not so easily lived up to. Just when Stephen takes pains to complete his theory of consubstantiality, Philip Drunk and Philip Sober appear to mirror his unconscious, to remind him that his lofty philosophical considerations do not amount to much when there is no one to buy the next round. This prosaic pair locates Stephen firmly in the world, a "foul and pestilent congregations of vapors" and stinking drunk.

Like Hamlet, Stephen struggles unsuccessfully to come to terms with the past. The father's admonition, like that of his mother, goes ignored but not forgotten by the son; and this disturbance of memory troubles the symbolic union of Bloom and Stephen, which purports to set forth a new myth and seemingly transforms religion to art. Joyce reminds us through his irony that it may not be so simple. Similar admonitions inform Heaney's relation to place and also find expression through ghostly visitations. The parade of ghosts that troubles Heaney's mind in "Station Island" echoes Hamlet's predicament by evoking feelings of disinheritance; for Heaney and Joyce, this disinheritance is cultural as well as familial. But Joyce and Heaney give different emphases to this condition of disinheritance. While Stephen pretends to reject from the outset any claims on him by his heritage, Heaney's penitent may second-guess his motivation for making the pilgrimage, but he has committed himself all the same to reconcile himself with the past. It is a critical difference insofar as Heaney is obliged to work from the inside instead of representing himself as exiled, removed from time and place in good modernist fashion.[6] In one sense the fact that Heaney situates himself in relation to tradition calls attention to the impossibility of escaping social and historical

6. The extent to which one finds that Joyce's irony undermines this enabling sense of exile draws him in under the rubric of postmodernism.

context and the forces hopelessly shaping poetic insight. But his location inside also makes possible Heaney's commitment to the "local":

> Once again, I hope I am not being sentimental or simply fetishizing—as we have learnt to say—the local. I wish instead to suggest that images and stories [emerging out of local traditions] do function as bearers of value. The century has witnessed the defeat of Nazism by force of arms; but the erosion of the Soviet regimes was caused by, among other things, the sheer persistence, beneath the imposed ideological conformity, of cultural values and psychic resistances of the kind that these stories and images enshrine. Even if we have learned to be rightly and deeply fearful of elevating the cultural forms and conservatisms of any nation into normative and exclusivist systems, even if we have terrible proof that pride in the ethnic and religious heritage can quickly degrade into the fascistic, our vigilance on that score should not displace our love and trust in the good of the indigenous, per se. ("Crediting Poetry" 1995, 31–32)

Heaney is concerned to give voice to and examine the value of cultural traditions, to excavate their origins, to determine their worth in the present. In this sense the pilgrimage through Station Island both embraces and disavows tradition at the same time.

On the one hand, Heaney's pilgrimage serves to question the conventionalized understanding of religious faith and, by extension, the mythological trappings of a nationalist tradition associated with it. Those mythologies no longer enable him to see more deeply into the order of things; instead he must understand the world without reference to any preconceived order. On the other hand, it is Heaney's "backwards look" that affords this insight as he records his encounters with those who live local tradition, whose identities are shaped by that context, and whose honest lives deny abstraction and require the poet's attention to difference. Childhood memories come to life before him, first in the guise of that old "Sabbath breaker, Simon Sweeney," who tells him to "Stay clear of all processions!" just when Heaney's penitent is caught up and carried off by a group of shawled, praying women.

> "I know you, Simon Sweeney . . ."
> "Damn all you know," he said,

his eye still on the hedge
and not turning his head.
"I was your mystery man
and am again this morning.
Through gaps in the bushes,
your First Communion face
would watch me cutting timber.
When cut or broken limbs
of trees went yellow, when
woodsmoke sharpened air
or ditches rustled
you sensed my trail there
as if it had been sprayed.
It left you half afraid."
    (Heaney 1990, 224)

The allusion to Sweeney, an Irish mythic figure for the displaced artist who has broken all cultural and religious ties to home, conveys a sense of secular communion that overlays the holy one—what the old man directs the speaker through as a child in a moment of eye contact. Unlike that of the church, Sweeney's sacrament is grounded entirely in the speaker's earthly awareness—so much so that it is translated into the sense of smell.

This earthly awareness, which relies on the senses as opposed to spiritual direction, is also promoted by the ghost of William Carleton, who is for Heaney a figure paradigmatic of someone who broke with cultural heritage and challenged the hypocrisy of Catholic tradition. In fact Carleton's story "The Lough Derg Pilgrim" is a model for the "Station Island" sequence, and the tension in Carleton's narrator, who is half peasant, half scholar, is captured in Heaney's voice. Carleton reminds the speaker of the artistic importance of holding others accountable regardless of any ties to home or cultural allegiance the poet and audience may share:

It is a road you travel on your own.
I who learned to read in the reek of flax
    and smelled hanged bodies rotting on their gibbets
    and saw their looped slime gleaming from the sacks—

> hard-mouthed Ribbonmen and Orange bigots
> made me into the old fork-tongued turncoat
> who mucked the byre of their politics.
> If times were hard, I could be hard too.
> I made the traitor in me sink the knife.
> And maybe there's a lesson there for you.
>           (Heaney 1990, 227)

But Heaney's speaker is reluctant to accept the advice: "The angry role was never my vocation." Rather, it was the "Obedient strains" of the "last marching bands of Ribbonmen / On Patrick's Day" playing "their Hymn to Mary" that "tuned" him first, "not the harp of unforgiving iron the Fenians strung." Carleton's ghost suggests that the questioning eye of the poet is capable of providing a glimpse beyond ourselves, allowing us to sense that other "life that cleans our element" (1990, 228).

At the same time, the speaker charges Heaney with the task of preserving tradition, providing a record of what goes on: "you have to try to make sense of what comes. / Remember everything and keep your head." But to record this world, in the eyes of those victims of sectarian violence that the penitent also confronts, means taking a side. When the speaker is confronted by the ghostly vision of their ravaged bodies, the distance between Heaney and his speaker collapses. It is the poet who seeks forgiveness directly, as Heaney seemingly reflects back on critical reaction throughout his career that indicts him for not taking a stand.[7] Most visibly out from behind the mask of his speaker's persona, Heaney reflects on the danger he faces confusing "evasion and artistic tact." In his words to one victim he confronts, " 'Forgive the way I have lived indifferent— / forgive my timid circumspect involvement' " (1990, 237). But this guilt never compromises Heaney's tensional relation to place, which requires an awareness of how the space of home is "utterly empty, / utterly a source, like the idea of sound." That space is utterly empty insofar as it is always written over by multiple perspectives and histories; but it is also a source in the sense of being an unavoidable shaping force on poetic imaginings, one that requires his attention. Like the "king of the ditchbacks,"

---

7. Seamus Deane and others have raised this concern.

the poet's role requires that he "live in his feet / and ears, weather-eyed, / all pad and listening, / a denless mover." In this Stephen Dedalus-like figure, Heaney suggests an attitude toward language that recognizes and vigilantly interrogates its shaping effects on identity.[8]

When Heaney reminisces in the poem about his childhood, it is the memory of words *as such* that often evokes his reverie, like "the dream words *I renounce*" or the strangeness of "robbing the nest / of the word *wreath*." The young Stephen also revels in the "queerness" of words, often testing the reality of experience against its adequate expression in language. Remembering lines from his spelling book in *Portrait*—"Wolsey died in Leicester Abbey / Where the abbots buried him" (*P* 10)—Stephen's evaluation of them as poetry takes precedence over their function as referential language or mnemonic device designed to reinforce grammatical rules. Instead Stephen constructs the world according to the rules of his imagination, where even green roses might grow.

But the world of language gives rise to a romanticism in Stephen that he soon learns to distrust. If his vision of the world early on is colored by *The Count of Monte Cristo,* he eventually comes to question this tendency to idealize experience through abstractions like love or nation. After his deflating performance in the play, which makes him conscious of his tendency towards self-dramatization, Stephen painfully senses the difference between his romanticized self-perception and the squalor of his surroundings. This realization is brought home profoundly when he chases after E. C. after the play is over; like the boy in "Araby," Stephen recognizes himself as a "creature driven and derided by vanity." Only this time Joyce denies his subject in *Portrait* even the consolation of melancholy in cadence and tone. The language of epiphany now evokes no more than the stench of horse piss burning Stephen's eyes. The language of romance merely evokes dreams of a world beyond the squalor of experience. It locates him firmly in the world, just as the "foetus" scrawled on his father's old desk in school reminds him with horror that he is locked into the cycle of generations, that the misery of his father's life will someday be his. Like Simon, like Stephen.

Similarly, Heaney's poetry evokes both the materiality of language—

8. From "King of the Ditchbacks" (Heaney 1990, 221).

often in terms of its historical and social sedimentation—and the desire to escape the limits it imposes on consciousness. In Wallace Stevens's phrase, the language of poetry for Heaney should push back against the pressures of reality.[9] This preoccupation with language—in poems such as "Anahorish"—enables a postcolonial critique for some readers who make much of the poet's attempt to reclaim place names altered through a history of colonization as their etymologies are traced back to recover buried origins. But his archeological searches give rise to a paradox—one that makes possible a deconstructive reading of his poetry—in the way that voice seems grounded in Heaney's poetry and groundless at the same time, a paradox most visibly explored in Heaney's "bog" poems.

In *Portrait* this appreciation of language finds expression when Stephen encounters the seabird girl. Even though Stephen thinks his epiphany transcends language, Joyce's "Uncle Charles" principle suggests that the passage reveling in the girl's sensuality depends on language to make of her a symbol of artistic freedom, to change her from a girl to a "strange and beautiful seabird." Just after he escape the hangman's noose of the priesthood, Stephen experiences and celebrates a revelation of "mortal beauty": "Her image had passed into his soul for ever and no word had broken the holy silence of his ecstasy. Her eyes had called him and his soul had leaped at the call. To live, to err, to fall, to triumph, to recreate life out of life! A wild angel had appeared to him, the angel of mortal youth and beauty, an envoy from the fair courts of life, to throw open before him in an instant of ecstasy the gates of all the ways of error and glory. On and on and on and on!" (*P* 172). If Stephen fails to break from the controlling frame of Christianity in his conception of the artist, having recourse only to language imbibed with Christian reference—as suggested in this passage, or in the vilanelle he writes later—Joyce's vision of the artist and his understanding of language at least imagines the space for that freedom. Only by understanding the relationship between the two, between the creative force of language and its material ties to a shaping historical and social context, can the artist maintain any faith in the possibility of artistic expression.

9. See Heaney's "From the Frontier of Writing" in his recent collection of essays, *The Redress of Poetry* (1995).

In his recent collection *The Spirit Level,* Heaney embodies this under-standing of language in the figure of St. Kevin, whose ghost very well might have been one of those Heaney encountered in his pilgrimage to Station Is-land. There Heaney evokes the shaping force of history, in his focus on the body of the saint, while at the same time suggesting the force of language to resist that contextualized body. Through his prayer and meditation, the saint keeps him still enough to allow birds to make of his shoulders and arms a perch that he is reluctant to disturb. Through experience grounded in the local, subjective perception of time and space is altered; the world has assumed different coordinates as the saint's body in prayer is transformed and merges with the world around him. While the poet self-consciously frames that prayer as part of an oral tradition that is reliable—as in the opening line, "And then there was St. Kevin and the blackbird"—that trustworthiness grounded in place reflects only the poet's desire; myth gives way to a "prayer his body makes entirely / For he has forgotten self, forgotten bird / And on the river-bank forgotten the river's name"—a prayer that embodies the poet's desire to be removed from an awareness of time and space (1990, 20–21).

Yet this self-forgetting bears the trace of desire, that which marks the body's location in the world. If the distinction between subject and object breaks down, freeing subjectivity from the limits imposed on consciousness, it is this desire that relocates the subject in history. At one level, this works to shut down access to the world by calling attention to the interests that mark desire beyond conscious reflection. But the poet also seeks to identify his po-sition in relational terms, as negotiating those interests he values with those that potentially escape the full light of consciousness. The poet's interest lies in an engagement with community such that the blurring of subject and ob-ject is not one that he may claim ahead of time. Heaney reads the world as shaping his experience of self rather than the reverse. Living this awareness at the level of community, for Heaney, depends on moving beyond the feeling of resentment to imagine a space traversed by different interests. But this plural-ism is negotiated—in order always to *read* and contextualize difference rather than make a fetish of it—negotiated and read against an historical context, that which situates the national subject and demands to be read.

This making a fetish of difference, as Seamus Deane suggests, reflects the revisionist tendency to celebrate the multiplicity of claims to Ireland's past while eliding the specific effects of its history as a record of colonial dispossession and occlusion of voices:

> Revisionism defends itself against those who describe it as simply another orthodoxy, created in accord with the political circumstances of the moment, by claiming to have revealed such a degree of complexity in Irish and Anglo-Irish affairs that no systematic explanation is possible. It has effectively localized interpretation, confining it within groups, interests, classes, and periods; any attempt to see these issues as variations on a ghostly paradigm, like colonialism, is characterized as "idological" and, on that account, is doomed. Ultimately, there may have been no such thing as colonialism. It is, according to many historians, one of the phantoms created by nationalism, which is itself phantasmal enough. (Deane 1990, 7)

On the one hand, it is politically enabling for Deane that there is no longer any overarching Name in Rieland (colonialist or nationalist)—no ultimate metaphysical claim to unify identity. But this condition of namelessness leaves itself open to appropriation by those in power, leading to a society that can only perpetuate the effects of imperialism, of which Ireland's history (and present problem) of sectarian division is the most visible.

It is on this point, which reflects more generally the tension between cultural nationalism and postmodern theories of history, that the ghost of Joyce in "Station Island" responds most directly to the poet. When Stephen contemplates the reality "underneath" appearance, walking down Sandymount Strand with his eyes shut, his attempt to read the "signatures of all things" struggles to affirm the order of the world underneath "the ineluctable modality of the visible" (*U* 3.31), and he commits himself to a *lex eterna* in which the consubstantiality of the father/son relationship exists beyond the mere physical act of coition. But like Shem the Penman's corporeal artistic expression in *Finnegans Wake,* at the end of the chapter Stephen is left to contemplate the world as having reality only as an extension of his own being, his body in particular—the world that appears while urinating, which mirrors the "fourworded wavespeech," "flows purling, widely flowing, floating foampool, flower unfurling" (*U* 3.41). This moment marks a tension that Heaney feels as well, the tension between Stephen's earlier desire to transcend the material limitations of his body (recognizing the divine order underlying experience) and the desire to create the world anew in the poetic act.

At the end of "Station Island," as Heaney's penitent concludes his pilgrimage, Joyce's ghost offers advice to the poet to help resolve Stephen's conflicting aesthetic attitudes. He tells him:

> The way to cement
> community is the dolphin's way: swim
> out on your own and fill the element
> with signatures on your own frequency, echo-soundings, searches, probes,
>     allurements,
> elver-gleams in the dark of the whole sea.
>     (Heaney 1990, 245)

Joyce's advice reflects the need to understand the world without reference to any preconceived order, exactly that which Heaney struggles with as a sense of obligation to tribe or cultural tradition. The dialogue that Heaney imagines with Joyce allows him to transform the nationalist, mythic grounding of place; instead of seeking its pre-given coordinates, Heaney's backwards look now attempts to maintain the fictional status of home. The distinction between "myth" and "fiction" is one that Terry Eagleton develops to apply to nationalist discourse, borrowing from Frank Kermode's definition of the terms. On the one hand, myths have "mistaken their symbolic worlds for literal ones and so come to naturalize their own status" (Eagleton 1991, 191). On the other hand, fiction is a "symbolic construct ironically aware of its own fictionality: The dividing line between the two is notably blurred, since fictions have a tendency to degenerate into myths. . . . To place one's credence in [a] slogan as rhetorically valid is to perform a fictional act, whereat to take it literally is to fall victim to a myth" (Eagleton 1991, 192). Heaney's Joyce embodies this shift from myth to fiction in conceptions of place and national identity.

Heaney's conception of home attempts to engage tradition as fiction, to question the authority of the past as being capable of ordering the present. This often occurs through the image of the father, a trope loaded with cultural implications. In an early poem "Digging," Heaney expresses a desire to follow after his father through the craft of poetry, to "dig with it" in a way similar to his father's working the earth. But now he asserts a more ambiguous relation to the father, as in the moving short poem, "The Strand."

> The dotted line my father's ashplant made
> On Sandymount Strand
> Is something else the tide won't wash away.
>> (Heaney 1996, 62)

The figure of Stephen Dedalus is evoked here as it is in "Station Island," but his legacy is given different emphasis than that expressed in the early advice to go off "the dolphin's way," alone and free from cultural ties. What the poet claims as certain and permanent amounts to an assertion he may only manage ironically in the image of a "dotted line" in the sand. The imagistic quality of this memory, claimed against time and the tide and evoking an immediacy of experience, is belied by the syntactical dependence on the poet's assertion that the past is true. Unlike imagism in a modernist poetics, which would avoid any syntactical dependence on the utterance or sense of the speaker limited in time and space *performing* speech, in this instance the poet's act of asserting the past as permanent calls attention to itself as poetic construction. This ironic awareness of the past is never celebrated in Heaney's poetry as an end in itself. Rather, Heaney's irony works to engage and rewrite the past through the frame of the present, a view of the past newly contextualized and sensitive to the different interests shaping community. In this sense, Heaney holds on to the trope of the father to rework its significance.

Remaining both outside and inside tradition, the Joycean artist for Heaney must confront what it means to maintain artistic authority in order to address community. For a critic like Linda Hutcheon, this doubled position only thinly disguises the author's belief in his autonomous ability to shape social forces rather than be shaped by them. But Hutcheon's definition of parody as an attribute of postmodernism should certainly extend to Joyce as well (1989). Joycean parody complicates the possibility that a position of authority exists; for that position, to borrow Hutcheon's terms, is always shown to be complicit with the world it sets itself above to comment on, as seen in the figure of Stephen Dedalus. If Joyce's use of parody works to undermine the mythological forces driving the Citizen's nationalism, for Heaney it also speaks to the desire to imagine the nation differently. This parodic aspect of Joyce's work influences other contemporary Irish poets such as Paul Muldoon, who finds in Joyce's example the techniques to vacate completely the space of subjectivity, to show the subject hopelessly dislocated in relation to place. Whatever mythic significance the Wakean thunderwords may have, for instance, in Muldoon's *The Annals of Chile* (1994) they are made the product of a desperate memory belonging to a frustrated persona so unsure of himself that he stutters when conveying details of a lover. History elides memory and encloses the subject in ways from which he can "no more deviate . . . than the map of Europe / can be redrawn" (1994, 109).

If Muldoon's poetry turns inward in order to emphasize the subject in history or the hopelessly private nature of reference in language—to demystify the romance of communal ties to home—Heaney turns inward in order to turn outward again. In "Station Island," Stephen Dedalus figures this more convincingly for Heaney than *Ulysses*'s other likely candidate, who might have conveyed this tension equally well. Leopold Bloom's proximity to the sights and sounds and smells of the body certainly contrasts with Stephen's more lofty desire to transcend the modality of the visible. One could argue that Bloom is just as invested in coming to terms with his past, with finding a place in Dublin that depends on different categories of understanding than those the Citizen holds where Bloom is concerned. But given Bloom's relation to language, which follows from his physicality, figured so often in terms of misrecognition or misinterpretation, Heaney must turn to someone who has just as much faith in artistic expression, however naïve or misguided. In any case it is hard to imagine Heaney and Bloom having much to talk about.

Joyce's modernist legacy is certainly different from that which Yeats leaves behind, and Heaney's poetry may be understood as caught between the two. For T. S. Eliot the "familiar compound ghost" of Yeats ironically comments on the promise of poetry, which involves only "the rending pain of re-enactment / of all that you have done, and been; the shame / of motives late revealed, and the awareness / of things ill done and done to others' harm / Which once you took for exercise of virtue" (1970, 142). Still, the frustrated purpose remains to "purify the dialect of the tribe," as both Heaney and Eliot interpret Yeats's legacy. But this restoration may no longer come with Eliot's "refining fire / Where you must move in measure, like a dancer." Heaney's Joyce does not promise this purifying transformation. Rather, like Joyce's Stephen, the poet only affirms the possibility of turning inward in order to turn outward again. It is Stephen's desire to transcend place, his tensional awareness of his locatedness in the world, and the faith this inspires in poetic language, that Heaney's poetry conveys.

# PART 2

## Dear Dirty Dublin

# 6

# Dublin Boy and Man in "The Sisters"

STANLEY SULTAN

I believe an important reason why the story with which James Joyce began *Dubliners* belongs in its initial place is the general declaration it makes about Dublin, through both its unnamed boy's experience and the narrative about that experience by the man the boy became. Joyce's judgment on his native city in "The Sisters" can be elicited by tracing what he did with the two memorable details he placed, one in each of its first two full paragraphs of exposition: the set of three italicized words in the story's first paragraph and, in the paragraph after the boy learns that Father James Flynn is dead, the memorable dream the boy has of the priest's disembodied smiling face confessing to him and his own responsive smile.

The three italicized words "had always sounded strangely in my ears," the man reports for him. That adverb "strangely" is not slovenly English, but describes his auditory experience when the man was the boy and signifies his actual young ears' hearing of the sounding of those three words; both memorable details indicate that things experienced by a Dublin boy constitute the essence of "The Sisters." My procedure will be to first trace out what Joyce did with the other detail, then discuss the three italicized words.

The pair of smiles the boy dreams inaugurates a pattern in the story, a series of four linked elements he experiences: the first dreamed, the next he recollects, the third he sees, the last he hears. And the difference between the order in which he experiences the four elements of the pattern and their historical chronology—the order in which they actually occurred—is significant for the story. Finally, one element of the series of four linked experiences inaugurated by the dreamed pair of smiles is central to the boy's experience of each of the four specific components of the armature of Joyce's story. In sequence: his ambivalent attitude toward Flynn, his remembrance of Flynn as his religious teacher, Flynn's corpse, and how other adults regard Flynn.

## I

The pattern begun by the dreamed pair of smiles and the set of italicized words are two important changes Joyce made when in 1906 he transformed the mediocre first story of the original 1905 *Dubliners* into a miniature masterpiece. A third important change related to both of the important elements was his turning a datum of the early version into an open question. I mean the fact, asserted by "old" Cotter and confirmed by Flynn's sister Eliza, that Flynn "was always a little queer," in her words, "even when we were all growing up together." He changed it in 1906 into imputations by Cotter and Eliza that late in life the priest *became* demented. Joyce took pains to change a datum of the original story into characters' opinions because nothing in his eventual portrayal of Flynn establishes that Flynn is other than completely sane.[1]

In the second component of the armature, the boy recollects his experiences of Flynn as his teacher. It is no ordinary parish priest, but this sane and learned old product of the Irish College at the Vatican who asked him disturbingly finical moral questions, went on to characterize to him as Flynn did the library of Catholic scholasticism that addresses such questions, then smiled the first of a second pair of smiles—both accompanied by nodding and both Flynn's. The details of the familiar passage are important enough to quote. "Sometimes he had amused himself by putting difficult questions to

---

1. For comparison, see the 1905 and 1906 holographs transcribed on facing pages in *Dubliners*, G124–57. (Subsequent changes to the latter were slight; see G165–74.) In her long study of changes beginning with the *Irish Homestead* text of 1904, "Joyce's 'The Sisters': A Development" (1973), Florence Walzl observes that "Joyce eliminated from the late versions of 'The Sisters' virtually all material dealing with Father Flynn as a mental case" (392 93).

me. . . . His questions showed me how complex and mysterious were certain institutions of the Church (*D* 13).

A long sentence and another follow:

> The duties of the priest towards the Eucharist and towards the secrecy of the confessional seemed so grave to me that I wondered how anybody had ever found in himself the courage to undertake them; and I was not surprised when he told me that the fathers of the Church had written books as thick as the *Post Office Directory* and as closely printed as the law notices in the newspaper, elucidating all these intricate questions. Often when I thought of this I could make no answer or only a very foolish and halting one upon which he used to smile and nod his head twice or thrice. (*D* 13)

If the attitude toward their prodigious volume of the former student of those writings by the church fathers in fact was simply respectful, why did he smile and nod at the boy's dismayed response to his description of them? And why did he decline to provide answers—the "elucidating[s]" contained in the so "thick" and "closely printed" books—to the "intricate questions" he had put?

Flynn's first nodding smile seems to have involved antithetical religious instruction. If he was exploiting the boy's puerility for his own pleasure on those occasions, he would have "amused himself" more by revealing the answers to his questions. But he was not acting reprehensibly as a teacher, for he responded to the boy's bewilderment as though it is sound and sensible; a nodding smile as response suggests mild mirth and affirmation.

Because I share Joyce's hostility to institutional religion, it would be gratifying to be able to persuade myself that he has expressed it through his old priest—made Flynn not only sane but also a skeptic or even an apostate. However, to infer criticism of the church fathers by Flynn may be, in the words of one of them, *"praeter necessitatem"* ("Occam's razor"). The state of mind the priest reveals may have been pathetic rather than combative.

This possibility would be consonant with the general mode of Joyce's portrayal of the adult denizens of Dublin in the volume. Flynn's attendant nodding could have signified simply that his smile was not mocking patristic casuistry, but was rueful: he shared the boy's bewildered response (nodding smile) to the voluminous writings of the church fathers. For he himself was unable to derive secure guidance about "intricate questions" from them. So Flynn did not provide the answers to the "difficult questions" he had put because he could not. He was unable to construe what a priest should do in those circumstances.

With this interpretation of Joyce's portrayal of Flynn, the Irish College detail functions in the story to signify that Flynn knows patristic doctrine well. And the boy's recollection shows he knows it thoroughly enough for his knowledge to have incapacitated him as a priest. The samples of his knowledge reveal to the boy the extreme "grav[ity]" of his office, the "courage" it requires and has required of him, a man of moral imagination and fastidiousness who also possesses his knowledge. With this interpretation, Joyce's criticism of the church is more rich and subtle than the creation of a partisan; his priest is a victim, not a rebel.

That the significance of Flynn's conduct with the boy is ambiguous is one aspect of the account of their sessions in the first story of *Dubliners* that deserves to be noted; another, linked to the ambiguity, is the fact that the enlightening passage also portrays a stage in the boy's own enlightenment.

The boy's enlightenment derives from his *experience of* his recollection of his sessions with Flynn. The account given is unlike, for example, the physical description of Flynn in that the account is not the narrator's report. The boy is actively recollecting, in the present time of the story, while he is "walk[ing] away [from the dead house] slowly along the sunny side of the street," feeling "annoyed" by his "sensation of freedom" and "wonder[ing] at this for . . . he had taught me a great deal" (*D* 12–13). The account of his sessions with Flynn follows these reflections and occupies the remainder of the paragraph and is followed by another paragraph that begins, "As I walked along in the sun."

The fact that these two passages in the present time of the story bracket his recollection indicates the boy has been thinking about the sessions while he walks. The account must be the narrator's report of his memory of the sessions when a boy; but what he is reporting is the boy's active recollection of the sessions—he is depicting experience, similar to the phrase "sounded strangely" for the three words. This fact is signified promptly by the consequence of the boy's experience; he is certain no longer of what he has characterized at the beginning of his recollection as Flynn's having "amused himself by putting difficult questions." For the second paragraph begins, "As I walked along in the sun I remembered old Cotter's words and tried to remember what had happened afterwards in the dream"; the last words of the paragraph are, "But I could not remember the end of the dream" (*D* 13—14).

What the boy is unable to remember is the first element in the series, Flynn's continually smiling and confessing face and his own responsive face, "smiling feebly as if to absolve the simoniac of his sin." His experience of recollecting the sessions as he walks seems to have blocked out his sense of Flynn's sinfulness, expressed just before his recollection in his "sensation of freedom" and shortly after it begins by his belief that Flynn "had amused himself" with the questions.

In a fine touch of characterization, young Joyce presents a boy learning negatively, realizing inchoately from his recollection of their sessions that Flynn may deserve not reproach but sympathy, and that he himself does not know what the truth is. Flynn's second nodding smile of this second pair, the "pensive" one while he "put me through the responses of the Mass, which he made me learn by heart," is relevant here; for it concerns "the Mass," "The duties of the priest towards the Eucharist." The boy is yet to learn that this priest's "courage" failed him with respect to "the Eucharist" on one notorious occasion. He learns it as his signal experience, which is the fourth element in the pattern, the one he is told about. This is the fourth and last component of what I have called the story's armature, the one that provides his experience of how other Dublin adults regard Flynn, and why.

The third element in the pattern, the one he sees, is what the boy experiences when he sees Flynn's corpse; it is constituted by one word, probably the most important single new word in young Joyce's transformation of "The Sisters": "truculent."

The boy declares the experience he expects: "The fancy came to me that the old priest was smiling as he lay there in his coffin." However, the third element in the pattern is antithetical:

"But no. . . . His face was very truculent, grey and massive" (*D* 14; G144). Flynn's surprising fierce expression in death is an increment in the knowledge about him that the boy takes to the Flynns' "little" parlor, the scene of the major part of the story. There it almost immediately contributes to his knowledge about the other adults of his Dublin world.

As we know, the boy's experiences implicating Flynn comprise only one element, and not the defining one, in the compound experience that constitutes his story. The boy's witness to the attitude toward Flynn of his adult world occupies about two-thirds of "The Sisters," including its early scene during the family supper and its final and longest scene.

Comprising almost half the story, the final scene culminates the prior experience the boy brings to the parlor. It provides him with knowledge of the adults' view of three things about Flynn: his death, his mental state, and its etiology. The first of these is the view the boy learns about almost immediately, when he witnesses this exchange, begun by his aunt:

> —Did he . . . [sic] peacefully? she asked.
> —O, quite peacefully, ma'am, said Eliza. . . . He had a beautiful death, God be praised.
> —And everything. . . ?
> —Father O'Rourke was in with him a Tuesday and anointed him and prepared him and all.
> —He knew then?
> —He was quite resigned.
> —He looks quite resigned, said my aunt.
> —That's what the woman we had in to wash him said. She said he just looked as if he was asleep, he looked that peaceful and resigned. No one would think he'd make such a beautiful corpse.
> —Yes, indeed, said my aunt. (*D* 15)

This gross misrepresentation of Flynn's truculent expression in death, which is the third element in the pattern of four, the boy experiences at the beginning of the long parlor scene. Its final element occurs at the end of the story in combination with the climactic revelation to the boy about the other Dublin adults. The fourth and final element of the pattern of linked experiences begun by the dreamed smiles is, of course, the boy's hearing that Flynn had sat laughing in his confessional.

"The Sisters" ends when Eliza repeats, after an interpolated paragraph of exposition, the climax of her narrative of her brother's late dementia, and adds a significant surmise by the colleagues who discovered him:

> And what do you think but there he was laughing-like softly to himself?
> She stopped suddenly as if to listen. I too listened; but there was no sound in the house; and I knew that the old priest was lying still in his coffin as we had seen him, solemn and truculent in death, an idle chalice on his breast.
> Eliza resumed:
> —Wide-awake and laughing-like to himself. . . . So then, of course, when they saw that, that made them think that there was something gone wrong with him. (*D* 18)

The richness with which he invests the conclusion to "The Sisters" anticipates the mature Joyce. In the paragraph of exposition, "I knew" and "idle" echo the initial paragraph of the story: "I had thought his words idle. Now I knew they were true" (*D* 9). As "vanity" in the last sentence of "Araby" means not only self-importance but also futility, so "idle" has two of the word's principal meanings. That it is not in use is almost redundant for a chalice placed in the hands of a corpse; the functional meaning of the word is the evaluative one invoked in the initial paragraph: for this priest, a chalice is without worth or significance. The other echo from the initial paragraph reveals a second thing about the boy's state of mind at the end of the story, which otherwise must be inferred from what he has experienced. Eliza's histrionic silence after her revelation, *"as if* to listen" for Flynn's laughter, prompts the boy really to listen, although he "knew" futilely.

Flynn's disembodied face smiles "continually" while it confesses in the boy's dream; he smiles in response, and in the boy's recollection of their sessions together Flynn smiles in two successive sentences, first while nodding to the boy's bewilderment, then "pensively" when the boy "pattered" his memorized responses to the Mass. And Flynn's smile—which the boy in his dream believes irreverent and ambivalently both reproves and sympathizes with, then recalling their sessions realizes he cannot judge—the dead Flynn replaced, to the boy's surprise, with its exact opposite: an expression of fierce anger. The boy knows at the beginning of the story that the death is imminent; before the story's end he knows it occurred neither as he had expected it nor as the adults around him have represented it. Finally, just before the story ends, the boy learns the ultimately "solemn and truculent" Flynn's frequent and different smiles had been preceded by almost hysterical laughing. Promptly he judges the appropriateness of a chalice for Flynn's corpse and observes that the adults knew ("we had seen him") Flynn's attitude at his death. Eliza's concluding speech augments what he has been learning.

Flynn's smiling, which the boy dreams about and then recollects, oc-curred between Flynn's almost-hysterical laughing at his predicament and his anger when dying. The boy hears about and sees in reverse sequence this laughing and anger when he accompanies his aunt on her condolence call. In addition, Eliza's account and the conversation of the adults have disclosed to him the misperception—or misrepresentation—of elements of the truth about Flynn, made by Eliza, the woman who laid Flynn out, his own aunt, the churchmen. To Eliza's final words, the long parlor scene in which the story culminates enlightens the boy far more about the adult Dubliners' representa-tion of Flynn than about Flynn himself.

In that culminating scene of "The Sisters," the boy enters the Flynns' par-lor knowing the attitude of his "old friend" in death. There, he hears the adults around him inaccurately characterize Flynn as having died "resigned." After that, he learns they believe Flynn to be mentally "queer." Then he learns of the sequence of events that led to their misapprehension: Flynn dropped the chalice while celebrating a Mass; in consequence he "began to mope"; eventually he was discovered laughing in his confessional. The final element of the boy's enlightenment, provided by the last sentence of the story, is the au-thoritative origin of the adults' misapprehension.

Knowing about Flynn's doctrinal perplexity from their sessions, the boy can discern that his previously dropping the chalice, moping, and laughing, record stages in the incapacitation of an Irish priest, who then hinted the cause to him with questions and nodding smiles. Hence, the boy knows that the sig-nificance of those stages has been misconstrued by the adult Dubliners around him. Finally, he learns it was the respected churchmen making the discovery in Flynn's confessional—types of the principal authorities in his world—who er-roneously inferred from Flynn's "laughing-like softly to himself" there that he must have become—who originated the belief their fellow-priest was—mentally unstable.

## II

An extensive bibliography exists of interpretations of the meaning in and for "The Sisters" of the three italicized words. My particular concern is their function for what Joyce was declaring in the story about Dublin.

While sitting in Flynn's chair, with the boy in his "usual chair in the corner" (*D* 14), Eliza is in the place of his late instructor; conducting the proceedings, she unknowingly instructs the boy. Before entering the parlor he was aware of the smiling then finally truculent Flynn's troubled history with two of the four sacraments of the church relevant to one of its priests: Holy Orders and Extreme Unction. In the parlor, she reveals Flynn's troubled history with the other two, Communion and Penance (his "nervous[ly]" dropping the chalice and laughing in his confession box). But Eliza functions for the boy there as *gnomon,* in the broad sense of "that which enables knowledge," less for this reason than for being the instrument of his learning that the adults already know, or learn with him, all he learns from her about her brother and refuse or are unable to acknowledge its significance.

He knows the adults misperceive or deny Flynn's truculent end and attribute Flynn's treatment of Communion and Penance to mental debility. Beyond the hints in "idle" and "I knew," the narrator does not reveal how he reacted, when he was the boy, to his experience of the failures of perception and understanding, or of candor, by Dublin adults, including churchmen and his own surrogate parent, with respect to Flynn's late life and death. However, he has directed his story of himself when a boy toward, and ended it with, that experience; this fact indicates how the most prominent of the three italicized words may function in "The Sisters."

At the end of its first paragraph, he reveals that the "being" whose name *paralysis* "sounded to me like" when a boy "filled me with fear, and yet I longed to be nearer to it and to look upon its deadly work" (*D* 9); promptly the boy hears at home that he will not succeed with the literal paralysis of Flynn's final illness.

However, he realizes during the story that Flynn was confounded—

metaphorically paralyzed—by his strict (i.e., orthodox) conception of the duties of the priesthood. More to the point, the boy learns in the story that the other adults, explicitly Cotter, Eliza, and the churchmen, consider Flynn and not their church to be the cause of his predicament; they have been incapacitated for acknowledging the truth about a priest broken by his profound grasp of the extreme demands of his—and their—church. The story portrays a boy learning, as Phillip Herring points out in "Structure and Meaning in Joyce's 'The Sisters,'" that Dublin adults are mentally immobilized—metaphorically paralyzed—by their conformity to a hegemony of Roman Catholic piety (1982, 131–44). For them, the legitimacy of the Irish Church is a categorical given. Although the narrator the boy has become does not reveal whether he recognized at the time this etiology for the metaphorical paralysis of these Dublin adults, manifestly the grown man recognizes it, for what he tells is his boyhood experience of "be[ing] nearer to it"; as a boy he had, at the end of the story he has begun with the word in italics, "look[ed] upon [the] deadly work" of Catholic Dublin's intellectually paralyzing religious hegemony (*D* 9).

If the symbolic Eucharist that Joyce created for the story is considered in the context of this metaphorical paralysis of a community, its signification ceases to be problematic. The sherry and crackers symbolize the sacrificial wine and wafer, not to invoke Communion directly, but to effect a highly appropriate social trope on the religious rite the communion the sisters' wine and crackers admit one to, and the aunt receiving them participates in, is that of pious Dublin Catholic adults, who misperceive and misinterpret things that are contrary to the religious ideology that has absorbed them and so has immobilized their intelligence.

The narrator's report of his ambiguous response to the proffered social communion when he was the boy points to his complicated place in the story he tells. While telling his thoughts and dream in bed the previous night those many years ago, the narrator calls Flynn "the paralytic," then in the same passage makes his explicit judgment, "the simoniac." Both his epithets have their limited truth, but both obfuscate; as "The Sisters" creates a significance for *paralysis* different from the one he invokes, so it does for *simony*. After the boy has forgiven Flynn in his dream, he learns of the priest's failed struggle to perform his office and its pathetic conclusion. The narrator knows that in this context Flynn committed trivial simony; he learned it when he was the boy. I will try to show that both italicized words that the narrator obfuscates the significance of, that "had always sounded strangely in [his] ears" when a boy, Joyce's story applies to him and *gnomon* as well.

Not only Eliza, but Flynn before her and even his aunt, are gnomons for the boy in the broad sense of the term. That sense does not enrich the story particularly; "*gnomon* in the Euclid" invokes explicitly its geometric sense, of the remainder of a parallelogram after a similar one had been taken from one of its corners; the shape of the remainder reveals (provides *gnosis* of) that of the removed corner. The rich significance of *gnomon* in the story is indicated by an early instance of the functional comic wit Joyce used increasingly in *Ulysses* and the *Wake*.

In the original story, Nannie is seated not "behind her sister" but "in a corner" (G144) and the boy's location in the parlor is not specified. When Joyce revised it in 1906, the boy as well as Nannie is precisely situated. In that culminating scene, he is explicitly where he sat when being tutored by Flynn: "I groped my way toward my usual chair in the corner" (*D*14). It is "in the corner" that he previously learned about the baleful effect of the church on the most admirable kind of priest, the erudite and conscientious Father Flynn; and it is there he learns about the distorted consensus of the adults. Not sharing that consensus, he is the piece taken out of the whole. "Let him learn to box his corner," his uncle specifies at the beginning of "The Sisters", and by its end he has done so.

The remainder of the parallelogram, not the removed corner, is the gnomon defined by Euclid; in the story it is the adults around the boy who reveal their nature to him precisely because he is not part of their adult Dublin Catholic "communion." Being the boy grown up, the narrator also has *gnosis* of that gnomon whose nature the boy apprehended; yet the narrator speaks as part of it. The reason is that a gnomon reveals by its own shape the shape of the removed piece. Eventually, "The Sisters" turns toward its teller, the Dublin Catholic adult the boy became.

The narrator provides reasons why both the boy's inability to pray in the dead room and his later declining the crackers of the adults' symbolic communion are innocuous actions; he preserves his own reputation as a pious Catholic boy. The reasons sound like lame excuses, but the narrator presents them as the boy's conscious reasons and specifies that he did sip his wine.

Moreover, there is a pattern of increased withholding of the boy's reactions to his four crucial experiences as the story progresses; it is the narrator of a story who reveals or withholds. Of the four components of the story's armature, the boy's silent outrage at Cotter and subsequent ambivalence about Flynn that night and the next day are fully articulated; there is a brief account of his reaction to his memory of the sessions with Flynn. Of his reaction to his discovery that the face on Flynn's corpse is not only not smiling but "truculent," the narrator tells nothing more than that he "groped my way towards" his seat in the corner, providing only this physical symptom of his state of mind; at the end of the story, after telling that the adults shared what "I knew" about Flynn and quoting Eliza's reiteration of the almost lurid climax and conclusion of her account of her brother, he withholds almost totally his reaction when the boy.

Possibly nothing in "The Sisters" before it points as insistently to the narrator as does the conclusion of the story. In both of the other childhood stories in *Dubliners,* the boy's reaction to his culminating experience provides closure, even though the narrator knows, and has shown, more about its significance than he was aware of when a boy. In "The Sisters," the reaction of the boy to Eliza's revelation about the extent of adult misapprehension in his Catholic Dublin world can be inferred easily enough. It is the narrator's action in essentially withholding what he realized about the adults when he was the boy that calls for scrutiny. That action, his declining to articulate what he realized, relates to his conventional piety in the story and explains his inconsistency; in spite of what he knows about a priest's disablement by his church and about the intellectual paralysis of Dublin's adult Catholics when confronted with it, as an adult he has joined them. The gnomon reveals the shape of the (once-)removed piece. Hence, at the end of his narrative he refrains from disclosing his boyhood reaction to the derogatory truth about Dublin's adult Catholics that has been revealed to him. His withholding the reaction he had when the boy recalls the beggar-playwright's changing the ending of his play, also to gain public approval, in Gay's *The Beggar's Opera;* in both cases, his act makes the agent the subject.

This is why all three italicized words in the first paragraph of "The Sisters" not only relate, as critics have pointed out, to the adults in the story and to the boy, but also ultimately relate to the narrator. The adults in his world when a boy are afflicted with intellectual paralysis; they are the boy's gnomon of that fact. But excepting Flynn they are not guilty of any simony. In contrast, the grown man who tells his boyhood story accommodates himself to the hegemony of Catholic Dublin. In doing so, he subverts truth for his convenience as the simoniac does faith. He knowingly conforms to the paralysis afflicting Dublin's adults and so joins them as gnomon of it. His knowing accommodation to the pious community is prudential, of course; Joyce is signifying by it that a man could not remain in that society otherwise. But it is still self-interested, an act of metaphorical simony against the truth, however understandable. In the context of the power in Dublin of Irish Catholicism, Father James Flynn and the man the boy became are foils.

Each of the two subsequent childhood stories in *Dubliners* presents a man telling about how his Dublin Catholic environment influenced his growing self; in "An Encounter," the influence is its class snobbery and violence; in "Araby," its sexual repression. Each narrator's understanding of the formative boyhood experience he tells of is part of young Joyce's story; implicitly, the knowledge has been salutary to him. But although the narrators are characterized to different degrees, the stories essentially are about the boys' formative experiences.

While this narrator's story also is about his formative experience when a boy, Joyce made "The Sisters" eventually about him and so turned his narrative into a revelation of how he has coped with that experience. The Dublin man's prudential submission to the environmental pressure on him affirms the force of that pressure. Joyce made the inaugural story of his volume an eloquent introduction to the baneful power of the Irish Church over the minds and lives of the Dubliners the volume portrays.

# 7

# A Pedagogical Note on "The Dead"
# of *Dubliners*

VIVIAN VALVANO LYNCH

**M**y topic emerges from my concerned reaction to a pedagogical situation. Recently, the English Division in which I teach at St. John's University adopted a literature anthology for use in our first two required courses.[1] The courses, Composition and Rhetoric I and II, resemble numerous like-minded courses elsewhere: they aspire to assist freshmen in the improvement of their formal, expository writing skills. In the first semester, students read essays and short stories from whence to model their own efforts and that may serve as topical foundations for rhetorical arguments; in the second semester, students read poetry, drama, and one short novel or novella on which expository assignments are based. The anthology in question, *Literature: Reading Fiction, Poetry, Drama, and the Essay,* edited by Robert DiYanni (1998), includes James Joyce's "The Dead" as a short novel. (Faculty members may, and several do, assign a short novel from outside the anthology;

---

1. I extend my thanks to the following colleagues who responded to my invitation to the Division of English and Speech in the College of Professional Studies of St. John's University to discuss this project with me and who offered comments and ideas: Reverend Michael Callaghan, C. M., Elena Grievo, Thomas Kitts, Joseph Marotta, George McCartney, Barbara Morris, and Claire O'Donoghue. Special thanks to Tom Kitts for facilitating my communication with Robert DiYanni.

Kafka's *The Metamorphosis* is the only other example included in DiYanni's volume.) This is the anthology's fourth edition; previous editions do not include "The Dead."

Certainly, considerable criticism exists that labels "The Dead" as a short novel or novella. Some critics argue strenuously for that categorization while some more conservatively suggest that the text is a short story that may also be considered a novella. Indeed, some critics simply utilize the terms "short story," "novella," and "short novel" interchangeably, implying comfort with each. However, the anthology in question does something that startles me. It includes no mention at all of *Dubliners* in connection with "The Dead." After a brief introduction on the short novel as genre, which emphasizes the allowance of "a slower unfolding of character, incident, idea" (DiYanni 1998, 214) than the short story and the "greater efficiency and sharper focus" (1998, 214) than the novel, the editor cites Henry James, Vladimir Nabokov, and Irving Howe on the benefits of the novella. " 'In masterpieces of the genre,' " he quotes Howe, " 'the action forms a harmonious equivalent to the motivating idea' " (1998, 215). He concludes, "Two short novels worthy of such high praise are Franz Kafka's *The Metamorphosis* and James Joyce's *The Dead*" (1998, 215). Neither footnotes nor explanatory apparatus of any kind accompanies Joyce's ensuing text. No copyright acknowledgment is necessary, *Dubliners* being out of copyright in the United States. "The Dead" is not only treated as a novella here; its original existence as part of *Dubliners* is ignored, or perhaps more accurately, metamorphosed. Figuratively, in our context of discussion of "Joyce and the City," I think of it as rezoned. "Araby" and "The Boarding House" also appear in the anthology, included in the short-story section. Copyright acknowledgment is noted for "Araby," since that story is reprinted from an earlier edition of the anthology when *Dubliners* was still in copyright in the United States, but not for "The Boarding House," which, like "The Dead," is an addition to the 1998 edition.[2]

---

2. I am indebted to Robert Spoo, former editor of *James Joyce Quarterly,* who generously reviewed with me the status of copyright regarding *Dubliners.* He notes, "since the Estate no longer has control, in the U.S., over whether one copies the *Dubliners* stories, it does not have any say in how one characterizes it either (i.e., as a novella)." Robert Spoo, e-mail to the author, 12 Feb. 1998.

The decision to anthologize "The Dead" in this manner does not simply intrigue me; it causes me some uneasiness and alarm. My primary interest is not whether it is wise or even justifiable to call "The Dead" a novella, although I will necessarily examine that issue. I am more interested in the advisability, justification, and repercussions of so labeling "The Dead" within an educational anthology, one obviously intended for the college classroom, in such a gaping void—in the complete and utter absence of the facts of its original publication. It seems to me that editorial ellipsis, aided and abetted by end-of-the-millennium copyright law, has created a gnomon with which I am not entirely comfortable. Is Joyce adequately served by such a decision? Moreover, is the contemporary student of literature adequately served by such a decision? As Joycean academics, we quickly discover Joyce's oft-quoted expression of regret in his 25 September 1906 letter to Stanislaus, prior to composition of "The Dead":

> Sometimes thinking of Ireland it seems to me that I have been unnecessarily harsh. I have reproduced (in *Dubliners* at least) none of the attraction of the city for I have never felt at ease in any city since I left it except in Paris. I have not reproduced its ingenuous insularity and its hospitality. The latter "virtue" so far as I can see does not exist elsewhere in Europe. I have not been just to its beauty: for it is more beautiful naturally in my opinion than what I have seen of England, Switzerland, France, Austria or Italy. (*Letters* 2: 166)

Joyce's statements have engendered much critical commentary. One of the most comprehensive warnings against taking Joyce's epistolary contrition strictly at face value comes from Vincent P. Pecora. In " 'The Dead' and the Generosity of the Word" (1986), Pecora reminds us that Joyce's frequently quoted statement of apparent remorse is immediately followed by this possible disclaimer: "And yet I know how useless these reflections are. For were I to write the book as G. R. suggests 'in another sense' (where the hell does he get the meaningless phrases he uses) I am sure I should find again what you call the Holy Ghost sitting in the ink-bottle and the perverse devil of my literary conscience sitting on the hump of my pen" (*Letters* 2: 166). Pecora goes to great lengths to prove that Gabriel's "generosity" throughout the story is ironical and that the ultimate "generosity" with which he looks west is partic-ularly suspect. Pecora concludes,

> In fact, Gabriel in no way overcomes or transcends the conditions of his exis-tence. Rather, he merely recapitulates them unconsciously in this self-pitying fantasy. If the guests he has addressed at the party, and Dubliners as a whole, value those "dead and gone great ones" to soothe their apprehension of cul-tural inferiority, and beyond that their metaphysical discontent, then Gabriel hardly rises above this petty, bourgeois attitude. To avoid being further hu-miliated by others, Gabriel must of course humiliate himself. In the name of Michael Furey, his legendary hero and personal saint, Gabriel sacrifices him-self to the past, and to the dead, more profoundly than any of his compatriots does. (Pecora 1986, 243)

As Joycean academics, we fastidiously follow the gestation of Joyce scholar-ship and note that it has yielded numerous considerations of "The Dead" as deliberate coda to *Dubliners* as well as numerous considerations of "The Dead" as a distinctly cohesive and independent text. This essay cannot digress into a summation of that formidable critical record. Let us note that the field ranges from the extreme position of Brewster Ghiselin, who argues in a 1956 essay that the unity of *Dubliners* is so unshakable that the entire book is "both a group of short stories and a novel, the separate histories of its protagonists composing one essential history, that of the soul of a people" (quoted in Schwarz 1994, 67) to the conversely extreme position of Colin MacCabe, who in his pioneering 1979 *James Joyce and the Revolution of the Word* argues against overweening order amongst the stories and opens new doors of inter-pretations of each of the stories as idiosyncratic texts. Both positions, as well as numerous intermediates, are amply represented in the contemporary arena. One need only look at the recent special *Dubliners* number of *Studies in Short Fiction* (1995) to ascertain the vibrancy of arguments across this critical spec-trum. David G. Wright, in "Interactive Stories in *Dubliners*" (1995) discusses the collection as an interrelated whole even as he maintains that its Dublin cit-izens do not, after all, know much about each other. Emphasizing Joyce's in-terest in "interaction," Wright adds that the "conclusion of the *Portrait* echoes the conclusion of *Dubliners*" (Wright 1995, 287). He finds in the final moments of Gabriel Conroy and Stephen Dedalus a mutual qualification as "Gabriel subordinates his ego almost completely in the face of the world, while Stephen subordinates the world to his ego" (1995, 287). Conversely, in the same volume C. Roland Wagner discourses on the connections between "The Dead" and "the traditional theme—Christian and art-historical—of the Annunciation" (Wagner 1995, 447) without treating the story as a coda. Still later in the volume, Sean P. Murphy provides a Lacanian reading of the story in which he avers a negative aspect of considerations of "The Dead" as a terminating story that casts light on all those that precede it (Murphy 1995). He argues that critics are led into such a reading "because Joyce's tempting linear narrative construction hails them into a position similar to Gabriel's. That is, they are interpellated into a position within a symbolic network that satisfies their desire to feel 'whole,' total, totalized" (Murphy 1995, 469). Murphy's subsequent discussion contends that such a reading is problematic. He concludes, "Joyce does not allow readers to experience the traditional sense of closure at the end of 'The Dead,' for Gabriel does not recover the *jouissance* that existed prior to his entrance into the symbolic order (castration). Rather, he (like the critics) places his hopes of attaining perfect unity or 'wholeness' in an alternative Other (the west) to provide legitimation for his own faulty sense of unity" (Murphy 1995, 472).

I am certain that many undergraduates, not fluent with critical particularities such as the few I have mentioned, minimally know of Joyce's *Dubliners* before they approach it, or any of its individual stories, in class. However, I teach students who are not English majors.[3] I teach some students who are

---

3. My university is divided into several component units, each labeled a "college" or a "school." While the liberal arts unit, St. John's College of Liberal Arts and Sciences, holds an English Department that offers both undergraduate and graduate degrees in the discipline, my unit, the College of Professional Studies, offers baccalaureate programs in several areas that the University deems as professionally oriented. Communication arts, computer science, criminal justice, health care administration, hospitality management, journalism, paralegal studies, and sports management are examples of baccalaureate majors for which my Division of English and Speech provides required English courses as well as electives. I frequently teach an elective course titled "The Literature of Ireland from the Irish Literary Revival of the 1890s to the Present," a course that examines representative literature against the political, social, and cultural history of the is-

not avid readers. I teach some students who have never heard of *Dubliners* and some who have never heard of Joyce. Truth to tell, some will never read Joyce again. Notwithstanding any information that I as professor might furnish, should they be "officially" presented with the text that first appeared as the final story of *Dubliners* as if it never existed as anything apart from an independent construction categorized as a short novel?

In considering these problems, I wrote to DiYanni. He graciously replied, noting that, professionally, he has been inclined to present literature primarily without instructional apparatus or historical background in books intended for introductory courses. He emphasized that competent teachers can provide students with information deemed essential, but he also noted that, prompted by my concerns, he will think about a different example of the novella for his next edition. At one point in his message to me, he called "The Dead" "a long story," which is as good a point as any to talk a bit about the critical labeling of "The Dead."[4]

Critic A. Robert Lee provocatively asks, "Do we help or hinder in the understanding of a given text by assigning it to a generic category?" (Lee 1989, 7). With respect to "The Dead," we can see that moving it from its traditional generic category has provided a substantial scholarly forum. As early as 1939, David Daiches discussed "The Dead" in *The Novel and the Modern World*. Howard Nemerov, in his influential 1963 essay "Composition and Fate in the Short Novel," offers an adjudication to help define the short novel:

> whereas the short story extends to rest upon action, a combination of circumstances to which the characters must very readily conform, while the novel, especially in English, goes toward the opposite pole and tends to produce "characters" as an independent value, the short novel strikes a very delicate and exact balance between motive and circumstance; its action generally speaking is the fate of the agonists, and this fate is regarded as flowing

---

land. In such a specialized elective, "The Dead's" existence within *Dubliners* readily becomes apparent, and the class productively considers it both as coda to the collection and as an individual artistic performance. My concern is the student faced with "The Dead" *sans* the rest of the collection in the nonspecialized introductory course.

4. Robert DiYanni, e-mail to the author, 16 Sept. 1998.

demonstrably and with some precision and in great detail from their individual natures, which accordingly are developed at considerable length. (Nemerov 1985, 66)

Gabriel Conroy follows Aschenbach, Captain Delano, and The Man from Underground in Nemerov's examples. Mary Doyle Springer, in her 1975 *Forms of the Modern Novella*, discusses the aims that she believes the 15,000- to 50,000-word prose fiction known as the novella can achieve—all of them tied in some way to purposeful character revelation (1975, 9–13). "The Dead" appears on her list of "Serious Plots of Learning (or Failed Learning)" along with entries such as Saul Bellow's *Seize the Day*, Elizabeth Bowen's *Ivy Gripped the Steps*, Anton Chekov's *A Boring Story*, Stephen Crane's *The Red Badge of Courage*, D. H. Lawrence's *The Fox*, Philip Roth's *Goodbye Columbus*, and Lionel Trilling's *Of This Time, Of That Place* (Springer 1975, 163–64). One can occasionally find "The Dead" presented in a collection as a short novel. One of my colleagues found on his shelf a beat-up copy of a 1959 Dell paperback, *Six Great Modern Short Novels*, which includes "The Dead." However, the book's brief introduction paradoxically announces, "His [Joyce's] work ranges from a slim volume of verse: *Chamber Music* (1907); to a great volume of stories: *Dubliners* (1914) (from which 'The Dead' is taken)." The most comprehensive and meticulous treatment of "The Dead" as a novella is Thomas Loe's in his 1991 *James Joyce Quarterly* article, " 'The Dead' as Novella." Loe argues vigorously that the following characteristics all help to render the piece a novella: prevalent concern with theme, ambivalence of meaning, distinctive shifts in point of view, numerous ironies, development of Gabriel's character in tandem with his relationship with others, and relinquishing of Gabriel's former self as values previously antithetical to Gabriel (i.e., the values of the traditional Ireland associated with Michael Furey) are infused into Gabriel's consciousness (Loe 1991, 485–90). Loe reinforces Nemerov's implications: "its resonance comes as a result of the complexity resulting from the analogical mix of realism and metaphor, not merely because of slightly more extended action. The novella's distinctiveness accrues, in Nemerov's words, because 'every detail balances another so as to produce great riches of meaning not so much symbolically in a direct sense as by constellation and patterning' " (Loe 1991, 490–91). Loe's marshalling of such an extended argument has inevitably been answered by opposing critics. Peter J. Rabinowitz, for example, advancing a reader-response approach to "The Dead," charges the following:

> particular intertextual and etymological connections themselves sometimes bring ambiguity in their wake. Thus, for instance, qualities of ambiguity in the intertexts are sometimes carried over into "The Dead" as if by infection. This contagious ambiguity is seen, for instance, when Thomas Loe not only sees "The Dead" as a novella, but also treats this generic placement as grounds for comparing it to all other novellas (including future novellas such a Franz Kafka's *Metamorphosis,* Katherine Ann [sic] Porter's *Pale Horse, Pale Rider,* and even Saul Bellow's *Seize the Day,*) and for assuming, in part, that the ambiguities he finds in those texts must also be characteristic of Joyce's story as well. (Rabinowitz 1994, 144)[5]

However, painstaking labors like Loe's do not even need a focused riposte such as Rabinowitz's to stand contested. They are, indeed, undercut by what I am beginning to think of as the "rose by any other name" syndrome that is readily apparent in contemporary discussions of "The Dead": a simple inter-jection of the term "short novel" even as one more often uses the term "short story." Daniel R. Schwarz, in both his "Introduction" and his " 'The Dead': A Case Study in Contemporary Criticism" in the valuable 1994 volume on "The Dead," which he edited for the Bedford Books Case Studies in Con-temporary Criticism series, almost unfailingly calls "The Dead" a story. A few samples of his plentiful comments: "We should think of *Dubliners* as an evolv-

---

5. Despite the fact that Rabinowitz's choice of language makes me fear that Joyce's story has been infected by a computer virus, rather than by a genre controversy, his point is well taken. To be sure, Springer's (1975) book on the novella indicates the cul-de-sac destination toward which comparisons within a critic-defined genre can lead. Springer ends with a four-page appen-dix that compiles "novellas" from varied countries under the topic headings "Apologues," "Ex-ample Apologues," "Satires," "Degenerative Tragedies," "Serious Plots of Character Revelation," and (as previously cited with respect to "The Dead") "Serious Plots of Learning (or Failed Learning)." This appendix is titled "A Formal Listing of Novellas" and carries the caveat, "Let the buyer be wary. Yet not so wary as to miss a new light which might be cast on some hith-erto obscure novella by reason of seeing it afresh in relationship to other members of its kind" (Springer 1975, 161–64).

ing series of stories, a kaleidoscope in which each story takes turns as the centerpiece in the pattern" (Schwarz 1994, 9); " 'The Dead,' composed in 1907, was the last story Joyce completed for his collection *Dubliners*. Joyce had planned the story in Rome in 1906–7, but it was completed while he was living in Trieste" (63); " 'The Dead' has been read both as the last story of a closely integrated collection entitled *Dubliners* and as a separate story in its own right" (67). It would seem, then, that Schwarz considers "The Dead" a short story. However, Schwarz twice alters the nomenclature without discoursing on the reasons. He writes, "Isn't Gabriel Conroy, the protagonist of 'The Dead,' another figure who falls off the ladder of his hopes and illusions only to awaken and recover in his final epiphany of the common humanity that binds human beings together? Our focus in this volume is on 'The Dead,' that magnificent short novel of tenderness and passion but also of disappointed love and frustrated personal career expectations" (Schwarz 1994, 19). Later he offers, "To conclude: 'The Dead' is among the most read short novels in English" (Schwarz 1994, 81). In the midst of somewhat murky waters, it may be wise to recall Frank O'Connor's lucid comments from his 1963 study of the short story, *The Lonely Voice*. O'Connor patently notes the uniqueness of "The Dead" as measured alongside the other stories of *Dubliners*, concluding that within it lie signals that Joyce was leaving "storytelling" and embarking on the work of a novelist:

> One of his main passions—the elaboration of style and form—had taken control, and the short story is too tightly knit to permit expansion like this. And—what is more important—it is quite clear from "The Dead" that he had already begun to lose sight of the submerged population that was his original subject. There are little touches of it here and there, as in the sketches of Freddy Malins and his mother . . . but Gabriel does not belong to it, nor does Gretta nor Miss Ivors. They are not characters but personalities, and Joyce would never again be able to deal with characters, people whose identity is determined by their circumstances. (quoted in Charters 1987, 1266)[6]

6. Readers may also wish to heed W. B. Yeats, who wrote to the Secretary of the Royal Fund in July 1915 that Joyce's "book of short stories *Dubliners* has the promise of a great novelist and a great novelist of a new kind" (*Letters* 2: 356).

I like O'Connor's reference to Joyce's "original subject." I am not certain whether it is still unfashionable to consider an author's intentions or whether that tide has turned somewhat, but I want to consider Joyce's intentions. For Joyce, *Dubliners* was a book. Of course, individual stories could be published separately; he so published "The Sisters," "Eveline," and "After the Race" in 1904 and would have published more had circumstances been fortuitous. He was aware of American printings of "The Boarding House" and "A Little Cloud" in 1915 (*Letters* 2: 337). But throughout the voluminous Joycean correspondence; from the time of the composition of the first stories in 1904 through the periods of refinement from the originally planned ten stories to twelve, to fourteen, and finally with the composition of "The Dead" in 1907 to fifteen; through the torturous and tortuous history of the publication of *Dubliners*, which did not reach culmination until June 1914, one certainty emerges. *Dubliners* was not simply a collection of completed works of fiction; *Dubliners* was Joyce's book with which he would present "Dublin to the world" (*Letters* 2: 122). Repeatedly in the course of the letters, Joyce refers to "my book." Certainly, during the period of the Richards and Maunsel controversies that followed the composition of "The Dead" Joyce had plenty of time and opportunity to remove the piece from the collection and handle it as a separate text totally apart from the others. It was not one of the pieces engendering controversy with publishers or printers. He had ample time to try to market it as a novel or a short novel. He did not do so.[7] Repeatedly, beginning in 1915 he scrupulously refers to *A Portrait* in his letters as "my novel."[8] Had

7. For exemplary comments by Joyce on his book *Dubliners*, see especially *Letters* 1: 55, 60; and *Letters* 2: 111, 134, 122, 308, 324, 327, 328, 329, and 332.

8. For Joyce's distinction of *A Portrait* as "my novel," see, for example, *Letters* 2: 337, 338, 339, and 398. I am not trying to present an absurdity, that is, that *A Portrait* is a novel as opposed to a book, or that Joyce never called *A Portrait* a book. I am merely trying to point out an obvious but overlooked fact: Joyce labeled *A Portrait* by genre as a novel, but not "The Dead." Indeed, I particularly note Joyce's 1917 letter to J. B. Pinker in which he recounts, once again and more concisely than he was wont to do elsewhere, the publishing history of *Dubliners*, noting with evident exasperation, "The book cost me in litigation and trainfare and postal expenses about 3000 francs: it cost me also nine years of my life. I was in correspondence with seven solicitors, one hundred and twenty newspapers, and several men of letters about it" (*Letters* 2: 398). With all his careful use of numbers, never once does Joyce mention one novel or one short novel

he wished to, he certainly could have categorized "The Dead" as a novel or a short novel. But "The Dead" was not a novel or a short novel to Joyce. "The Dead" was the conclusion to his book, *Dubliners*. "The Dead" terminated the book about which he wrote to Nora from Dublin in 1912; despairingly, at this moment of the Maunsel controversy, he refers to himself as "thinking of the book I have written, the child which I have carried for years and years in the womb of the imagination . . . and of how I had fed it day after day out of my brain and my memory" (*Letters* 2: 308).

I think students should know that. Afterwards, knowing that, it is perfectly acceptable and even invigorating, challenging, and stimulating to embark on the critical argument that "The Dead" can be interpreted separately, without attention to the other stories in *Dubliners*. In conducting such hermeneutics, if it makes one more content to call it a short novel, so be it, though I would hope for an avoidance of the strained systematic comparisons proffered by Springer. But it serves no purpose to ignore "The Dead's" original existence. If it is, to some readers, formally a short novel, if as A. Nicholas Fargnoli and Michael Patrick Gillespie succinctly state, "in length and density, it is in effect a novella," it is also, and, most importantly, it was first, as they accurately state, "the last and longest story in *Dubliners*, often viewed as a coda to the collection" (Fargnoli and Gillespie 1995, 53). Students embarking on a study of Joyce and students who may never meet Joyce again should simply be presented with accurate information.

Susan Sontag gained a fair degree of fame for boldly asserting, "It doesn't matter whether artists intend, or don't intend, for their works to be interpreted" (Sontag 1967, 9). I am open to that. But occluding the facts of composition—even given the possibility that perhaps a fastidious and diligent teacher (and let us make no mistake: all teachers are not fastidious and diligent) will fill in the blanks—from inexperienced or naïve students is a far cry from interpretation. It is an error of omission. An error of omission can unfairly prejudice one's interpretation. Joyce is entitled to accurate presentation of information. Students embarking on a study of Joyce, as well as students

---

within *Dubliners*. In the same letter, he reminds Pinker, with equally careful designation, "My novel *A Portrait of the Artist us a Young Man* was refused by every publisher to whom you offered it."

meeting him for the first and perhaps only time in a Freshman comp course, are entitled to accurate presentation of information. Readers outside a classroom perusing a volume ostensibly published as a textbook are entitled to accurate presentation of information. Copyright intricacies have been the bane of many a scholar's existence, and we all cheer when a text under study goes out of copyright because it makes our work so much easier. Nevertheless, reflecting on what happened to "The Dead" of *Dubliners* in 1998, its metamorphosis in the DiYanni anthology into an independent short novel with no known attachments, I am somewhat sobered by the current Joycean copyright situation in the United States. Even in the absence of introductory material, a copyright notification would serve to state the fact of original composition as part of *Dubliners*, and Joyce and his city could be more content.

# 8

## Political Memorials in the City of "The Dead"

MICHAEL MURPHY

Gabriel Conroy, like James Joyce, inclines to the continent of Europe. He knows, consciously or unconsciously, that the culture of Gaelic Ireland died in the late seventeenth century on battlefields at the Boyne and Athlone and further west, at Aughrim and Limerick, all of them defeats for the Irish at the hands of the armies of William of Orange. Gabriel's unconscious (and ours) is regularly if only slightly stirred by the sight of memorials to defeat, conquest, and frustration, monuments that dot the city and punctuate the story. Like many of the other inhabitants of the Pale that is Dublin, he has become accustomed to those monuments and has perhaps accepted them as part of his landscape and mindscape. The public monuments are brought into the story much as they are distributed through the city, adding nothing obvious to the plot or to the town, barely noticed, in fact, by most readers or travelers, and much the same is true of the more private monuments. Joyce's intention appears to have been to make the memorials function something like unobtrusive symbols or musical motifs, almost subliminally. I will outline the references to the monuments offering a little commentary along the way, and at the end also offer a tentative reason for their presence.

At one point fairly early in the party, while Mary Jane is playing her difficult showpiece, Gabriel's eye catches a couple of pictures on the wall above the piano. One is of Romeo and Juliet, the other is a picture "of the two murdered princes in the tower which aunt Julia had worked in red, blue and brown wools when she was a girl" (*D* 186). Readers of the story were, of course, expected to know that *the* princes were the two young sons of King Edward IV of England who were supposedly murdered in the Tower of London by order of his brother their uncle, Richard Crookback, who thus became King Richard III. This story was a sentimental staple of English history textbooks and illustrators then and for years after, but why was it considered a suitable topic on which Irish girls should exert their needlework skills? And why would an Irish girl keep it on her wall into old age? The presence of the thing on the wall testifies to the efficacy of the syllabus in Irish schools at the height of the British Empire that taught *English* history of that kind, a tribute to the lasting effect of what started as Tudor propaganda and continued as a kind of historical romance with tenuous relevance to Ireland or Irish people who, of course, did not have any history of their own worth telling! The sad, sentimental English story of the little princes, whether it was real *history* or not, was woven into the minds of these Irish girls where it remained to old age, as much a part of the fabric of the minds in this maiden household as the Shakespeare play about Romeo and Juliet.

Even in the Irish Jesuit school to which Stephen goes in *Portrait,* the classroom teams into which the boys are divided are York and Lancaster, and they wear little white and red silk badges to represent opposing sides in the *English* Wars of the Roses, in which good Henry Tudor finally triumphed over bad Richard III. It was in the reign of good Henry VII that the two murdered princes in the tower came to life again briefly in the form of Lambert Simnel and Perkin Warbeck, one of whom was crowned in Dublin, a kind of futile anti-king. But like most rebellions in Ireland, before and after, this too fizzled, and King Henry's lieutenant Sir Edward Poynings put through a law that effectively subordinated the very summoning of the Irish parliament and any of its decisions to the will of good King Henry and his council in London, an act that stayed in effect until the abolition of the Irish parliament completely with the Act of Union in 1800. It is doubtful that Aunt Julia or Aunt Kate could have related any of that history, for the Morkan girls probably learned as little Anglo-Irish history as did the boys in Mr. Deasy's school, although in *Ulysses* Warbeck and Simnel are briefly on the mind of Stephen, the product of Clongowes (*U* 1.314–16). But whether or not all this confused history is implied by the picture, or just the sentimental story of the two slaughtered innocents, the embroidery, like the silk badges and like almost all the other monuments we speak of here, proclaims Ireland as "West Britain." "You could not have a green rose," young Stephen had thought. "But perhaps somewhere in the world you could." (*P* 12). Somewhere, perhaps. Not in Ireland, though.

Later during the party in "The Dead," Gabriel thinks of an English monument of a more public kind than the embroidery and the picture: the Wellington Monument, a tall obelisk in the Phoenix Park commemorating the victories gained for Britain by that Dublin-born soldier Arthur Wellesley, Duke of Wellington. Now, there seems to be no reason of plot or character development why Gabriel should think of that memorial, either while he is going over his speech or again when he is just about to deliver it in the Morkan house.[1] In both cases he "sees" the snow on the memorial to Wellington, the final victor over the French from whom the Irish had hoped for help in another hopeless rebellion in 1798, one hundred years after the defeat at Aughrim and the fall of Limerick. Wellington was a man so ashamed of his Irish birth that he had notoriously declared that calling him an Irishman was like calling a man a horse because he had been born in a stable: "Willingdone, bornstable ghentleman," as Joyce put it in *Finnegans Wake* (*FW* 10.17). Is the reader expected to know this about Wellington, and if so, what does the knowledge add to the story being told?

Gabriel has just been accused by Miss Ivors of being a West Briton, for Miss Ivors, in her somewhat self-righteous way, is trying with her brooch and a couple of Irish phrases to build a monument in the form of a bridge to defeated Gaelic Ireland. So, if one does know about Wellington's status as a successful British warrior but a reluctant Irishman and Dubliner, one can make the association between the story and a monument to one of the most famous of West Britons, a man annoyed by the detail that he had been born in that West and wanted just to be a Briton, with no desire to be of any help in improving that stable, the land of his birth. But the monument is not introduced in a way that shows any kind of obvious alliance between Gabriel and what it

---

1. Peter Rabinowitz calls this kind of occurrence a Rule of Rupture: "Any time a detail is mentioned when there seems to be no apparent reason for it, the surface of the text is ruptured; most of the times such ruptures are appropriately treated as signals to pay attention" (Rabinowitz 1987, 66).

represents; the monument appears to be a prominent but neutral landmark on which snow accumulates. We are not told that the obelisk was visible through the window. Indeed, because it is dark outside, it is unlikely that he could have seen the monument unless it was floodlit, a very remote possibility at the time. The language of both passages makes it reasonably certain that what Gabriel sees is in his mind's eye: "the snow *would be* . . . *forming* a bright cap on the top of the Wellington monument" (*D* 192), and later "he raised his eyes *to the chandelier* . . . the Wellington monument wore a gleaming cap of snow that flashed westwards" (*D* 202).

"Why the mention of the monument?" Marvin Magalaner and Richard Kain (1956) sensibly asked in their book more than forty years ago. Less sensibly they answered that "it is eminently if somewhat tritely suitable as a phallic symbol in the context of the narrative, just as Nelson's Pillar is phallic in the Aeolus episode of *Ulysses*. . . . Joyce is always equating love and death" (Magalaner and Kain 1956, 97). Apparently the phallic symbolism in both instances is supposed to be so obvious that no effort is made to demonstrate it. (Incidentally, Nelson's Pillar is noticeably absent from "The Dead.") But, after all, a pillar or an obelisk is sometimes just a pillar or obelisk, and it is not at all clear why a phallic symbol should come to Gabriel's mind "in the context of the narrative"; he is giving or about to give a speech at a family gathering.[2]

I think it is more likely that Joyce intended to imply subtly that the constant presence in Dublin of that silent and now invisible obelisk honoring a Dubliner who became famous by going abroad has had the equally subtle and unconscious effect on Gabriel that it was meant to have, what Ivors has just accused him of. In saying irritably "I am sick of my own country," he has seemed to concur with Wellesley. But even for the informed reader the connection has to be quite indirect.

Another public monument is brought to our attention later, again with Gabriel prominently involved. As the party is breaking up, Gabriel tells an an-

2. Marvin Magalaner and Richard Kain, *Joyce: The Man, The Work, The Reputation* (1956). Indeed it is absurdly easy (and quite fair) to parody a suggestion acknowledged even by its authors to be trite. Just look slightly aslant at the words quoted at the end of the previous paragraph: "the Wellington monument wore a gleaming cap of snow that flashed westwards." A phallus with a cap of *snow*? *Flashing* westward?

ecdote about Patrick Morkan, his grandfather, and King Billy (that is King William III of England and Prince of Orange), whose armies, as we have said, were victorious over the Irish at Aughrim, the Boyne, and Limerick, and whose image was still taunting a defeated people in the middle of the major city of their own land 200 years later. In a well-known and much-cited article (1965), John Kelleher interpreted the anecdote to damn Gabriel, however faintly, for *unintended* disrespect to his grandfather, a taboo-breaking or "sin" for which he is later punished by Gretta's sexual rejection.[3] But it is fairly clear that Gabriel's story about his grandfather is a yarn that everyone there knows already, certainly all those related to the Morkans. It is an old family joke that Gabriel could have heard only from his mother or from his aunts, the daughters of the said Patrick, who are part of his audience, and one gets the impression that it is one of Gabriel's party pieces. Kelleher says that Gabriel "mistells it. He hasn't the key" (Kelleher 1965, 427). If this is so, why then does everyone enjoy the story, greeting it with "peals of laughter" (D 208)? And since everyone present is thereby complicit in the irreverence, are we to assume that they were all punished? And was it sexual punishment, and if so why would that be appropriate? After all, Gabriel the alleged West Briton has also referred irreverently to a British monarch as King Billy, and the British gods were decidedly more jealous and certainly more effective than the Irish gods. Surely Kelleher oversteps the mark when he compares the "offence" of Gabriel's lighthearted storytelling to the "hubris that overcomes a tragic hero," for "the offended dead are already at work" (Kelleher 1965, 428).

This overreading comes of insisting on too close a relationship to the old Irish legend that, he says, lies at the back of the story , as well it may. Kelleher is very well aware of the danger of "triumphantly discovering more than exists or even what isn't there at all" (Kelleher 1965, 424).[4] But he takes the chance,

3. Kelleher, "Irish History and Mythology in James Joyce's 'The Dead' " (1965). Much of the rest of my paper is framed as a response to Kelleher, whose essay is a convenient point of departure because it has so often been cited as canonical and because he gives attention to some of the same historical references in the story, although not to all, and rather differently, as should become clear.

4. The Gresham might be an example. Gabriel and Gretta stay at a good hotel named for who-knows-what English lord Gresham. In one of his longer stretches, Kelleher turns the hotel

and suggests that Gabriel was breaking a taboo, however unintentionally, by telling this vaguely funny and lightly irreverent story about his grandfather and the English king. Now, taboo of this kind makes sense in a world of heroic myth and saga where the narrative method accepts or demands breadth, excess, exaggeration, and where brush strokes are big and bold, not the work of a miniaturist. A rash promise or the breaking of an arbitrary-looking taboo will do nicely to keep the story going in the direction that the narrator wants it to go. Verisimilitude or details of rational motivation do not count for much. But the conventions of the twentieth-century short story are different. In the world of Joyce's Dublin, portrayed by the artist with scrupulous meanness, the writer, unlike the epic tale teller, has to devise his scenes and characters with rather more plausibility.[5]

But Kelleher is right about one thing: he tries to make sense of the appropriateness of this particular anecdote in this particular story. Clearly, Joyce wanted a reference to the statue of William of Orange, perhaps as light as the one to Wellington, but he chose to give it as a story told at considerably more length than the Wellington reference and, like it, apparently unconnected with what immediately precedes or follows except by the thinnest of threads. The thread might go something like this: Shortly *after* Gabriel has told his story someone starts singing a song; a little after *that* we learn that the song is called the "Lass of Aughrim," and Aughrim was the name of a famous defeat of the Irish by the army of the King about whose memorial we have just heard. Considerably later still, in the second part of the story, we and Gabriel learn that his wife had had a boyfriend who died young, and who used to sing that song. Aughrim is in Galway and the boy and Gretta lived in Galway.

On a re-reading, this network of references *might* give to King Billy's

---

into the mythical Da Derga's hostel of the saga because of its red brick and other real or fancied resemblances to Da Derga's place.

5. One knows what Kelleher probably intended to provide by his parallels: "atmospherics," "pale wandering flashes" of allusion, as he puts it (1965, 433). But the paper ends up being more than the series of light allusions that he seems to have had in mind, for he uses the saga as a fairly close and detailed parallel to some of the incidents in "The Dead" and tries to account for what happens to the major character of the short story by reference to sin and broken taboo, after the fashion of heroic saga tradition.

statue a different kind of significance. "The Lass of Aughrim," which could have been just the name of a sad song sung long ago by a boy in the West that gives Gretta a sad reminiscence, could also, in the company of King Billy and the later "mutinous Shannon waves" (*D* 223), take on the character of a historical memory in the minds of Irish readers who recall the history even dimly, a subconscious memorial meant to have a quiet, almost unnoticed effect more emotional than rational, and which is not complete until the end of the story, or indeed until one re-reads it.[6] But this perhaps is to read ulyssesly.

Kelleher, of course, sees the possible connection between song and battle, but his interpretation of the King Billy narrative is that old Morkan is patriotically annoyed at the horse who goes round and round the statue, because the animal shows signs of the kind of servitude to King Billy that the Irish were reduced to after the battle of Aughrim. But Patrick was going out in his Sunday best to see the military review, a display of British martial might, and doing so in the company of "the quality," inevitably pro-British. Hence, there seems little reason to see him as a patriot angry at the servile behavior of his horse. Moreover, since Joyce was not among the patriots either, it seems unlikely that he would arrange his story to punish a mocker of Patrick's hypothetical patriotism. He was a fair mocker of Irish patriotism himself.

In the fuss of Mr. Browne's departure with Freddy and Mrs. Malins, still another monument is mentioned—three times in ten lines—Trinity College, the front of which looked straight at King Billy's statue nearby (*D* 209). The college is, to be sure, being used merely as a landmark to guide the cabby, but such persistent harping on the name needs to be explained in terms of narrative. The whole incident is quite irrelevant for any development of the central story about Gabriel and his family, but it brings to the fore for a moment that academic foundation and symbol of the Ascendancy still doing at the time of the story what Queen Elizabeth had founded it to do and what the victories of

---

6. For the extraordinarily powerful effect that the memory of Aughrim can still evoke in modern times, see the narrative and meditative poem "The Battle of Aughrim" by Richard Murphy, a Protestant who was born in Ireland but educated at exclusive British schools as the son of a very senior British diplomat. He is a man of precisely the kind of divided loyalties that Ireland has inevitably produced in large numbers. The poem has been put to music by Sean O'Riada.

King Billy and Wellington ensured it would go on doing: educating the Protestant ruling class to misgovern Ireland.

Two other public monuments in the next part of the story are indirectly related to each other. As Gabriel and company walk and drive home they see the seat of British law: "The Four Courts, stood out *menacingly* against the heavy sky" (*D* 213). Then the carriage passes the statue of Daniel O'Connell, the only monument to an Irish patriot that is mentioned.

O'Connell had had to agitate hugely and fight bitterly inside and outside court buildings for the restoration of what we would now call the civil rights denied to Catholics in a largely Catholic land during the reign of King Billy and through most of the eighteenth century. O'Connell's fight was never violent, but he secured emancipation where military efforts had repeatedly failed. He was from the West, County Kerry, but there was nothing simple about him; a skillful lawyer and a forceful speaker, he represented his fellow countrymen masterfully in the law courts and in the British House of Commons. He was a native speaker of Irish who was also a considerable orator in English; he shunned the use of force but organized Irish Catholic opposition in massed battalions of peaceful rallies that struck more fear into British leadership than Irish arms did. But, in spite of the fact that because of men like O'Connell the Penal Laws were no longer in full force in turn-of-the-century Ireland, the effects of hundreds of years of oppression and memorials to that oppression were still around them in late-nineteenth-century Dublin. Gabriel, whom Ivors has called a West Briton, salutes only the monument to O'Connell: "Good night, Dan" (*D* 214).

Kelleher needlessly transmutes the visible snow on the statue into imaginary starch from old Patrick Morkan's mill and, obediently followed by some others, turns Gabriel's cheerful wave and whimsically affectionate greeting to O'Connell's statue into an "unwitting impertinence to the mighty dead." Gabriel "has sinned a third time, and there is no escape for him" (Kelleher 1965, 429). Because Kelleher wants an explanation for what happens or does not happen to Gabriel in the hotel, he has sensibly if tacitly asked the reasonable question: Why put in this greeting to O'Connell at all? Why not just mention that they had passed his statue, a well-known landmark? He has provided an answer of sorts, one that some readers have found adequate: if there is a punishment, there must have been a sin, and the "irreverent" greeting to O'-Connell is the second sin after the irreverence to Patrick Morkan.[7] But one can see Gabriel's lighthearted salutation as an "unwitting impertinence" only if one is wearing saga-colored spectacles of the kind that might appeal to Molly Ivors. And "sinned" is exactly wrong.

There is one other British monument that gets some space in the story, but the space is left so tantalizingly empty that, as is usual with Joyce, critics have rushed in to fill it. This is the gap left by the quotation from Browning that Gabriel toys with but does not finally use, and we are never told what the quotation is. Here again Joyce draws attention to a British monument—literary this time, and more nearly contemporary than the others—only to let the reference drop, so that it provides an irresistible inducement to speculation for some critics. This literary device of marking an absence is one that Joyce became very skillful at using in *Ulysses*.

An even more tantalizing gap for anyone thinking of political monuments in "The Dead," but one that has drawn little or no speculation, is the absence of any reference to Nelson's Pillar, perhaps Dublin's most prominent and pre-eminent monument to British ascendancy. It was almost outside the Conroys' window at the Gresham, much closer to the hotel than the Wellington monument to the Morkan house, and was quite visible in gaslight. The omission is all the more noticeable to a reader of *Ulysses* because Joyce, as was mentioned already, makes Nelson's Pillar figure very prominently as a monument to British conquest in the Aeolus episode of his novel.[8]

---

7. Mary Reynolds in *Joyce and Dante* (1981) tells us what Kelleher would probably have been reluctant to claim: that he had *discovered* "that Gabriel's misfortune in the final incident . . . is a punishment—a reprisal for having sinned against his kinfolk and his country" including "a disrespectful salute to the statue of O'Connell. . . . The action is a denial of his origins" (Reynolds 1981, 161). I think Kelleher would have been happier with "speculated" rather than "discovered." See also Mitzi Brunsdale, *James Joyce: A Study of the Short Fiction* (1993), 36–51. One should also look at Powers's comment in Glasnevin Cemetery in the Hades episode of *Ulysses,* when he and Simon Dedalus pass the monument over OConnell's grave: "He's at rest, he said, in the middle of his people, old Dan O' " (*U* 6.86.643). I know no critic who has found that comment derogatory or lacking in respect and affection.

8. The point is developed within the episode in Stephen's story, "A Pisgah Sight of Palestine or the Parable of the Plums." See Michael Murphy, "Parable and Politics" (1997), 31–34.

What is the effect of the introduction (or pointed omission) of all these memorials to British conquest and Irish collaboration or resistance? They hint at a political element that remains undeveloped in a story that is largely about personal and familial relationships. As I have said, the physical monuments are introduced astutely enough, much as local landmarks might be mentioned, to give the story a local habitation in the names. But they quietly insist on being more than that in a number of ways: they are selectively chosen, at least two of them occupy otherwise inordinate space, and their structural function is not obvious.[9]

The allusions do not begin to amount to a central political theme, but they are nagging rather than fleeting. They are the occasional reminders to alert readers of the tale, as they were constant and half-noticed if unwelcome reminders to the citizens of Dublin, that some of the departed were far from dead—indeed were still quietly powerful—in the laws and institutions they had established, in the language they had imposed, in the habits of mind their successful oppressions had ingrained, in the education they had allowed to some, in the persona of Gabriel Conroy, in the person of James Joyce.

Those people from the past who are still most effectively alive are those who created the Dublin and Ireland of the Conroys and who are memorialized for the achievement: O'Connell, a man occasionally condescended to by the conqueror and allowed a few victories, still living at least to Gabriel, who familiarly (Joyce's word) but not disrespectfully calls him "Dan" and bids him "Good night" (D 214). But most potently present are the truly victorious: Queen Elizabeth, King William, Lord Gresham, Lord Wellington, even conspicuously unmentioned Lord Nelson—royal, aristocratic, British. They are not really dead.

At the end of Joyce's story, Gabriel hears the call of the West of Ireland—O'Connell's response, perhaps, to Gabriel's own recent greeting to that unashamed West-of-Irelander—a still small voice, to be sure, something associated largely with defeat, the frequent lot of the Irish before and after King William of Orange, before and after O'Connell. For Miss Ivors, who taunts Gabriel with being a West Briton, the call of the West is stronger or at least

---

9. A simple test of this last statement might be to consider whether the story would miss its major effect if it did not mention these monuments.

louder, with an ideological intellectual timbre; for Gretta it is a rain-soaked emotional murmur. Ivors is a woman of the Dublin Pale trying to touch or grow Irish roots; Gretta, a woman whose roots are in the West, who may never have become fully reconciled to the Pale of Dublin. Gabriel is a man until now unreconciled to the Pale in a different way, for he has not hitherto been interested in the West of Ireland either; his interest has been in the Continent, in urban culture, not in roots.

Michael Furey, who used to sing *The Lass of Aughrim,* may have died for Gretta in Galway, as many another Mick had died for Cathleen ni Houlihan at the battle of Aughrim, defeated by the army of King Billy after earlier defeats at the river Boyne, and at Athlone on the mutinous river Shannon. The last of the resistance of the Irish to King Billy was further down than Athlone and further west along the mutinous Shannon: the siege of Limerick. That town finally surrendered also, a defeat that led to one of the most savagely bleak eras in the history of a land that had known little else for more than one hundred years, including three military invasions of near-genocidal proportions in one century: the Elizabethan, Cromwellian, and Williamite. It was to know more. Limerick, where the last hope of Catholic Gaelic Ireland died in 1691, was still occupied in 1921 by the army of the king, whose troops murdered George Clancy, mayor of that city, because he would not give up the same cause for which his ancestors in that city had fought and died. Mayor Clancy had been Joyce's friend at the university and was the model for Davin, Stephen's near-friend in *Portrait.* His murder took place a few years after the publication of "The Dead" and *Portrait* and while Joyce was still finishing *Ulysses.*[10]

Joyce had no intention of giving his life to Clancy's passionately held views any more than Stephen did to Davin's or Gabriel to Miss Ivors's more dilettantish opinions. Gaelic Ireland was dead except in the hopes of men like George Clancy, who hated everything that most of the Dublin memorials represented and whom Joyce would not join—a choice for which critics typically praise him and Stephen but castigate Gabriel. As far as I know, Joyce wrote no

---

10. Clancy was not at all the dull-witted, well-intentioned peasant that Joyce portrays Davin as being. Peasants of any kind did not get anywhere near a university in Joyce's day, when a university education was a rare privilege indeed. Clancy came from a fairly well-to-do Limerick family in much better economic circumstances than Joyce's own family at the time.

lament, no memorial, for his old friend George Clancy, who *did* "pass boldly into that other world in the full glory of some passion," although, like Gabriel (and Joyce), he was a married man with children. It would probably be too kind to Joyce to think of the allusions to the call of the West at the end of "The Dead" as his awkward tribute to the influence of his old friend from the West, an attempt at a kind of memorial to that friend's ideals *before* his death in the old cause that Joyce would not serve with his person or his pen.

The mighty Dead whom we have mentioned, royal, aristocratic, British or West British historical figures, are powerfully if allusively present in the story. Powerfully if somewhat pitifully present also are the Dead with *un*remarkable memorials: the fictional Michael Furey buried under a headstone in Oughterard and in the heart of Gretta; the Lass of Aughrim present in a song still sung and also perhaps in the person of Lily—poor, plebeian, Irish. And maybe, just maybe, joining the voice of O'Connell, ever so faintly calling, not through the universe, just from the West of Ireland, across the dark mutinous Shannon waves where he was to die—the spirit of George Clancy.[11]

Translation of the memorial to George Clancy:

Pray for the soul of
George Clancy
Mayor of the City of Limerick
murdered on the 7th day of March, 1921.

11. That Joyce had not forgotten Clancy is clear from the entry in his Trieste notebook remarking that he had not managed to meet him on either of his Irish trips in 1909 and 1912: "I wonder where he is at the present time. I don't know is he alive still." Apart from the Irish quality of that last sentence, so typical of Davin, Joyce's thought is quite striking. He was about the same age as Clancy—around thirty at this point. Why would he wonder about Clancy's possible death (*P* 292)? There *are* a couple of physical memorials to Mayor Clancy: a plaque in his parish church in Limerick inscribed in Irish, and the street named after him that runs between the church and the modestly comfortable house in which he lived and was murdered and which still stands. Both buildings overlook the nearby river Shannon and the bridge over it, still called the Wellesley bridge in Clancy's day but since named for Sarsfield, the hero of the siege of 1691. The monuments to Nelson and King Billy have long since been violently removed by Irishmen who found their presence in the center of Dublin deeply offensive.

Mercenaries (troops) of the English crown committed the crime (did the treachery).

It is in the (hope of) the betterment of Ireland and in honor of him that his friends have raised this pulpit and this plaque to him (his memory).

# 9

# "The Dead"
## Joyce's Epitaph for Dublin

DESMOND HARDING

The dearest of all things in Ireland is the memory of the past.

Stanislaus Joyce, My Brother's Keeper

As the broad domain of human history records, there has always been an immemorial sense of patrimony given over by civilizations in a variety of architectural, cultural, social, and spiritual forms to the reverence—and placation—of the dead. Speaking in the broadest cultural and historical terms, urban historian Lewis Mumford contends that, beginning with the ritualistic practices of the earliest human settlements, over time the city has come to symbolize the ceremonial meeting place that serves as the goal for pilgrimage: "a site to which family or clan groups are drawn back, at seasonable intervals, because it [the city] concentrates . . . certain spiritual or supernatural powers, powers of higher potency and greater duration, of wider cosmic significance, than the ordinary processes of life" (Mumford 1961, 10). Consonant with the magnetic pull of "the city of the dead [as] the forerunner, almost the core, of every living city" (Mumford 1961, 7) is the fact that the origins of language itself can also be traced back to the pre-alphabetic signs of ancient burial sites as well as later alphabetical inscriptions engraved on funeral monuments located at the heart of the city in history. Yet while epitaphs manifest themselves in

123

many forms beyond engravings or hieroglyphs on tombs or gravestones, as acts of commemoration their shared sources of feeling solemnize our human points of origin and tendency *sub specie aeternitatis*. Inseparable therefore from civilization as we have come to know it, epitaphs speak to that liminal space separating the worlds of the living and the dead; they have the power to reconcile our belated claims on life while reminding us, ultimately, of that final journey we must ourselves one day make beyond the world of the living.

The modern city James Joyce presents in *Dubliners* (1914) constitutes a signal shift in urban ideology. The old idea of the spiritual city, founded on a consecrated burial place with a centrally located sanctuary, has given way to the vision of a rationally organized metropolis radiating out from the Duke of Wellington Monument, the heart of imperial and commercial Dublin. But Joyce's city is more than the sum of its turn-of-the-century mercantile and colonial parts, for in the midst of this modern community of souls a vestige of the sacred cities of the past remains alive in the symbiotic relationship between Dublin's living and dead. While Joyce's representation of Dublin invites a range of fertile associations with Mumford's urban-historical paradigm, for the purposes of this discussion I would like to restrict my remarks to a consideration of the appropriately titled "The Dead" as a text subsumed in elegy, and in particular William Wordsworth's notion of the epitaphic mode, a language and logic of feeling and expression used by the poet throughout his poetry and prose to mediate competing conceptions of historical consciousness. What is unique about "The Dead" is the way in which, in keeping with the parameters of Wordsworthian epitaph, Joyce braids into language a consolatory sense of historic space or doubling of consciousness that holds in creative tension the complex realities of the organic city of the living with the inorganic and encroaching community of Ireland's dearly departed. Moreover, as the story brilliantly dramatizes, "The Dead's" epitaphic framework further dramatizes the tensions underpinning the narrative by unveiling Joyce's antagonistic response to contemporary Nationalist pastoral narratives that demarcated the cultural and spiritual locus of the nation to lie beyond, and often in opposition to, metropolitan Dublin. An act of imaginative pilgrimage, finally, "The Dead" thus enabled Joyce to return once more to his native city, condensing and reiterating in manifold terms the paradox of Dublin as a vital phenomenon circumscribed by the past, the dead, and their enduring significance for the living.

In typological terms, Richard Lehan notes that from F. Scott Fitzgerald to T. S. Eliot, the "funereal moment" in modernist literature is a common staple denoting that "one's fate in the city often starts or ends with the grave" (Lehan 1998, 272). At the same time, modernism's fascination with death masks a hidden history, the roots of which can be traced back to the shared discourses of nineteenth-century theologians and creative writers concerning the four last things: death, judgment, heaven, and hell. Michael Wheeler, for example, has shown in his investigation of religious experience, belief, and language in Victorian Britain, that despite the wide range of contemporary responses to the subject of death there was in fact a "shared vocabulary" common to imaginative literature and theological discussions that constituted "a Victorian cult of death" (Wheeler 1990, 25).[1] Central to these discussions on death—in particular between theologians and preachers, poets, novelists, and painters—was the difficulty in coming to terms with what Wordsworth in *The Excursion* (1814) termed "death and its two-fold aspect":

Death and its two-fold aspect! wintry—one,
Cold, sullen, blank, from hope and joy shut out;
The other, which the ray divine hath touched,
Replete with vivid promise, bright as spring.
         (*Poetical Works* 1949, 5: 171, 554–57;
         quoted by Wheeler 1990, 25).

1. In *Death and the Future Life in Victorian Literature and Theology*, Michael Wheeler maintains that, "at the center of these concerns [the nature of religious experience, belief and language, as they relate to the processes of death and bereavement in Victorian deathbed and grave-yard scenes] lies a tension between what can broadly be defined as 'horizontal' ontological and epistemological models, which tend to be anthropomorphic, historical, experiential, and gradualist in orientation, and 'vertical' models, which are often theocentric, eschatological, scriptural, and catastrophist. . . . The horizontal dimension of temporal process and deferral comes to the fore in the Victorian novel, and the 'sense of an ending'; in millenarian epic poems on the 'course of time'; and in doctrines of purgatory and the 'intermediate state' between death and the last judgment, whereby final dispensations are deferred" (Wheeler 1990, xiii).

According to Wheeler, "these conflicting ideas and emotions associated with death in its two-fold aspect or paradoxical nature—as the first of the four last things, as terminus and point of departure, or as loss and gain—often focused upon two *loci* in the nineteenth century: the deathbed and the grave" (Wheeler 1990, 27). Of core importance for "The Dead" as an extension of the nineteenth century's obsession with death (and the burden of Wordsworth), I would like to argue, is Joyce's incarnation of Wordsworth's epitaphic mode. In particular, Joyce transplants the provincial contours and scenes of these debates concerning the ambiguous and conflicting duality of death and transfers their *loci* to the modernist city.

From a literary and critical perspective, the epitaphic mode is centrally associated with Wordsworth's three "Essays upon Epitaphs."[2] In the "Essay upon Epitaphs" (1810), for example, Wordsworth roundly critiques Augustan and early nineteenth-century attitudes towards language, death, and burial by taking Dr. Johnson to task for writing in his *Life of Pope,* "To define an Epitaph is useless; everyone knows that it is an inscription on a Tomb" (*Prose Works* 1974, 2: 29). Basing his argument upon the authorities of nature and ancient burial practices, Wordsworth isolates the soothing efficacy of a traditional "parish-church, in the stillness of the country," as a "visible centre of a community of the living and the dead," in contrast to the "busy, noisy, unclean, and almost grassless churchyard of a large town" (*Poetical Works* 1949, 5: 449–50). But as critics Frances Ferguson and Alan Liu have discovered to varying degrees and in radical contexts, in addition to the value of the "Essays upon Epitaphs" as cultural critiques, Wordsworth's exegesis of the epitaphic mode provides not only for provocative statements on poetic language but more importantly highlights the mode's more penetrating and self-reflexive application.

While Wordsworth ostensibly uses the epitaphic mode for occasional verse commemorating those individuals who have passed away—what Liu refers to as "Wordsworth's version of the return of the dead . . . from a transformed world" (Liu 1989, 384)—in generic terms the mode actually consti-

---

2. Wordsworth's "Essay upon Epitaphs" was first published in 1810 in *The Friend,* then again as an appendix to Books V-VIII of *The Excursion* in 1814. The latter two were published after Wordsworth's death in 1850.

tutes "a ubiquitous, multi-form presence" (Ferguson 1977, 155) throughout Wordsworth's poetry and prose that permits the poet to continuously renegotiate the bonds between the "past" and "present" in their infinite guises. In *The Prelude,* for example, the mode manifests itself whenever Wordsworth speaks of his present state of consciousness in relation to a former "self":

> so wide appears
> The vacancy between me and those days
> Which yet have such self-presence in my mind
> That, musing on them, often do I seem
> Two consciousness, conscious of myself
> And of some other Being.
> ( *Poetical Works* 2: 28–33;
> quoted by Ferguson 1977, 155).

Wordsworth's use of epitaph allows the consciousness of the poet to turn back upon itself "across vacancies almost as wide as those between the living and the dead" (Ferguson 1977, 155) in order to locate and/or recall dramatically the traces of former selves adrift in the continuum of space and time. The result in poetic terms is a spiritual autobiography grounded in "self-epitaphic history" (Liu 1989, 381). Furthermore, in keeping with the rhetoric of Wordsworth's romantic landscapes as a function of space and place, the mode mediates competing conceptions of historical consciousness between the poet and his relationship with rural northern England, the chosen venue for his use of the mode. In nature, therefore, Wordsworth coins the engraven image of his own soul.

The triduum that constitutes Wordsworth's "Essays" invariably resonates Mumford's identification of cities of the dead as endemic to the very idea of organized, living cultures. Moreover, in the same way that Mumford's numinous ancient city privileges a necropolis at its core, so Wordsworth's historical sense similarly underscores the cultural, social, and religious importance of epitaphs for protecting and memorializing the corporeal remains of a culture's dead. In historical terms, Wordsworth notes that "Almost all Nations have wished that certain external signs should point out the places where their dead are interred. Among the savage tribes unacquainted with letters this has mostly been done either by rude stones placed near the graves, or by mounds of earth raised over them. This custom proceeded obviously from a twofold desire; first, to guard the remains of the deceased from irreverent approach or from savage violation: and, secondly, to preserve their memory" (*Poetical Works* 1949, 5: 444). Likewise, the first requisite in an epitaph, Wordsworth advises, is that it "should speak, in a tone which shall sink into the heart, the general language of humanity as connected with the subject of death—the source from which an epitaph proceeds—of death, and of life" (*Poetical Works* 1949, 5: 451). Yet as Wordsworth goes on to note emphatically, epitaphs take their being not so much from the conjunction of "the principle of love" or the "faculty of reason" intrinsic to humankind but from the incarnation in language of a principle of immortality, "an intimation or assurance within us, that some part of our nature is imperishable" (*Poetical Works* 1949, 5: 445).

Conceived in the "funerary reality" (Ellmann 1982, 225) of the disastrous sojourn in Rome from 1906 to 1907, "The Dead," as Richard Ellmann eloquently notes, not only forced Joyce to re-evaluate himself as an artist but also spurred him to reconsider the artistic and spiritual possibilities of his own past in relation to the haunting palimpsest of Dublin.[3] In many ways, we might well argue that it is Wordsworth who supplies the tantalizing logic behind Joyce's reconciliation of the paradox of Dublin as a sacred city comprising the living and the dead. And yet Joyce goes further by imaginatively engaging both the paradox of Mumford's analysis of the city and Wordsworth's consideration of language and death as functions of human civilization in which "origin and tendency" are "notions inseparably co-relative" (*Prose Works* 1974, 2: 35).

While Joyce's use in "The Dead" of epitaph and the self-epitaphic mode as a vehicle for the consideration of language, life, death, and memory is grounded primarily in the workings of Gabriel's consciousness, the story actually unearths a range of epitaphs held in suspension throughout the narrative.

---

3. As Richard Ellmann notes, "The obtrusiveness of the dead affected what he thought of Dublin, the equally Catholic city he had abandoned, a city as prehensile of its ruins, visible and invisible. His head was filled with a sense of the too successful encroachment of the dead upon the living city: there was a disrupting parallel in the way that Dublin, buried behind him, was haunting his thoughts" (Ellmann 1982, 244).

Of course any interpretive reading of "The Dead" must at some point engage Gabriel's final epiphany, an endeavor made all the more difficult given the entrenched tradition of critical responses that has variously declared the conclusion to either pronounce annihilation and death or intimate transcendence and spiritual life. Indeed, this hermeneutic quest for meaning has much to do with how Joyce manifests, and how we perceive, Gabriel from the beginning of the story. At the same time, embracing "The Dead" as a form of epitaph not only provides for a more complex reading of Gabriel but in the process presents us with a more radical consideration of the axiomatic relationship between the shifting signs of memory and mortality, life and death as they relate to Gabriel's (and Joyce's) position within "The Dead."

Nowhere is Wordsworth's epitaphic consciousness more colorfully presented than in Gabriel's extended dinner speech, in which the notions of human origin and tendency are variously negotiated. The speech, like the feast spread before the Morkans' guests, is truly one of the highlights of the story, with the theme of hospitality—that Irish quality Joyce unreservedly celebrates—the most successful subject Gabriel approaches. In the course of a polished delivery, Gabriel presents several topics: the homegrown tradition of hospitality as a "princely failing" among the "modern nations" (D 202–03), the relation of the past and its sense of hospitality to a present "hypereducated" and "thought-tormented age" (D 203), and the "sad memories" of the past (D 204). Praising the past at the expense of the present, Gabriel's remarks operate at the level of epitaph insofar as the speech invokes a range of private and public memories for those present at the table. Unfortunately, rather than drawing Gabriel (as narrator of the epitaph) into the consciousness of the group, his evocations of the past merely serve to highlight his own social, cultural, and emotional disconnection from the gathering.

Prior to delivering his speech, Gabriel seemingly withdraws from the party on the grounds that he wants to be alone: "Now that supper was coming he began to think about the [Robert Browning] quotation . . . and retired into the embrasure of the window." Secluded from the company, his thoughts subsequently turn away from his fellow Dubliners: "How pleasant it would be to walk out alone. . . . The snow would be lying on the branches of the trees and forming a bright cap on the top of the Wellington monument. How much more pleasant it would be there than at the supper table!" (D 191–92). More-

over, as the time for dinner draws closer, Gabriel further worries about his imminent "failure," given the "grade of culture" of the guests, to comprehend
his literary allusion, especially "the lines from Robert Browning." He admon-
ishes himself because in his mind, "He would only make himself ridiculous by
quoting poetry to them which they could not understand. They would think
that he was just airing his superior education. He would fail with them" (*D*
179). Yet despite his feelings of alienation, the toast to the Morkans' hospitality is the most genuinely energetic moment of the evening, providing as it
does the only point at which everyone at the party feels "in unison" (*D* 205).

The memories of the living aside, at the core of Gabriel's speech lies the
foreboding presence of the dead: "the past, of youth, of changes, of absent
faces we miss here tonight" (*D* 204). Gabriel's epitaph, however, unlike the
centripetal force of the company's earlier memories concerning the old days of
Dublin's "legitimate opera" (*D* 199) and its great singers gone by, is one to
which the narrative registers no response. Eschewing commemoration as
something fit only for morose sentimentalism, Gabriel states, "I will not linger
on the past. I will not let any gloomy moralising intrude upon us here
tonight" (*D* 204). Gabriel's rhetorical maneuver fails because his incarnation
of the past has no direct effect upon the members of his audience, whose own
memories and desires concerning the shades of the past define their present
thoughts and experiences. Perhaps one reason for Gabriel's failure here is that
he does not possess, in spite of his generous nature, an epitaphic sense capable
of bearing the weight of the past. From a Wordsworthian perspective, we
might even go as far as to say that Gabriel's epitaph fails because "only epitaphic historical consciousness, in sum, can lay the past to rest with acceptance
of loss because it lays to rest the present—with all its hopes and fears—as well"
(Liu 1989, 382).

Running counter to Gabriel's use of epitaph at this point in the narrative
is Aunt Julia's rendition of "Arrayed for the Bridal," a lyrical memorial performed to music. The song not only recalls Aunt Julia's musical past but also
is a virtuoso performance that generates romanticized passions—and dangers—within the borders of the text. Aunt Julia's age, however, belies the possibility of ever acting her part in the romantic Nationalist narrative she
continues to sing. Moreover, her captive audience is able to believe and join in
the sense of excitement that her song creates: "To follow the voice, without

looking at the singer's face, was to feel and share the excitement of swift and secure flight." So enticing is her performance that even Gabriel himself "applauded loudly with all the others at the end of the song" (*D* 193). If, as the text implies, Aunt Julia is yet one more of Joyce's symbols for Ireland, then her song may well be an epitaph for Nationalist Ireland—an old woman with "a vague smile of reminiscence playing on her face" who "wouldn't be said or led by anyone" (*D* 194) to recognize the reality of her past. But while Joyce may well be warning us against romanticizing a history of servitude and betrayal in Aunt Julia's song, the fact remains that the lyricism of her performance, unlike Gabriel's literary eloquence, is the first communication of the evening to create a sense of passion and communion between performer and audience.

It is left to Miss Ivors, who most fully embodies the ethos of the Nationalist movement, to call into question Gabriel's disconnection from Irish life and culture. In the first instance, she unnerves him by revealing her knowledge of his literary contributions to the Unionist *Daily Express,* a conservative publication opposed to the Nationalist cause. She also criticizes Gabriel's attendant refusal to join in the cause of his "own land . . . own people, and . . . own country" (*D* 189). Gabriel, however, responds with antipathy to such calls to duty: "—O, to tell you the truth, retorted Gabriel suddenly, I'm sick of my own country, sick of it!" (*D* 189). But Miss Ivors returns with a cultural and ideological taunt that rankles Gabriel for the rest of the evening: "—West Briton!" (*D* 190). The situation is made all the more frustrating for Gabriel because he "wanted to say that literature was above politics" but could not risk "a grandiose phrase" (*D* 188) with a woman who is his intellectual equal. Gabriel's subsequent rejection of his wife's entreaty to join Miss Ivors and her Nationalist friends on a "trip to the West of Ireland" (*D* 191) is still another call Gabriel refuses to consider, but as the narrative suggests the manner of Gabriel's refusal seems unnecessarily harsh.

It is not until the closing scene in the Gresham Hotel, when Gabriel learns of the tragedy of Gretta's past in the West of Ireland, that he finally realizes the extent to which her latent desires are determined by a history to which he has no authentic connection. Indeed, Joyce takes full advantage of the closing scene to underscore one of the core imperatives of the story: geography is a function of destiny. Consequently, in the wider provinces of the story the desires and passions associated with the West of Ireland constitute a phantasmagoric backdrop intimately bound up with the life histories of Gretta, Michael Furey, and Gabriel. If anything, Gretta's remembrance of Michael Furey's death betrays Gabriel's bourgeois pretensions by re-exposing his cultural antagonisms to the life of Ireland beyond the city. As a result, because he places himself in a position from which he cannot perceive, much less penetrate any part of Gretta's past or memory that is distinct from his own, Gabriel cannot comprehend her present passions, let alone her own sense of epitaphic consciousness.

Like Gabriel, Joyce also turned to the Continent in order to distance himself from the calls of Nationalist Ireland. In addition, Joyce also wrote periodically for the *Express,* a choice he felt "did not necessarily make him pro-English" (Manganiello 1980, 25). But as the narrative is often at pains to suggest, Joyce's reasons for escaping Ireland were quite different from those of Gabriel. In exiling himself from Ireland, Joyce made it patently clear that he was not rejecting his nation in favor of its colonial overlord. Rather, Joyce attempted to transcend the debilitating English-Irish binary by turning to a broader, more inclusive frame of reference: Europe. As the omniscient narrator Joyce manipulates the valency of this radical disconnection—Gabriel/Ireland versus Joyce/Ireland—to betray Gabriel's bourgeois pretensions at the expense of mythicizing his own. One instance of Joyce distancing himself from his epitaphic narrator is Gabriel's focus prior to the dinner on things particularly English: the iconographic symbol of English imperialism in the form of the Duke of Wellington monument—a civic memorial commemorating an Irishman who became an English hero—and English poet Robert Browning, whom Joyce blamed for Irish poet James Clarence Mangan's neglect.

In *Dubliners* Joyce consciously chose to turn his nicely polished looking glass for the Irish people in the direction of the city; as a consequence, he challenged the "dreamy dreams" (*CW* 151) of the Literary Revival, which, in Joyce's opinion, wallowed in a degraded romantic conception of Ireland's brutal past and present rural-urban realities. As Declan Kiberd and Seamus Deane (1990) have shown, stock cultural stereotypes such as the music hall Paddy, taken from the vaudeville repertoire of nineteenth-century British cultural discourses, were in time internalized, and indeed sentimentalized, by an emergent indigenous Irish social formation: the Irish Catholic middle class. Moreover, this bloc "installed the landless peasant, the superannuated aristocrat, and the urban poor as the new bearers of an updated mythology" (Kiberd 1996, 7). Too late perhaps, the culmination of this cultural turn inward was, as many Irish writers later discovered, nothing short of "a fake nostalgia for a pastoral Ireland . . . the false consciousness of the peasant periphery" (Kiberd 1996, 16). Joyce, however, who was writing even as this aestheticization of country people was being codified on the part of nationalists and their sympathizers, had already outlined in his 1902 essay on James Clarence Mangan a conception of history in direct opposition to that promoted by the revivalists: "History or the denial of reality, for they are two names for one thing, may be said to be that which deceives the whole world" (*CW* 81).

In Joyce's mind, a romanticized vision of history obscured the reality of the nation's oppressions; "The Dead," as a consequence, can be read as a form of self-epitaphic history that exposes the dichotomy between the (rural-urban) myth of romantic primitivism embodied in the West of Ireland and the culture of metropolitan Dublin. Furthermore, "The Dead" also highlights the fact that in *Dubliners* Joyce is clearly attempting to negotiate what "Ireland" and/or "Irish" might possibly mean for anyone, let alone himself. But having disconnected himself from his nation in the first fourteen stories so as to betray the realities of Irish life all the more clearly, Joyce nonetheless continued to feel that his picture of Ireland had been "unnecessarily harsh"—indeed, that he had not given a faithful account of his native country's "ingenuous insularity" and unique "hospitality" (*SL* 132). As the well-documented nostalgic tone of his correspondence to Stanislaus from Rome during 1906–07 reveals, this remove often came at the cost of isolating himself from the passions of his countrymen. In many ways, reconceptualizing Irish life and culture in "The Dead" allowed Joyce to recapture that sense of his former self he believed self-exile and progressive artistic diminishment had taken from him. Writing "The Dead," meanwhile, enabled Joyce to attempt a more tempered conception of his native city and its enduring significance for his life and work. In its totality, therefore, "The Dead" consummated a national countercultural discourse that allowed Joyce to re-evaluate the origins and tendencies of what he had earlier outlined in "A Portrait of the Artist" (1904) as "the word . . . the masses . . . and the nation that is to come" ("A Portrait of the Artist" 265–66).

At the end of "The Dead," the two-fold paradox of death that so troubled the Victorians in their many deathbed and graveyard scenes is once again re-cuperated to devastating effect by Joyce's appropriation of Wordsworthian epitaph (and epitaphic consciousness). Failing to turn Gretta's will to his own present sexual needs, Gabriel's attempt to undermine her commemoration of Michael Furey (D 219) serves only to reinforce further the pathos of her epi-taph as a profoundly affecting memorial. Joyce makes it abundantly clear that, instead of triumphing over the living and the dead, Gabriel is shamed: "Gabriel felt humiliated by the failure of his irony and by the evocation of this figure from the dead, a boy in the gasworks. While he had been full of memo-ries of their secret life together, full of tenderness and joy and desire, she had been comparing him in her mind with another" (D 219).

Gretta's epitaph for Furey in turn triggers Gabriel to now speak over the body of his wife as she lies physically exhausted on a bed saturated with the memory of death and loss. At this critical juncture Gabriel's sense of paralysis in the face of Gretta's confession is compounded by Joyce in two ways. First, the narrative confines Gabriel to resignation—"It hardly pained him now to think how poor a part he, her husband, had played in her life" (D 222). At the same time, Joyce follows on quickly with a vision of Gabriel's latent bitterness masquerading as pity: "a strange friendly pity entered his soul. He did not like to say even to himself that her face was no longer beautiful but he knew that it was no longer the face for which Michael Furey had braved death" (D 222). Meanwhile, Joyce's own moral anger towards Gabriel is dissipated somewhat by the latter's self-epitaphic confession of his own failings: "He [Gabriel] saw himself as a ludicrous figure, acting as a pennyboy for his aunts, a nervous, well-meaning sentimentalist, orating to vulgarians and idealizing his own clownish lusts, the pitiable fatuous fellow he had caught a glimpse of in the mirror. Instinctively he turned his back to the light lest she [Gretta] might see the shame that burned upon his forehead" (D 220).

In his mind Gabriel now foresees Aunt Julia's death, with himself "sitting in that same drawing-room, dressed in black, his silk hat on his knees. The blinds would be drawn down and Aunt Kate would be sitting beside him, cry-ing and blowing her nose and telling him how Julia had died. He would cast about in his mind for words that might console her, and would find only lame and useless ones" (*D* 222–23). The pathos of this premonition is made all the more complex by the fact that Joyce presents the reader with multiple wayward and flickering representations of Gabriel. On the one hand, these lines give the impression that, in keeping with his seeming nature, Gabriel is concerned more with the burden of once more having to lend significance to the ritual of death through his own formal incarnation of language rather than allowing himself free rein to respond emotionally to Aunt Julia's passing. But the passage also intimates that Gabriel is more than ever aware of his overreliance on language as a way of mastering and/or deceiving a reality that is otherwise too much for him. This unsettling disjuncture may well, as Vincent P. Pecora contends, have to do with Joyce's use of free indirect discourse in that "language in Joyce, even in *Dubliners,* is often *dispossessed* discourse—thought, feeling, or inner speech that never completely belongs to the speaker" (Pecora 1986, 234).

"The Dead's" famous coda ends as follows:

> The time had come for him [Gabriel] to set out on his journey westward. Yes, the newspapers were right: snow was general all over Ireland. It was falling on every part of the dark central plain, on the treeless hills, falling softly upon the Bog of Allen and, farther westward, softly falling into the dark mutinous Shannon waves. It was falling, too, on every part of the lonely churchyard on the hill where Michael Furey lay buried. It lay thickly drifted on the crooked crosses and headstones, on the spears of the little gate, on the barren thorns. His soul swooned slowly as he heard the snow falling faintly through the universe and faintly falling, like the descent of their last end, upon the living and the dead. (*D* 223–24)

Despite Joyce's reservations concerning Gabriel, it might well be argued that in the "lyric peace" (Liu 1989, 387) of this closing moment Joyce creates a link between his own aesthetic vision and the masses through Gabriel, who first recognizes the veiled power of romantic passion and then transcends the bounds of his own self in order to identify with the archae of that passion: Michael Furey and the symbolic Oughterard cemetery. Lying alongside

Gretta's prostrate body on the bed, Gabriel in his symbolic resting place collapses the boundaries between deathbed, grave, and beyond as he prepares for his own journey westward toward the hosts of the dead.

Given that the highest form of presence in "The Dead" is absence in the form of the past and the dead, Gabriel's final epiphany naturally has ramifications far beyond his connection to the world of the living. We are told that, looking westwards, Gabriel's "soul had approached that region where dwell the vast hosts of the dead. He was conscious of, but could not apprehend, their wayward and flickering existence. His own identity was fading out into a grey impalpable world: the solid world itself which these dead had one time reared and lived in was dissolving and dwindling" (*D* 223). As this passage reveals, the power of Furey's spectral presence, like a sentinel from beyond this world, engenders a kind of supernatural absorption (colored over as it is with Gabriel's "generous tears" [*D* 223]) in which Gabriel's sundered soul figuratively dissolves out into the collective presence (and memory) of the grateful departed. In the heart of metropolitan Dublin, Gabriel journeys toward death; he has found that "other" community of the living: the dead. And yet it is the very nature of this metaphysical journey, as mediated through Gabriel's consciousness, that remains enigmatic. Gabriel's westward gaze, it has been argued, is merely one final instance of "the social *ricorso* that eventually traps all who remain in Joyce's Dublin"—as if the city itself is the site of some "grand repetition compulsion by which the conflicts that trouble its inhabitants are constantly evoked and rehearsed, but never worked through" (Pecora 1986, 234).

While we would do well to keep in mind the rich tradition of critical responses as we read "The Dead," it seems more likely that in this final installment of *Dubliners* Joyce in fact re-forges a larger connection (however ambiguous) with his nation and his former self in the form of self-epitaphic history. As Liu pointedly remarks with Wordsworth in mind, "*self*-epitaph . . . allows the reader to pick up the bones of the dead in a different way. The nature of the self-epitaph is to trigger further stages of self-epitaphic consciousness in the reader" (Liu 1989, 381). In the course of working through his own sense of self-epitaphic history, it can be argued, Joyce turns his consciousness back upon his variegated points of origin and forward toward their approximate tendencies—but not necessarily through the eyes of Gabriel as his epitaphic narrator within the text. The larger significance of Joyce's use of epitaph is that, while it is inevitable that there will always be contending critical readings of "The Dead," the accommodating concept of the epitaphic principle provides a means of holding in suspension (mediating and/or negotiating) the multiplicity of responses (which invariably turn out to be reductive binary readings) without necessarily demanding conformity. Epitaph, in other words, enables the reader to take back "The Dead."

In broader terms, I would like to suggest further that "The Dead" both recycles and modifies the historicity of Dublin's past and present in keeping with *Dubliners* as a spiritual autobiography. In Wordsworth's case, the use of epitaph often exists in opposition to the very real deaths of the individuals he memorializes, for as Wordsworth notes "the Writer of an epitaph" performs his act of remembrance "by the side of the grave" (*Poetical Works* 1949, 5: 152). By the same token *Dubliners* itself, in keeping with Wordsworth's dictum, similarly commiserates with very real people by poeticizing the diachronic realities of Irish life that have engendered a deathlike state of living paralysis.

There is also a concentric beauty in Wordsworth's use of epitaph in that the *Essays* collectively move beyond specific characters and communities to embrace the anonymity of the deceased as a function of epitaph's ability to commiserate at a universal level. According to the poet, the rationale for the move beyond immediate passions is "so that what was peculiar to the individual shall still be subordinate to a sense of what he had in common with the species, [and] our notion of a perfect epitaph would then be realized" (*Poetical Works* 1949, 5: 453). In commiseration Wordsworth aims to defuse an affective response; consequently, the universal affections of the writer are their own justification, and thus an appeal to the reader's affections is avoided. For Wordsworth, therefore, the importance of epitaphs is that as incarnations in language they radically implicate the consciousness of the reader. As a consequence, Wordsworth's epitaphs adopt a series of mutually informing mediations grounded in the act of reading with the result that a complex structure of interacting relationships arises comprising the poet, reader, and the deceased through which "the stranger is introduced . . . to the company of a friend" (*Poetical Works* 1949, 5: 456). Interestingly, a similar system of informing relationships is apparent in Joyce's use of epitaph. In reading "The

Dead," we invariably reach the terminus of Wordsworth's sense of the epitaphic mode, for, "out of the discontinuities of both language and life," Joyce,
like Wordsworth, brokers "a poetry of memory" (Ferguson 1977, 31).

As the dramatic framework supporting Gabriel's epiphany unravels, the
consciousness of the reader is inevitably drawn into a series of reciprocal relationships mediated by Joyce as the writer of the epitaph as follows: Joyce and
Gabriel; Gabriel and Gretta; Gabriel and the guests at the party; Gretta and
Michael Furey; Furey (and the hosts of the dead) and Gabriel; and, finally, the
reader and all of the above permutations. In the course of these reciprocal relationships, the use of epiphany is a necessary component in the process of
representing "reality" as the thing-in-itself, as revealed "truth." Yet as Joyce's
use of epiphany reveals, the incarnation of language-as-epiphany (or linguistic
incarnation) does not necessarily correspond to Gabriel's, Joyce's, or even the
reader's own transfiguration. One reason for this state of indeterminacy is that
the danger with incarnation is that it is not always absolute. The self-epitaphic
mode also adds to the lack of resolution in that it triggers further stages of self-
epitaphic consciousness in the reader. Wordsworth's epitaphs necessarily
throw the burden of consciousness back upon the reader in order to remind us
that, in the process of linguistic incarnation, "language is not a salvation for
the complexities of individual consciousness" and that "the life of language in
poetry, like the life of the individual, is radically implicated with death." (Ferguson 1977, 33–34). All the same, "The Dead" is as much the first cry of a
newborn spirit as it is the last gasp of a dying soul. What we are left with is
Joyce's guarded confession that the artist and the common people can only
meet through their passion on a spiritual rather than a political plane. Yet even
in this final point lies the irrevocable pathos at the heart of all forms of epitaph,
Joyce's included: "the incarnation into language comes always ex post facto,
too little and too late" (Ferguson 1977, 31).

# PART 3

# The Chamber of Words

# 10

## But on the Other Hand

### *The Language of Exile and the Exile of Language in* Ulysses

IGNACIO LÓPEZ-VICUÑA

James Joyce inhabits Dublin as a ghost, someone "who has faded into impalpability" (*U* 9.147) through exile. Because Joyce made self-exile a personal as well as an aesthetic choice, *exiles* permeate and repeat themselves in his texts. Joyce's heroes—Gabriel, Stephen, Bloom—are men who are not fully at home even at home. Exile is an essentially ambivalent form of absence—it means being there, but not altogether. If *Ulysses* dramatizes a quest to return to the home, then this return means coming to terms with the unfamiliarity of "home" and with estrangement as a precondition for finding oneself.

When Stephen "chooses" exile at the end of *A Portrait of the Artist as a Young Man*, this choice is a ruse to conceal the fact that in a sense he already is an exile. He is estranged from his family, his friends, his church, and his country, and hence has been forced into "silence, exile, and cunning" by the very powers from which he seeks to free himself. Writing as an exile, Joyce is acutely conscious of the extent to which language shapes affiliation and estrangement, and he highlights this dimension in Stephen's rebellion: "I will not serve that in which I no longer believe, whether it *calls itself* my home, my fatherland or my church, and I will express myself wholly and freely, using si-

*141*

lence, exile, and cunning" (*P* 238, my italics). This emphasis on what those cultural institutions *call themselves* points to the critical importance of words in shaping absence or exile. In drawing Gabriel, and particularly Stephen and Bloom, Joyce's language is consistently oblique and ambivalent; as alter-egos, these characters constitute self-parodies of Joyce and hence are cited with irony. This technique allows Joyce to recuperate his own voice ambivalently, thus evading assertion and straightforwardness. Furthermore, in *Ulysses* both Stephen and Bloom resist assertion in every possible way: their language is a language exiled from itself, always ambivalent, always undercutting itself. Through Stephen and Bloom, and through his own ironical distancing from them, Joyce engages in a micropolitics of language that employs obliqueness and non-affirmation as strategies not only to resist propaganda but also to critique the whole notion of conviction.

## Gabriel: Self Parody and the Recuperative Value of Irony

In a letter to Stanislaus of September 1906, Joyce wrote, "Sometimes thinking of Ireland it seems to me that I have been unnecessarily harsh. I have reproduced . . . none of the attraction of the city for I have never felt at my ease in any city since I left it except in Paris. I have not reproduced its ingenuous insularity and its hospitality. The latter 'virtue' so far as I can see does not exist elsewhere in Europe" (Ellmann 1982, 231). Joyce was referring to his collection of stories, *Dubliners*. He wrote "The Dead" as an afterthought to the rest of the collection and, according to some critics, this story marks the beginning of his reconciliation with Dublin. In the Christmas speech in "The Dead," Gabriel Conroy's words not only echo, but also mock, Joyce's: "I feel more strongly with every recurring year that our country has no tradition which does it so much honor and which it should guard so jealously as that of its hospitality. It is a tradition that is unique as far as my experience goes (and I have visited not a few places abroad) among the modern nations" (*D* 184). Gabriel is as insincere as he is contemptuous of his audience (he even omits from his speech a literary reference he knows will be "above his listeners"). But—one should ask—do Gabriel's insincerity and sentimental rhetoric invalidate his words? As is frequently the case with Joyce, the status of Gabriel's words remains ambiguous. However, reading the "Christmas speech" as a citation (and parody) of Joyce's own words provides one possible context for interpretation. Richard Ellmann, for example, views Gabriel's words as a token of Joyce's reconciliation with Dublin: "This was Joyce's oblique way, in language that mocked his own, of beginning the task of making amends" (Ellmann 1982, 245).

Although this narrative of estrangement and reconciliation is possible, I am more intrigued by the way Joyce's citations undermine the meanings they offer while allowing those same meanings to be recuperated. In other words, the status of Gabriel's speech, like that of Stephen's rebellion or Bloom's defense of universal love, is ambivalent. It expresses a meaning that remains under erasure, expressible only insofar as it is a parody of itself. Hence Joyce's irony towards his characters is double-edged and recuperative, as Harry Levin recognized (Levin 1960, 68). His characters' words activate contradictory, conflicting readings, whose reconciliation is possible but always uneasy. If there is irony in Joyce's citations, his irony works both ways, and thus defies closure.

## Stephen: From Silence to Paradox

What is an exile? one could ask, echoing Stephen's question "what is a ghost"? ("What is a ghost? Stephen said with tingling energy. One who has faded into impalpability through death, through absence, through change of manners" [*U* 9.147–49].) Joyce would seem to suggest that an exile is one who can no longer speak the language of the land; one for whom the words that express affiliation, love, loyalty, have become burdensome and constraining, like so many nets flung at him to keep him down. In *A Portrait*, Stephen arrogantly defies all these hindrances: "You talk to me of nationality, language, religion. I shall try to fly by those nets" (*P* 196). Joyce stresses dramatically the connection between exile and linguistic failure—the experience of being "at a loss for words." In particular, for Stephen "I will not serve" means "I will not say the words," as is evident in the opening episode of *Ulysses*.

In "Telemachus," Buck Mulligan castigates Stephen for refusing to "say the words": "—You could have knelt down, damn it, Kinch, when your dying mother asked you. . . . But to think of your mother begging you with her last breath to kneel down and pray for her. And you refused. . . . But a lovely mummer! he murmured to himself. Kinch, the loveliest mummer of them all!" ( *U* 1.91–98). Stephen, a "mummer" who forsakes his mother(land) through silence, offers a compelling image of the inescapable link between language and loyalty.

But loyalty, Joyce seems to be saying, need not be expressed through assertion. It can be expressed ambivalently, through paradox and parody. Hence Stephen's silence is not merely a refusal but indeed is a resistance to assertion and conviction. There are numerous examples of Stephen's resistance to assertion—through silence, paradox, irony, and disavowal. In *Stephen Hero*, the president of the university warns Stephen against paradoxes: "To support Ibsenism on Aquinas seems to me somewhat paradoxical. Young men often substitute brilliant paradox for conviction" ( *SH* 101). For Stephen, however, paradoxes seem to be one—and often the only—valid way of expressing conviction. Stephen's language, in particular, seems to function as a resistance to assertion and to certain models of forcefulness and masculinity of which Joyce is suspicious.

One of these models is Mr. Deasy, who states "firmly" that his motto is *"per vias rectas"* ( *U* 2.282). After paying Stephen his salary and duly lecturing him on the English virtue of thrift, Deasy concludes, "We are a generous people but we must also be just," to which Stephen replies, significantly, "I fear those big words . . . which make us so unhappy" ( *U* 2.263–64). (This is, again, a citation of Joyce's own words. Joyce once accused the poet Rooney of suffering from "one of those big words which makes us so unhappy." Arthur Griffith replied with the statement that the word Joyce meant was "patriotism" [Manganiello 1980, 233].) Through Deasy, Joyce exposes the underlying violence of those who speak in "big words." Deasy's anti-Semitic tirades are complemented by his self-acknowledged rhetoric in the letter about "foot and mouth disease": "I don't mince my words, do I?" ( *U* 2.331). While Stephen shuns "big words," Deasy "doesn't mince" them. By allowing Deasy to speak himself into obliteration, Joyce offers one eloquent example of how assertive speech can undo itself.

Another instance of self-damning speech is provided by Buck Mulligan. In "Telemachus" he taunts Stephen by summing up his theory on Shakespeare for Haines: "It's quite simple. He proves by algebra that Hamlet's grandson is Shakespeare's grandfather and that he himself is the ghost of his own father" ( *U* 1.555–57). Mulligan's clever parody of Stephen's ideas mocks them by presuming to state them straightforwardly. Of course this is ironic, but patronizingly so; Mulligan's cleverness assumes a certain air of familiarity whereby he can possess and control Stephen's knowledge: *it's quite simple.* By "Scylla and Charibdys," however, Stephen has passed from silence to paradox, from quiet suffrance of the slings and arrows of Mulligan's wit to an expansive display of brilliantly paradoxical rhetoric as he unfolds the mysteries of his "theory of Shakespeare." Mulligan is reduced to mimicking Stephen's wit, but less happily so. ("No . . . neighbor shall covet his ox or his wife or his manservant or his jackass.—Or his jennyass, Buck Mulligan antiphoned" [ *U* 9.790–92]. Later Mulligan is inspired by Stephen's idea that every man shall be a wife unto himself, and exclaims "Eureka!" as though he had himself come up with the idea [ *U* 9.1053].) Interestingly, Stephen does not assert his theory; when asked if he believes it, he answers "no" ( *U* 9.1066–67). By deauthorizing his own theory, Stephen puts it under erasure: he states and undercuts at the same time. Joyce seems to be saying that meanings can be expressed legitimately only if they are silenced or denied—paradoxically, contradiction seems to be the highest form of affirmation. (Also in the Library episode, the men discuss whether Wilde's *Portrait of Mr. W. H.* is merely a paradox [ *U* 9.542–44]. Joyce's wink to the reader here appears to indicate that even the idea that mockery is serious is not to be taken seriously.)

### Bloom: The Politics of Nonassertion

Bloom is aware of the dangers of assertion, and he continually resists a forceful assertion of self in words and deeds. Like Stephen, Bloom is conscious of how "big words" can confine and paralyze. In "Cyclops," Bloom is insistently provoked to assert himself forcefully "like a man" and resists as best he can. Challenged by the citizen to state what his nation is, Bloom replies unambiguously, "Ireland. I was born here. Ireland" ( *U* 12.1431). However, he complicates this statement by adding, "And I belong to a race too . . . that is hated and persecuted. Also now. This very moment. This very instant" ( *U* 12.1467–68). When asked if he is talking about "the new Jerusalem," Bloom responds that he is "talking about injustice," to which John Wyse retorts, "Right . . . Stand up to it then with force like men" ( *U* 12.1473–75). By invoking anti-Semitism, Bloom reminds his listeners (and readers) of his status as an *other*, an exile in his own homeland, a man at home yet never fully at home. Joyce seems to be showing here a particular way of inhabiting Dublin—as an exile, as an Irish Jew, as a native who is also at the same time an *other*, both familiar and unfamiliar, heimisch and unheimlich.

What makes the situation more poignant is the fact that Bloom is not even master of his own house; his wife Molly is sleeping with Blazes Boylan. Under this light, Wyse's challenge to "stand up with force like a man" might be read as an exhortation to stand up to his wife's lover and show him (and Molly) who is boss, somewhat like Odysseus, who slaughtered Penelope's suitors upon his return to Ithaca. As *Ulysses* makes clear, however, Bloom does not slay the suitor(s), but instead accepts his wife's desires. His acceptance can be read as a comment on sexual tolerance and a rejection of traditional models of male competitiveness. In Willy Maley's words, "In *Ulysses*, Bloom and Blazes Boylan share the bed of Molly Bloom. It would seem . . . that whereas [for Joyce] national betrayal is a bad thing, men—in particular—must learn to come to terms with sexual jealousy and the spectre of betrayal in the home" (Maley 1996, 8).

If there is a politics at work here, then Joyce seems to condemn machismo as much as he condemns nationalism and imperialism. But Joyce's politics are even more evident at the level of language—what Vicki Mahaffey calls "the micropolitics of language and narrative" (Mahaffey 1998, xiii). (Mahaffey borrows the term "micropolitics" from Deleuze and Guattari's *A Thousand Plateaus: Capitalism and Schizophrenia,* in particular, "1933: Micropolitics and Segmentarity" [Mahaffey 1998, xiii].) For example, Bloom is conscious of the underlying violence of "big words" such as "love," and is careful not to repeat the gesture of the citizen, who enounces *"Sinn fein amhain*! The friends we love are by our side and the foes we hate before us" (*U* 12.523–24). Hence, when provoked to "assert himself with force," Bloom appeals instead to universal love, and immediately realizes his mistake:

> —But it's no use, says he. Force, hatred, history, all that. That's not life for men and women, insult and hatred. And everybody knows that it's the very opposite of that that is really life.

—What? Says Alf.

—Love, says Bloom. I mean the opposite of hatred. (*U* 12.1481–85)

Aware that he has named one of "those big words which make us so un-happy," Bloom immediately rephrases it as "the opposite of hatred." But it is too late—the citizen and his buddies will ridicule Bloom as an apostle for "universal love." There is no reason to suppose Joyce is not citing Bloom with irony here; in fact, my point is precisely that a defense of love could not be ar-ticulated in *Ulysses* if it were not for Joyce's tongue-in-cheek presentation of the humane Bloom. As soon as Bloom leaves the pub, the citizen mocks him: "A new apostle to the gentiles. . . . Universal love" (*U* 12.1489). Not content with this, Joyce also has the narrator mock Bloom by chanting "love loves to love love." But rather than invalidate Bloom's statement, this parody merely allows Joyce to name love without sentimentality. In Richard Ellmann's words, "it is the kind of parody that protects seriousness by immediately going away from intensity. Love cannot be discussed without peril, but Bloom has nobly named it" (Preface to *Ulysses* 1986, xiii). Because love is such a "big word," it can only appear in *Ulysses* if it is at the same time erased (mocked, disavowed). (It remains a fine Joycean irony that the "word known to all men," which Stephen identifies as "love" in "Scylla and Charybdis," was liter-ally in a state of erasure from *Ulysses* until the publication of Gabler's recon-structed text. It is only then that "love" appears as the word Stephen demands from his mother in "Circe.")

   If it is true that Joyce's citations tend to undermine the meanings that they offer, then it makes sense to consider Bloom's statements as ironical per-formances of themselves. On this point I find Leo Bersani's discussion of *Ulysses* illuminating: "The question of point of view," he writes, "is essentially a question of citation—whose voice is the narrative quoting?" (Bersani 1990, 161). Bersani argues that Joyce objectifies the subjectivity of his characters by writing as the character himself would write if he had "performed himself with irony." In Bersani's view, this is a ruse that allows Joyce to escape points of view altogether and present the narrative as though it were a "quotation of es-sential being," and hence a presumed objectivity, which reaffirms both Joyce's virtuosity and his mastery (Bersani 1990, 161–63). Ironic self-performance is of course also a question of the status of enunciation: Joyce tends to splinter the enunciation into a voice and its mocking echo. But if Bloom's voice is cited with irony, it is the kind of ambivalent irony that undermines and recuperates at the same time. (L. A. Murillo in *The Cyclical Night* argues that Joyce's irony achieves a "poise" or "balance of attitudes" by both magnifying and mocking his characters [Murillo 1968, 38].) In "Cyclops," the voice that the narrative quotes is that of a one-eyed narrator, hostile to Bloom and unappreciative of his evenhanded rhetorical style. The narrator's irritation is evident every time Bloom's penchant for equanimity and prudence surfaces. When Bloom attempts to downplay the citizen's celebration of Irish sports by mentioning the risks of violent exercise, the narrator is incensed: "I declare to my antimacassar if you took up a straw from the bloody floor and if you said to Bloom, *look at, Bloom. Do you see that straw? That's a straw.* Declare to my aunt he would talk for an hour so he would and talk steady" (*U* 12.893–96); when Bloom tries to temper the citizen's blasting against British military discipline by suggesting that discipline is "the same everywhere," the narrator reduces Bloom's rhetoric to the absurd: "Didn't I tell you? As true as I'm drinking this porter if he was at his last gasp he'd try to downface you that dying was living" (*U* 12.1362–63). For the narrator, Bloom's persistent attempt to look at both sides of any question is as absurd as denying the simple facts that a straw is a straw and that death is not life. Bloom's voice is often not cited directly in this episode, but rather is refracted through the narrator's mimicry: "And Bloom with his *but don't you see?* and *but on the other hand*" (*U* 12.514–15). Bloom seems always to be able to find an "other hand." With Bloom, Joyce offers a humorous example of being of two minds, a sort of idealized equanimity or evenness of mind that, while remaining humorous, represents a political intervention to resist the language of assertion. In his endeavor to find a nonassertive and nonauthoritarian language, Joyce found in Bloom a jocoserious alternative.

## But on the Other Hand—

In "Circe" Bloom is introduced as "bisexually abnormal" and as "a finished example of the new womanly man" (*U* 15.1776, 15.1798). This characterization is not related so much to sexual ambivalence, I would argue, as to a humorous enactment of Bloom's desire to consistently look at the *other side* of things. For every "one hand," in Bloom's mind there must also always be an "other hand." It will be remembered that, according to Dr. Mulligan's diagnosis of Bloom, "Ambidexterity is also latent" ( *U* 15.1780). Bloom's psyche, then, typifies the kind of thinking that refuses to define itself; that says, it is but it isn't, an ambivalent positioning Freud called "disavowal": the ability to hold contradictory ideas in the psyche simultaneously. In Freud's analysis, the male is able to understand that women do not have penises while at the same time believing that (on the other hand) they may, a belief that explains fetishism (Freud 1963, 326). In this sense Bloom, like Joyce, evades straightforwardness.

Joyce's style is well characterized by Garry Leonard's words: "What teaching Joyce's fiction should teach everyone is that the 'truth' about his fiction is not what one comes to understand, but what defies explication" (Leonard 1993, 310) Joyce's ambivalent ironies and the contradictory readings he invites (and authorizes) defy being put straightforwardly (O rocks! Tell us in plain words). By means of paradox, ambivalence, self-parody, and, especially *jocoseriousness*, Joyce flies by the nets of straightforward assertion. The words Lynch's cap says to Stephen in "Circe" seem to me to illustrate Joyce's ambivalent disavowals magnificently: "Ba! It is because it is. Woman's reason. Jewgreek is greekjew. Extremes meet. Death is the highest form of life. Ba!" ( *U* 15.2097–98). Framed by dismissal (ba!), these words are disavowed, and yet they provide crucial interpretive keys to Joyce's text. The statement "Death is the highest form of life" is a mockery of Stephen's rhetorical use of paradoxes; but what makes it significant is that it is a citation (and parody) of words Joyce himself once wrote. In 1902 a very young James Joyce wrote that the poet James Clarence Mangan proclaimed, "the praise of life . . . and of death, the most beautiful form of life" ( *CW* 83). Joyce's self-indulgent use of paradoxes was also parodied at the time with the suggestion that absence was the highest form of presence, a joke Joyce remembered many years later. The cap's words in "Circe" therefore parody Joyce's early words and at the same time indirectly recuperate that other parody: the idea that absence is the highest form of presence.

I would like to suggest that, by means of his ambivalent disavowals, Joyce presents a way of being with oneself that presupposes never being fully of one mind. Such a choice is analogous to the way Joyce's ironic performances of himself—Gabriel, Stephen, Bloom—inhabiting Dublin: as exiles, as men who are there, but not altogether. This was the way Joyce himself inhabited Dublin; for him as well, absence was the highest form of presence. By undercutting, mocking, and disavowing every assertion, Joyce seems to be engaged in a politics of language that insists on taking things, not seriously, but jocoseriously. Like Oscar Wilde before him, Joyce was dead serious about not being serious; this is the reason why *Ulysses* (and *Finnegans Wake*) is a profound tribute to Ireland and is also a huge joke. It is as if Joyce were suggesting that, in any constructive project, one must be able to undercut every statement; one must be able to say, at any given moment, "but don't you see? but on the other hand . . ."

# 11

## Hosty's Ballad in *Finnegans Wake*
### *The Galway Connection*

MICHAEL BEGNAL

N ear Galway in July 1998, a sixty-eight-year-old mystery was solved when the body of Patrick Joyce was discovered in a bog ("The Strange Case of Patrick Joyce" 1998, 2). Patrick Joyce, no relation to James, had disappeared from his home at Barna, a village outside Galway, on October 15, 1920, presumably kidnapped and executed by soldiers of the IRA as an informer for the Black and Tans. The whereabouts of his corpse was unknown until now. As a reprisal for the crime, a month later Father Michael Griffin, attached to Saint Joseph's Church in Galway and a known IRA supporter, was murdered by the Black and Tans in retaliation for the killing of Patrick Joyce. The two cases became a cause célèbre and were front page news in all the British and Irish papers of the 1920s, also making many papers in the United States. Subsequently, an inquiry was publicly launched in the British House of Commons, which reached no significant conclusions. The incident would remain today as only a footnote in the bloody Irish struggle for independence, along with being a local curiosity when a body pops up in a bog, were it not for the details of the events that lead us back to several mysteries that exist in *Finnegans Wake*. Behind Patrick Joyce and Michael Griffin lies a web of coincidence and significance that would have appealed to James Joyce, and it seems almost impossible that he would not have known of them.

In book I, chapter two, the "Ballad" chapter of the *Wake*, Humphrey

151

Chimpden Earwicker, aka Persse O'Reilly, perhaps a Joycean surrogate figure, is exposed as a sinner, a liar, and a traitor. He is accused of a wealth of evils, before he is finally driven out and shot dead—"caught his death of fusiliers" (*FW* 47.10). Apparently, Earwicker also conspired with the British Black and Tan troops who ravaged Ireland—"And Gall's curse on the day when Eblana bay / Saw his black and tan man-o'-war" (*FW* 46.13). As a result, he receives the short shrift of a traitor's burial, and his body will never be found—"And not all the king's men nor his horses / Will resurrect his corpus / For there's no true spell in Connacht or hell / That's able to raise a Cain" (*FW* 47.26). The indictment of Earwicker is contained in a scurrilous ballad, written, printed, and distributed by a shadowy figure known only as Hosty—"the mann to rhyme the rann, the rann, the rann, the king of all ranns" (*FW* 44.16). This Hosty appears to be in league with Shem the Penman (a letter writer) and Shaun the Post (the mailman who delivers the letters),[1] and the episode contains the essential themes of *Finnegans Wake* that permeate the novel: letters, gossip, rumors, dirty dealings, trials, and reprisals. It is the tale of yet another disgraced and betrayed Irishman.

The ballad emanates out of HCE's unfortunate meeting with the Cad in Phoenix Park, and its author is "Hosty, (no slouch of a name), an illstarred beachbusker" (*FW* 40.21), who is in league with two more bar loungers, Treacle Tom and Frisky Shorty. Hosty's career as a street performer has been less than successful, and on this evening he is considering the two ways out that are left open to him—suicide or a permanent place in an indigents' hospital. But, upon hearing the gossipy tale of HCE, the next morning Hosty, "the rejuvenated busker" (*FW* 41.13), fortified by several hours of pub crawling with his new friends, gives up his latest idea of writing a letter for relief. "The small p.s. ex-ex-executive [recalling Shaun's "Exexex! COMMUNICATED" (*FW* 172.10)] capahand in their sad rear like a lady's postscript: I want money. Pleaseend" (*FW* 42.08). Instead, Hosty opts to make his fortune with "The Ballad of Persse O'Reilly." "The rhymers' world was with reason the richer for a wouldbeballad of which the world of cumannity singing owes a tribute for

---

1. After examining the *Finnegans Wake* notebooks, Danis Rose and John O'Hanlon write that "VI.B.14 208 identifies Hosty as one of HCE's sons: '[Shaun] = Hosty' " (*Understanding "Finnegans Wake"* 1982, 39).

having placed on the planet's melomap his lay of the vilest bogeyer but most attractionable avatar the world has ever had to explain for" (*FW* 42.12).

The contradiction inherent in "vilest" and "most attractionable" underscores the paradoxical nature of the ballad itself. Persse O'Reilly can be a hero or a traitor, depending on which verse we read, and the political situation and O'Reilly's affiliation are even more unclear. As was noted, Earwicker-O'Reilly is associated with the Black and Tans, but later, when Treacle Tom is called before the inquisitive Mamalujo, a different possibility emerges. Tom states that the ballad came about when "me and Frisky Shorty, my inmate friend . . . was glad to be back again with the chaps and just arguing friendlylike at the Doddercan Easehouse having a wee chatty with our hosty in his comfy estably over the old middlesex party and his moral turps" (*FW* 523.23). In the ensuing discussion, Tom will suggest that the fallen Earwicker "they say is a fenian on the secret. Named Parasol Irelly. . . . And peopling the ribald baronies with dans, oges and conals [Daniel O'Connell]!" (*FW* 525.15). If Earwicker-O'Reilly is a Fenian, why would he be attacked by the gang, who seem to be Fenians themselves: "the rascals came out of the licensed premises . . . wiping their laughleaking lipes on their sleeves, how the bouckaleens shout their roscan generally (seinn fion, seinn fion's araun)" (*FW* 42.07). Certainly, in any political discussion Joyce would have invoked a plague on both their houses, since he was always leery of any certitude. The fluid, multiple applications and associations of the ballad reveal the frightening truth that there is no certainty, that one can never truly know anything about anyone else. And, as we shall see, Joyce would apply such a premise to his own personal life.

So who, then, is this Hosty, who has been speculated about for so long? Martha Black, who has written extensively and ably about the balladeer, says that "Hosty is the host of the eucharist, his name is a deflation of the ideal of religious communion as well as an ironic comment on traditional Irish hospitality" (Black 1995, 347). This may be relevant, but names are a slippery business in the *Wake*, and Earwicker-O'Reilly is exhibit number one. Who he is depends on where one stands. "Some vote him Vike, some mote him Mike, some dub him Llyn and Phin while others hail him Lug Bug Dan Lop, Lex, Lax, Gunne or Guinn. Some apt him Arth, some bapt him Barth, Coll, Noll, Soll, Will, Weel, Wall but I parse him Persse O'Reilly else he's called no name at all" (*FW* 44.10). While one character appellation morphs slyly and confusingly into another, "in this scherzarade of one's thousand one nightinesses that sword of certainty which would indentifide the body never falls" (*FW* 51.04). But this tendency does not apply to Hosty, whose identity is stable and unchanging, and to ferret him out we will have to investigate the streets and pubs of Nora's Galway in the 1920s.

Returning to the murders of Patrick Joyce and Michael Griffin, we know to begin with that James Joyce was fascinated by others who shared his name, relatives or not. As early as 1907, he had written a piece for the Triestine *Piccolo della Sera* on the Galway Maamtrasna murder trial of 1882, coincidentally Joyce's birth year, where among the accused were Myles Joyce, probably innocent, yet another Patrick Joyce, probably guilty, and a victim named John Joyce ("Ireland at the Bar," *CW* 197–200). Throughout their years in Trieste, Zurich, and Paris, the Joyces were in constant touch by mail with Nora's family in Galway, so it is quite possible that they would have heard of the sensational events surrounding Patrick Joyce and Father Griffin. But in 1922 Nora returned to Galway with Giorgio and Lucia to visit her relatives, where the case would certainly have been an outstanding topic of conversation, especially given its details, its coincidences, and its personal connections to Nora. It is highly unlikely that Joyce would not have heard about all this, one way or another.

Focusing again on Patrick Joyce, apparently the IRA had been for some time suspicious of his activities and the possibility of his being an informer.[2] A clandestine IRA investigation was thus begun by one John Hosty (the name Joyce would use for his ballad writer), a local printer who worked in a Galway shop named O'Gorman's, noted as a publisher of broadsides and ballads, that had coincidentally employed Nora Barnacle when she was a teenager. (It should be noted, though, that this is not the first appearance of the distinctive Hosty name in this Galwegian labyrinth. Years earlier, Nora's father, itinerant baker Thomas Barnacle, was drinking illegally after hours one night in his favorite pub, Hosty's Public House on Bridge Street. When the pub was raided

2. For many of the following Galwegian historical details, I am indebted to two very interesting books written by local historian Padriag O'Laoi. Both were privately printed, and they seem to have been missed by most Joyceans: *Nora Barnacle Joyce: A Portrait* (1982) and *Fr. Griffin: 1892–1920* (1994).

by the constabulary, Barnacle escaped notice by hiding under the counter. The couplet he wrote to commemorate the incident became a Barnacle family favorite. "The whiskey was nice and so was the maker / And under the counter was Barnacle the baker.") Hosty was no stranger to the Barnacle family, and even today there are more than a dozen listings for "Hosty" in the current Galway telephone directory.

And the plot thickens. Desperate for information, John Hosty contacted a friend and fellow IRA man Joe Togher, who was employed as a mail sorter in the Galway General Post Office. Soon enough, Togher had picked out and stolen five letters, all in the same handwriting, addressed to the Black and Tan Command and to the British authorities. ("So why, pray, sign anything as long as every word, letter, penstroke, paperspace is a perfect signature of its own" [*FW* 115.6].) But these letters did have an incriminating signature, and Hosty and Togher discovered that all five of the communications were written by Patrick Joyce. The letters named scores of supposed IRA soldiers and their supporters in the town and surrounding countryside. Patrick Joyce urged that all of these people be arrested immediately, so that this lawless rebellion could be put down before it actually had a chance to begin. Thus, Hosty betrayed the betrayer Joyce, and the letter writer was brought down by the postman, perhaps yet another example of "the last word in stolentelling" (*FW* 424.35). A Hosty is the snake who reads your mail and discovers your secrets. Patrick Joyce was kidnapped forthwith, taken to the country, and executed, after being summarily court-martialed by four IRA judges named Michael, Morgan, Ned, and Tim (unfortunately, not Matthew, Mark, Luke, and John).

But one murder demanded another, and this leads to Father Michael Griffin, Nora Barnacle, and her old boyfriend or lover Willy Mulvey. The Black and Tans were infuriated that their prized informer Joyce had disappeared and had obviously met his end at the hands of the rebels. As was mentioned, soon enough Father Michael, who was rumored to have been present at Patrick Joyce's death (although this was never proven), was dealt with in exactly the same way. Coincidences continue. Father Michael was based at St. Joseph's Church, and Nora Barnacle, who was baptized there, also at one time worked next door as a porteress at the Presentation Convent, although she could never have known this priest. Further, on the night of Griffin's abduction, three men came to his rooms on Montpelier Terrace where he lived alone, sometime around midnight, and apparently persuaded him to come along with them.

The loud banging on Griffin's door at such a late hour awakened a neighbor, who peeked out his bedroom window at the commotion and secretly watched the proceedings. He stated that he could not identify the three men. That neighbor, who testified extensively at the military enquiry that was ultimately unable to discover any of the guilty parties, was Nora Barnacle's one-time paramour Willy Mulvey. Finally, Mulvey would only say noncommitally, sounding like a character out of *Dubliners*, "I was under the impression it was an ordinary raid, and went back to bed" (O'Laoi 1994, 49). Mulvey saved his skin and Father Michael was gone, but the priest was not forgotten. A monument was erected in his memory at Barna, another at Loughrea, a church was named after him at Gurteen, and a road in Galway still bears his name. Soon after, shades of Persse O'Reilly, a ballad was composed in Father Michael's honor, printed at O'Gorman's where Hosty worked, and was often sung at republican social events. The ballad ends, "A fair-haired saint is watching / from his kingdom in the skies / O'er the hills and vales of Ireland / with those gentle smiling eyes / 'Twas like the lamb that likewise / was by man so foully slain / who now leads to make of Erin / a proud nation once again" (O'Laoi 1994, 49).

Whether or not Nora Barnacle saw Willy Mulvey when she returned to Galway in 1922 is unknown (though apparently she did not tell James Joyce if she did). But Galway was still buzzing over these sensational events, as Nora must have heard from her mother, uncle, and sister Kathleen, who also was employed at O'Gorman's. While it is certainly true that Joyce did not engage in a point-by-point retelling of the Patrick Joyce–Father Michael Griffin story in *Finnegans Wake,* names and concurrent themes strongly indicate that there is a Galway connection to the ongoing saga that produces Hosty's "Ballad of Persse O'Reilly" and with the nefarious Father Michael Arklow, the alleged deflowerer of Anna Livia Plurabelle. The new story would have opened old wounds.

We know that James Joyce was always jealous and suspicious about Nora's romantic and sexual past, and he often quizzed her about it (Maddox 1988, 96). As early as 1904 in a letter to Stanislaus, the threatening duality of the priest and the lover first emerges as Joyce tells his brother what he has learned of Nora's history before she came to Dublin (Glasheen 1977, 192–93). Supposedly, when Nora was sixteen, a Galway priest, "a nice young man with black curly hairs on his head," took a fancy to her, pulled her onto his lap, and put his hand up under her dress. When Nora pulled away, the priest, who knew that she would have to admit the incident at her next confession, told her to say that it was a man, and not a priest, who did this. "Useful difference," comments Joyce. When Nora was nineteen, she was walking out with Willy Mulvey, but Joyce seems to accept her story, at least at this stage ("Says she didn't love him and simply went to pass the time") (*Letters* 2: 72). The relationship ended when her uncle found out that Mulvey was a Protestant and apparently beat her severely. The priest figure resurfaces in a 1909 letter to Nora written from Dublin, in which Joyce recalls that she rebuked him for saying that priests are repulsive and disgusting, an opinion he says that bursts forth "sometimes when that horrible story of your girlhood crosses my mind" (*Letters* 2: 255).

In 1912 a homesick Nora traveled from Trieste to Galway, and a lovesick Joyce followed soon after. It is clear, however, that before he got there jealousy was again getting the better of him. Held back by literary business in Dublin, he writes to her detailing the laudatory reviews that *Chamber Music* has received, and he boasts insecurely, "Can your friend in the sodawater factory or the priesteen write my verses?" Richard Ellmann says only that these two figures are "Unidentified Galwegians" (*Letters* 2: 304), but Father Padraig O'Laoi, in his memoir of Nora, has discovered who they are. The "priesteen" is the Galway curate from Nora's girlhood, and the friend in the sodawater factory is Willy Mulvey, who worked for many years as an auditor and accountant in Joe Young's Mineral Water Company (O'Laoi 1982, 36). James Joyce never forgot the past, or at least Nora's past, perhaps a nightmare from which he was trying to awake. The reappearance of Willy Mulvey ten years later would certainly have piqued Joyce's interest, to say the least, as would the murder of a Joyce, informer or not. So Joyce was unable to escape the spectres of the priest and Willy Mulvey, and the stories of Patrick Joyce and Father Michael Griffin in 1922 might well have seemed like déjà vu all over again, as Yogi Berra has said.

The Father Michael figure is never far from sight or memory when Anna Livia or Issy, or any female for that matter, are around. He is an omnipresent entity, multiple and mysterious in his various appearances, almost always a force of sexual seduction. For the young Anna Livia, he is a local priest and hermit ("Michael Arklow was his riverend name" [*FW* 203.18]), and he is rumored to have relieved Anna Livia of her virginity. He was excited by her "kindling curves you simply can't stop feeling, he plunged both of his newly annointed hands, the core of his cushlas, in her singimari saffron strumans of hair, parting them and soothing her and mingling it, that was deep-dark and ample like this red bog at sundown." The conclusion was inevitable. "He cuddle not help himself, thurso that hot on him, he had to forget the monk in the man so, rubbing her up and smoothing her down, he baised his lippes in smiling mood, kiss akiss after kisokushk (as he warned her niver to, niver to, nevar)" (*FW* 203.32). He may be carried away by passion, but his "niver to's" might also recall Nora's Galway priest's admonishments never to tell what went on between the two of them.

As well, Father Michael will resurface in the marital law case of Anita-Anna Livia and Honuphrius-Earwicker as the wife's confessor and seducer. "Anita has formerly committed double sacrilege with Michael . . . a perpetual curate. . . . Michael, who has formerly debauched Anita, dispenses her from yielding to Honuphrius who pretends publicly to possess his conjunct in thirtynine several manners" (*FW* 573.03). Again, the priest as thief, the alienator of affections—this is the irrational fear that would have upset Joyce so much. The priest is the deceiver, whether he leads the young girl into sin or alienates the affections of the once-dutiful wife. Any priest named Michael can raise the red flag, so why not Griffin as well? "Anita is disturbed but Michael comminates [threatens] that he will reserve her case tomorrow for the ordinary Guglielmus [William, Willy Mulvey?] even if she should practise a pious fraud during affrication [rubbing up against something or someone]" (*FW* 573.23). (We might recall Gabriel Conroy's jealousy over Gretta's first giving her love to *Michael* Furey, another boy from the West.)

Father Michael, guilt, and sex seem synonymous in the world Joyce is creating. Earlier, when the letter, or Anna Livia's mamafesta, is discovered in a dungheap, the effort to figure out its writer mirrors Hosty's and Joe Togher's ultimate discovery of Patrick Joyce as letterwriter. After a discussion of the handwriting, Father Michael is cited by the repressive narrative voice in a sexual digression that begins with a young woman's fall from her "bisexcycle," intentionally or unintentionally in front of a priest. The double entendres, which conclude with the girl's reply, begin with the priest, "who picks her up as gingerly as any balmbearer would to feel whereupon the virgin was most hurt and nicely asking: whyre have you been so grace a mauling and where were you chaste me child? Be who, farther potential?" (*FW* 115.17). Our stern narrator sees nothing funny about the situation, and, even though he may reveal his own desire for girls like this, he knows that Father Michael is not to be trusted. This narrator points to experts like himself for support— "we grisly old Sykos who have done our unsmiling bit on 'alices, when they were yung and easily freudened . . . could . . . tell . . . that *father* in such virgated contexts is not always that undemonstrative relative (often held up to our contumacy) who settles our hashbill for us and what an innocent allabroad's adverb such as Michaelly looks like can be suggestive of under the pudendascope" (*FW* 115.21).

A couple of lines from the aforementioned letter would seem to indicate that at least now the doubledealing priest is dead. Anna Livia concludes "with a beautiful present of wedding cakes for dear thankyou Chriesty and with grand funferall of poor Father Michael don't forget unto life's & Muggy well how are you Maggy" (*FW* 111.13). And there's the rub, since the funeral recalls "the grand fun for all," and a woman's memory is something a jealous lover can never erase. That memory is the worm at the core of the apple. The between-the-lines gist of Anna's letter is clarified to an even greater extent by the letter-valentine that Issy, Anna's avatar, hands to the departing Jaun in book III, chapter two.

Of course, engine dear, I'm ashamed for my life . . . over this lost moment's gift of memento nosepaper which I'm sorry, my precious, is allathome I with grief can call my own but all the same, listen . . . accept this witwee's mite . . . from my hands in second place of a linenhall valentino with my fondest and much left to tutor. X. X. X. X. It was heavily bulledicted for young Fr Ml, my pettest parriage priest, and you know who [Mulvey?] between us. . . . And, listen, now do enhance me, oblige my fiancy and bear it with you morn till life's e'en and, of course, when never you make usage of it, listen, please kindly think galways again or again, never forget, of one absendee not sester Maggy. . . . Of course, please too write, won't you, and leave your little bag of doubts, inquisitive, behind you unto your utterly thine. (*FW* 457.32)

The unfaithful temptress Issy admits that the letter-valentine was originally meant, with a great many hugs and kisses, for her tutor and paramour Father Michael, "my pettest parriage priest." Both her letter and Anna Livia's mention sister Maggy, and both insist on remembering what went on in the past— "don't forget" and "never forget"—the letter's "never" echoing Father Michael's "niver to, niver to, nevar," and adding a romantic dimension to the demand. Issy's letter would seem to tie the deception firmly to Nora, her adventures with priests and boyfriends, and the town where everything occurred—"please kindly think galways again or again, never forget." A jealous husband would not forget what might have gone on in Galway either. Her call for him to write, and not to be jealous, is not very reassuring to a Joyce who wrote to Nora during both of her Galway visits, especially when Issy asks him to sign his letters clearly "in case I couldn't think who it was or any funforall happens" (*FW* 458.21). (There is that "funeral," "funforall," again.) In her attempts to convince her current lover of her fidelity, she keeps returning to thoughts of Michael ("my sapphire chaplets of vingarosary I will say for you to the Allmichael" (*FW* 459.01). It remains unclear whether her phrasing is accidental, or an exercise in the Freudian slip—"I will long long to betrue you along with one who will so betrue you that not once while I betreu him not" (*FW* 459.20). Her outrageous explanation of why she would dally with Michael or someone else (Mulvey?), and whose name she will cry, takes the proverbial biscuit. "I just want to see will he or are all Michales like that, I'll strip straight after devotions before his fondstare . . . your name . . . will [Willy?] come forth between my shamefaced whesen with other lipth I nakest open my thight when just woken by his toccatootletoo my first morning" (*FW* 461.20).

A Joyce has his writing stolen, and is betrayed by a Hosty, or "enemy" in Latin. And then, as well, there is a beloved woman, who may or may not be a base betrayer. For reasons we cannot know for sure, Nora's last visit to Galway left a bitter taste in the mouth of James Joyce, from which he does not seem to have recovered. Writing to his aunt Josephine in 1922, with Nora and the children's narrow escape from a crossfire of civil war gunfire that whizzed through their railroad train compartment fresh in his mind, he said this.

No doubt you will see Nora some other time when she goes to revisit her native dunghill though it is doubtful if Giorgio or Lucia will go. The air in Galway is very good but dear at the present price. The only enlivening feature of their journey appears to have been their interview with my father who amused them vastly by the virulence, variety and incandescence of curses which he bestowed on his native country and all in it—a litany to which his eldest son says *Amen* from the bottom, that is to say, the nethermost or lowest part of his heart. (*Letters* 1: 191)

He says that Nora and the children are out, and he will ask them more about the Galway trip when they return, "but who knows whether they will be telling the truth or not? That's the point" (*Letters* 1: 191). Father Michael Griffin stands at one end of the continuum of distrust, Willy Mulvey at the other, with Patrick Joyce in the middle. (In a recent development that Joyce might have loved, Patrick's granddaughter refuses to believe that the found body is that of her grandfather, because coins in the corpse's pockets are too shiny ["The Body in the Bog" 2000]). These figures loom behind the central concerns that would find their way into the pages of *Finnegans Wake*.

# 12

## *Tambour,* the "Revolution of the Word," and the Parisian Reception of *Finnegans Wake*

MARK MORRISSON

> "THE REVOLUTION IN THE ENGLISH LANGUAGE IS AN ACCOMPLISHED
> FACT."
> "THE IMAGINATION IN SEARCH OF A FABULOUS WORLD IS
> AUTONOMOUS AND UNCONFINED."
> "PURE POETRY IS A LYRICAL ABSOLUTE THAT SEEKS AN A PRIORI
> REALITY WITHIN OURSELVES ALONE."
> "THE LITERARY CREATOR HAS THE RIGHT TO DISINTEGRATE THE
> PRIMAL MATTER OF WORDS IMPOSED ON HIM BY TEXT-BOOKS AND
> DICTIONARIES."
> "THE PLAIN READER BE DAMNED."

These are some of the battle cries of literary modernism proclaimed in "Revolution of the Word" in the June 1929 issue of Eugene Jolas's Parisian magazine, *transition.* This manifesto, signed by expatriates including Kay Boyle, Caresse and Harry Crosby, Hart Crane, and Eugene Jolas, is a famous (and easily accessible) proclamation of modernist aesthetic autonomy, as well as formal and linguistic experimentation. The final salvo, "THE PLAIN READER BE DAMNED," notoriously and memorably shifted the onus of interpretation squarely onto the shoulders of the reader and, like some pre-World War I manifestos, the "Revolution of the Word" advertised and distinguished itself using a rhetorical opposition to mass audiences.[1] Indeed, *transition* published James Joyce's most difficult writing—*Finnegans Wake* (then still known as *Work in Progress*)—for almost ten years, and, as Jean-Michel Rabaté puts it, "Even if Joyce did not endorse the most extreme statements of the manifestoes announcing the 'Revolution of the Word,' in *transition* there were enough points of contact to let the main contributors to the magazine stand as the official interpreters of the *Wake,* and to give Joyce a renewed sense of rootedness in Paris" (Rabaté 1997, 98).

The "Revolution of the Word" manifesto was signed by two such interpreters of *Work in Progress,* Harold J. Salemson and Stuart Gilbert, who were also, however, writing for *Tambour,* a little magazine published and edited in Paris by Salemson from February 1929 to June 1930. In 1930 Salemson penned an equally noteworthy but largely forgotten rejection of the "Revolution of the Word." His manifesto, titled "Essential: 1930," called into question many of the ideals of the modernism espoused by *transition* and looked toward the socially and politically engaged writing of the 1930s. Other magazines, like V. F. Calverton's *Modern Quarterly* in America, also took up the debate with *transition* and, as Jeffrey Segall has shown, in America *Ulysses* was frequently invoked in contentious intellectual and political struggles: "during the twenties and thirties, *Ulysses* was at the center of a broader debate about the social or political unity of literature. One's opinion of the novel became something of a litmus test defining a critic's position in the cultural tug-of-war taking place at the time" (Segall 1993, 7–8). Segall notes that before the Woolsey decision in 1933 legalizing the American publication of *Ulysses,* and before the New Critical espousal of modernism helped effect its eventual canonization in the 1940s and 1950s, *Ulysses* was attacked from the Left (by Soviet critics and henchmen like Andrey Zhdanov and Karl Radek and by Communist Party-controlled magazines like *The New Masses*) and from the Right (by New Humanists like Paul Elmer More) as well as from the liberal "middle" (writers like Archibald MacLeish and Van Wyck Brooks) while it was defended by "Dissident Left" writers like Edmund Wilson, Dwight MacDon-

---

1. See Janet Lyon (1992) for an account of such rhetorical practices in pre-World War I manifestos by British Vorticists and Suffragettes and Italian Futurists.

ald, and James T. Farrell who upheld modernism and a kind of independent Trotskyist Marxism.

But in Paris at the end of the 1920s, the litmus test was *Work in Progress*—a text largely written in that city. *Tambour* helps us situate Joyce's work in relationship to both American reception—and I emphasize expatriate American reception in Paris, not specifically the cultural circuits that Segall describes—and French reception. *Tambour*'s rhetorical about-face is especially interesting in that it emerged from the modernism of late 1920s Paris (rather than from, say, the Greenwich Village socialism of *The Liberator* or *The New Masses*) and therefore challenged some of the assumptions of formalism and aesthetic autonomy of its own milieu. I will use *Tambour* as a lens through which to view, not how the discussion of modernism in Paris shaped *Finnegans Wake*, but rather how *Finnegans Wake* shaped debates about modernism in Paris at the end of the "roaring twenties."

*Tambour* was published during the midpoint of Joyce's stay in Paris, and 1930, as Rabaté notes, marked the close of a particularly productive period for him (1997, 89). The years 1929 and 1930, during which *Tambour* was published, saw the transformation of *Work in Progress* from primarily magazine publication (in the *Transatlantic Review, Criterion, Navire d'Argent, This Quarter,* and, most steadily and prolifically, in *transition*) to major book publication and translation into French. In August 1929 American expatriate Caresse Crosby's Black Sun Press published *Tales Told of Shem and Shaun* in Paris; the French translation of *Ulysses* appeared in 1929; in 1930 Jack Kahane published *Haveth Childers Everywhere* in a beautiful expensive edition in Paris and New York; and, most importantly, in June 1930 Faber & Faber published *Anna Livia Plurabelle.* Moreover, in December 1930 Joyce began working with several people, including Paul Léon, Eugene Jolas, Ivan Goll, and Philippe Soupault, on the French translation of *Anna Livia Plurabelle,* which appeared in the May 1, 1931, issue of one of the key French literary magazines of the day, *La Nouvelle Revue Française* (see Richard Ellmann 1982, 632–33, and Rabaté 1997, 89–90).

While American critics continued to fight cultural wars over the still-banned *Ulysses,* in Paris *Work in Progress* was clearly a central text for critical scrutiny, and as a phenomenon it deeply affected *Tambour* and a manifesto titled "Direction," written by Harold J. Salemson, Richard Thoma, and Samuel

Putnam in 1930 (after *Tambour* had folded). Examining *Tambour* in relationship to *transition* (with which *Work in Progress* will always be associated) offers us a more complicated vision of the expatriate modernist scene in Paris at the end of the 1920s. *Tambour* challenged *transition*'s "Revolution of the Word" vision of modernism in two ways: first (and implicitly), by emphasizing film, *Tambour* acknowledged a crucial turn in modernism—from the revolution of the word to the revolution of the image—at a key moment in Parisian modernism during which surrealists were beginning actually to make their own films; and second, by explicitly attacking what had come to seem a pure formalism, *Tambour* urged a concomitant move toward a more accessible and socially engaged literature. Understanding these currents within modernism helps us to gain a more nuanced account of Joyce's Parisian reception, offering a context for understanding the quasi-surrealist descriptions of *Work in Progress* and the conflict over "unintelligible" modernism that *Work in Progress* helped provoke.

Because *Tambour* has yet to be reprinted and is only available in a few rare-book rooms, let me supply a brief sketch of the magazine. Many American little magazines have been praised for their international flavor, including *transition,* which published some French and German literature; but *Tambour* was more international and polyglot than most. Unlike *transition,* which almost always translated European literature into English for the American readers it targeted, *Tambour* not only published contemporary French literature in its original French but also translated some American work into French. Editorial leaders appeared side by side in both French and English, and the magazine was much more committed than other little magazines to bringing contemporary French writing to both American and French audiences.

*Tambour* created a discursive space that combined disparate scenes of writing at the end of the decade; as one might expect, present are American expatriate modernists in Paris (Paul Bowles, Ralph Cheever Dunning, Ludwig Lewisohn, Richard Thoma, Charles Henri Ford, Countee Cullen, Maxwell Bodenheim, Samuel Putnam, and Salemson himself). But American southwestern writers, like Witter Bynner and Norman Macleod, also contributed. Several famous American authors saw some of their earliest publication in *Tambour.* Paul Bowles published six of his earliest poems in the magazine, and some of his pieces have not appeared in any of Bowles's poetry collections.[2] Moreover, two early stories by James T. Farrell and an early and uncollected Elder Olson poem, "Two in a City," also saw publication in *Tambour*.[3] But beyond these Americans, many of the most significant French writers and artists of the day, including Blaise Cendrars, Philippe Soupault, André Spire, and Jean Cocteau, appeared in *Tambour*, and Richard Thoma's work on the life and writing of Cocteau was also published in the magazine.[4]

*Tambour*'s attention to French and American arts also drew it closely into contemporary French magazine genres. It is an interesting hybrid, combining the modernist expatriate little magazine of the 1920s with a traditional French "revue" magazine—like the *Mercure de France, Nouvelle Revue Française,* or *Revue des Deux Mondes.* (Salemson himself temporarily took over Jean Catel's "Lettres Anglo-Américaines" section of the *Mercure*'s "Revue de la Quinzaine" from February 15, 1929, through August 15, 1930.) The "Revue de la Quinzaine" section, which had taken up more than half of each issue of the *Mercure de France* since the 1890s, divided the world as it interested the French reader into different departments. These departments reviewed foreign and French literature, history, moral and religious issues, politics, psychology, the sciences, and other intellectual fields, as well as the art galleries, the circus, the theater, and the cabaret. The emergence of the "Revue de la Quinzaine" section, in fact, changed the fortunes of the *Mercure*—which had

2. "Poem" in *Tambour* 4 and "Hymn" in *Tambour* 6 have not been published in any of Bowles's collections of poetry. Two others, which were published together in the eighth issue under the joint title "Moonward"—individually titled "Dream" and "Slow Song"—have been published in his books, but "Dream" has been renamed "Prelude and Dance." The two poems were never again published consecutively and have lost their original pairing as "Moonward."

3. Farrell never reprinted "In the Park," although "My Friend the Doctor" appeared as "The Doctor" in his *Fellow Countrymen: Collected Stories* (1937).

4. Moreover, its seventh issue included an admirable selection of contemporary Italian poetry, including poems by Massimo Bontempelli, Eugenio Montale, and others. The magazine also supported the modernist chinoiserie of the day, including Witter Bynner's "Chinese" poems, Stuart Gilbert's story "The Whispering Pagoda: A Burma Night's Entertainment," and translations of poems by Liang-Tsong-Tai. Cocteau, at around the same time as Thoma's series on him in *Tambour*, was also the subject of John Charpentier's "Figures: Jean Cocteau" in the *Mercure de France*.

been primarily a symbolist little magazine in the 1890s—and allowed it to continue publishing avant-garde literature while becoming an authoritative and fairly centrist institution of French culture.[5] *Tambour*'s version of the "Revue de la Quinzaine," titled "Notes," ended each issue with a fascinating document of American and Parisian cultural and intellectual life—modernism and mass culture—at the end of the 1920s. It included reviews of art and literature, but it also reviewed theater, musical performances, new phonograph records, and film.

This savvy combination of American expatriate little magazine and French revue gave *Tambour* a distinction not enjoyed by any of the other American expatriate magazines in Paris: it was reviewed and followed by the French revues. Charles-Henry Hirsch reviewed four of the eight issues of *Tambour* in his column, "Les Revues," in the *Mercure*'s "Revue de la Quinzaine," sometimes quoting extensively from *Tambour*.[6] *Tambour* reaped the rewards of not simply publishing obscure avant-garde literature, as its special Anatole France issue drew a long review in the January 15, 1930, *Mercure* (430–33).[7] Both the *Mercure* (June 1, 1930) and *Nouvelle Revue Française* (June 1930, 933), noted Salemson's "Essential: 1930" manifesto in the May 1930 issue of *Tambour,* and Hirsch's *Mercure* review mentioned the bilingual publication of the manifesto and its critique of "modernisme chercheur de forme" (the modernist seeker of form) (415). Both the *Mercure* and the *Nouvelle Revue Française* generally only reviewed French magazines in their revues sections, and *Tambour* was the only American expatriate little magazine to garner this kind of attention.

5. The institution that the *Mercure* had become appealed to Ford Madox Ford as he began his *English Review* in 1908, and also to Ezra Pound and Richard Aldington, who shared Ford's dream of a central critical institution embodying what they imagined to be a cohesive French culture.

6. Hirsch noted *Tambour* issues in the following *Mercure de France* issues: 1 Apr. 1929: 208; 15 Jan. 1930: 430–33; 15 Mar. 1930: 687; 1 June 1930: 415; and 1 Aug. 1930: 703.

7. *Tambour* 5 was a postmortem on Anatole France five years after his death that solicited assessments of his work from dozens of French and American authors, ranging from Andre Gide, Andre Maurois, Paul Morand, Blaise Cendrars, and Jean Catel to Theodore Dreiser, Waldo Frank, Zona Gale, H. L. Mencken, Bertrand Russell, Bernard Shaw, Edmund Wilson, and William Carlos Williams, among others.

The relatively new art of film was one of *Tambour*'s strong suits, and this trait kept it strongly in the fold of Parisian journalism and Parisian life. Immediately after the war audiences had flooded movie houses in Paris, and moviegoing continued in an upward trend throughout the decade of the 1920s, with such post-war movie houses as the Gaumont Palace at the Place Clichy seating 5,000 people with space for an eighty-piece orchestra. The Gaumont Palace and the Marivaux brought in more than four million customers in each year of the 1920s, and by 1924 ten Parisian cinemas had each reached more than two million viewers per year (Monaco 1976, 18–19). As Paul Monaco notes, "In 1921 paid admissions to cinemas accounted for 23 percent of total entrances to all 'attractions' in the city. By 1929 the percentage had risen to just over 40. The percentages are all the more impressive because they relate cinema admissions to *all* other public attractions. These included paid admissions not only to legitimate theaters, concerts, and operas, but also to circuses, music halls, cabarets, sporting events, recreational areas, public museums and historical monuments" (1976, 19). Cinema revenues escalated through the decade, cinema coaches were added to trains, films were shown on board ocean liners, and in 1922 the Paris Conservatory even began offering courses in cinematography (Monaco 1976, 22).

Important French reviews also lent legitimacy to cinema; in 1920 the *Mercure de France* published a series of lengthy film columns by Léon Moussinac, and the *Nouvelle Revue Française* began featuring film in 1926 (Abel 1988, 196, 322). As Georges Sadoul notes, in the wake of Moussinac's column, "nearly every published paper, from the major reviews to the dailies and weeklies, made way besides its section of drama criticism for a section devoted to film. Henceforward, the cinema became a subject of dinner-table conversation like the novel or the play, and there emerged a group among the intellectual *élite* for whom it was a major preoccupation" (Sadoul 1972, 34). Indeed, 1929, the year *Tambour* started publication, was the year that cinema caught up to and surpassed theater in returns in post-war France (Crisp 1993, 8). In 1929 the talkies also took off in France, and a momentary escalation of French-speaking films in Paris between 1929 and 1932, although short lived, returned French films briefly to pre-World War I production highs (Sadoul 1972, 60).

Like the French journals, *Tambour* kept up with cinema, including figures like Charlie Chaplin who were important to the surrealists; the "Notes" section regularly reviewed film journals like *Experimental Cinema, La Revue du Cinéma,* and expatriate English-language film magazines like *Close-Up,* which was begun by Bryher and Kenneth MacPherson and distributed at Shakespeare and Company and which Noel Riley Fitch claims was the first English-language magazine entirely devoted to film (1983, 266). *Tambour* brought commentary on American cinema to French audiences,[8] including Francis Ambrière's columns on films by King Vidor, Charlie Chaplin, and others; and Salemson's notes on L'Herbier's *Forfaiture* and on pioneering French filmmakers like Georges Méliès, whom Salemson pronounced "inventeur du spectacle cinéma-fantastique" ("Cinéma-Théâtre" n.d., 73) and whose *Voyage À La Lune* (1902) could rival surrealist films of later decades.

*Tambour*'s bringing of film discussion into modernism occurred just as surrealist film was coming to fruition. Although surrealists had been interested in the cinema since around 1920, and although Breton and Jacques Vaché had spent much of their free time during military service going from one movie house to another, it was not until the mid-1920s that they began to explore the possibilities of the medium more systematically.[9] The surrealists were fascinated by the potential of horror movies like Wiene's *Caligari* and Murnau's *Nosferatu* as well as Hollywood movies like *King Kong,* in addition

8. Harold J. Salemson was himself an important link between Parisian audiences and Hollywood film. After returning to America, from 1931 to 1940 he worked in Hollywood for one of Paris's leading evening newspapers, *L'Intransigeant,* and its weekly movie magazine, *Pour Vous.* He was the Hollywood Bureau Manager for the *Paris-Soir* from when it bought *L'Intransigeant* until the fall of France in 1940. (Salemson, "Professional Background" n.d.). Harold Salemson went on to write various Hollywood columns for several magazines and papers, including the *Sydney Sunday Telegraph;* after fighting in the war, he went back to Hollywood in 1946 to become Director of Publications for the Screen Writers' Guild and publisher of its magazine *The Screen Writer,* "transforming it from a house bulletin to a magazine internationally recognized in the field" ("Professional Background" n.d., 2). At this time he again became Hollywood correspondent for *France-Soir* and *L'Ecran*—successors to *Paris-Soir* and *Pour Vous*—and went on to work for a variety of film publications and film companies.

9. See J. H. Matthews's account of surrealist interest in film (1971). Robin Walz notes that surrealists "also engaged in a variety of viewing practices, from roaming indiscriminately from screen to screen and interrupting audiences by eating picnic lunches in movie houses" (Walz 1996, 51).

to more experimental work. They wrote film reviews, and, as Robin Walz notes, "In their own cinematic bids, Antonin Artaud, Blaise Cendrars, Robert Desnos, and Philippe Soupault wrote surrealist film scenarios, and a limited number of surrealist films were made by Man Ray, Salvador Dalí, and Luis Buñuel" (Walz 1996, 51).

Several of these figures, including Cendrars, Cocteau, and Soupault, contributed to *Tambour*, and Cocteau and Cendrars, at least, were subscribers to the magazine (others may have been also, but a complete subscription file has not survived). Although Cocteau was in a rivalry with the surrealists and saw himself, as Frederick Brown puts it, "as the underdog in a political contest [with the surrealists] for the suffrage of Youth" (Brown 1968, 293), his early film style owed some debt to surrealist film. Indeed, in *Tambour*'s first year, on July 10, 1929, Cocteau saw a private screening of what some call the first surrealist film—Luis Buñuel and Salvador Dalí's *Un Chien Andalou*—and Cocteau's first film, *Le Sang d'un Poète* (1930), borrowed heavily from Buñuel's film (Brown 293). Michel Arnaud, who directed Cocteau's *Le Sang d'un Poète,* contributed a long verse drama, "Onan," to *Tambour* 6, and a story to *Tambour* 2—an issue in which a drawing by Cocteau also appeared. Film was examined in both the "Notes" section and in articles, and *Tambour* discussed Hollywood films for Parisian audiences.

Discussions of film provide an important context for understanding conflicts over the status of modernism at the end of the 1920s. Max Eastman, a staunch American critic of Joyce's *Work in Progress* and of Stein, Cummings, Eliot, and Edith Sitwell, used film metaphors to complain that modernism was becoming too visual—he complained that audiences must *"see* [Cummings's] poetry because it is composed so largely of punctuation that it cannot be heard. In fact we shall soon have to exhibit Cummings in a projection-room" (Eastman 1935, 59). But *Tambour* and its contributors were more sanguine about film's possibilities for creating an important modernist medium. Surrealists saw the power of the visual register of film to rearrange and reorder reality, to have the "power to disorient [son pouvoir de dépaysement]," as Breton put it, and Breton and Desnos spoke of it in terms of "mystery," "miracle," and "dream" (Matthews 1971, 2, 3), some of the same terms in which *Work in Progress* was understood. Although Joyce himself was wary of surrealism and saw in it a kind of sloppiness (Rabaté 1997, 95; Levitt 1979, 126), Herbert Gorman, in his defense of the "Revolution of the Word" in the *Modern Quarterly,* explicitly cast the verbal reconstructions and rearrangements of reality in *Work in Progress* in visual terms very much like those used in the surrealist discussion of the psychological depth to which filmic images can penetrate: "But the revolutionized word, the remoulded, reconstructed vocable, must be used only where it is necessary—in that peculiar type of creative literature whose best exemplar is James Joyce. To capture the exact nuance, to merge several meanings into one word so that that word like a finely cut precious stone dazzles the eye of the mind with several facets at once, to express at once a surface meaning, a sub-meaning and a super-meaning, that, I think, is the true function of the revolutionized word" (Gorman 1929, 292).

But, although the writers in favor of the "Revolution of the Word" used visual metaphors that might have evoked filmic associations, and the manifesto itself had, quoting Rimbaud, called for "the rhythmic 'hallucination of the word,' " it was still a manifesto about words per se, not one about film. *Finnegans Wake*'s oneiric qualities could suggest visual corollaries, but film was not held up as a weapon of the "Revolution" in the *transition* manifesto.[10] *Tambour,* then, tacitly challenged the "Revolution of the Word" by bringing film—both experimental and mass-market film—into an implicit conversation with the modernist literary texts in which the journal had invested much of its cultural capital, just at the time when silent film was fading away and words and image could be blended even more accessibly in the "talkies."[11]

But even as it affirmed the significance of film (even mass-market film), *Tambour* also mounted a more explicit challenge to the "Revolution of the Word" vision of literary modernism, a challenge that made *Work in Progress* a central issue. Although they both signed the *transition* manifesto, Salemson

10. The relationship of film to *Finnegans Wake* and *Ulysses* has been oft remarked, and several articles have appeared in the last few decades discussing the November 1929 meeting in Paris of Sergei Eisenstein and James Joyce, along with their interest in the formal innovations of and relationships between their verbal and visual media. See R. Barton Palmer (1985), Gosta Werner (1990), and William V. Costanzo (1984).

11. In a move presaging Aldous Huxley's "feelies" in *Brave New World* (1932), Stuart Gilbert in a *Tambour* article even predicted that "just as the 'movies' have been ousted by the more lifelike 'talkies,' very soon, I suppose, we shall go still one better and crowd to eye, ear and nose the '*smellies*' " ("Marching On" n.d., 46).

and Stuart Gilbert were uncomfortable with aspects of it. Gilbert wrote privately in his diary for May 9, 1929, "And Eugene [Jolas] the word-killer wishes me to sign a manifesto, praising the New Word! Why don't they learn the old ones first?" (Gilbert 1990, 13). Salemson made his critique explicit in his manifesto "Essential: 1930," arguing that modernism is a sort of belated romanticism continuing the "projection of the artist's personality into the world about him," but only differing from romanticism in its variation of forms. He rebels against the tenor of the "Revolution of the Word," arguing that "Modernism, a research of form, is exhausted" (1930a, 5), that the new path "must ignore form, since all forms and antiforms are at its disposal. They are waiting to be used" (6), and that, taking the place of a reification and deification of form, "the first place belongs to ideas" (6). This re-emphasis was meant to tie the artist back to the world: "As for the modern projection of the personality of the artist into the outside world, we replace it by the world without the artist, the world as it is in 1930, a world the artist must recreate (which does not suppose any obligatory realism) according to the contemporary way of seeing things" (Salemson 1930a, 7).

Of course there is a vagueness so common to manifestos that makes it unclear exactly how Salemson wanted to change modernism since he was still largely committed to publishing it in his magazine, but, again, Joyce took center stage in this discussion, and his appearances in *Tambour* give us insight into Joyce's Parisian reception. First of all, Joyce and Joyceiana were commonly discussed in *Tambour*. The Morel, Larbaud, Gilbert French translation of *Ulysses* was noted, as well as appearances of it in *Nouvelle Revue Française*, and Salemson often praised Joyce as a sort of measure of new fiction: "The extracts from James Joyce's new work are lucid fragments which bring out the great virtuosity of the Irish master. They seem unequal but are beyond the judgment or criticism of the ordinary mortal" ("From Magazines" n.d., 57). *Tambour* repeatedly affirmed Joyce's mastery of his medium.

But *Tambour* also contradicted the "plain reader be damned" attitude of *transition* by asserting the need to explain and interpret Joyce's work to make it more accessible. The magazine emphasized and advertised the first major push (since Larbaud's 1921 lecture on *Ulysses*) to explicate and interpret Joyce's later fiction. Stuart Gilbert's book, *James Joyce's "Ulysses,"* was, of course, discussed, as was the first major collection of essays on *Work in*

*Progress.* As Salemson noted, "Two volumes appear in Paris to help the reader of James Joyce's new work. One contains three fragments of *Work in Progress, Tales Told of Shem and Shaun* (Black Sun Press) and a preface by C. K. Ogden; the other is a collection of commentaries on Joyce's new novel, entitled *Our Exagmination Round his Factification for Incamination of 'Work in Progress'*" ("James Joyce" n.d., 75). Salemson and Stuart Gilbert certainly felt that elucidation and accessibility to Joyce's work was preferable to mere hyperbolic enthusiasm, and another regular *Tambour* contributor, Edouard Roditi, had even been hand picked by Joyce to contribute to *Our Exagmination,* but declined due to illness (Roditi 1990, 171). In his August 15, 1929 *"Lettres Anglo-Américaines"* column in the *Mercure de France,* Salemson had also discussed *Our Exagmination,* tempering what he saw as hyperbolic claims about *Work in Progress,* but largely praising *Our Exagmination's* value in helping readers through the "disconcerting" new work: "Tous louent la nouvelle œuvre de Joyce et nous regrettons de ne pouvoir repredendre leurs arguments en détail. Quoi qu'il en soit, *Work in Progress* est un document déconcertant qui, bien qu'il ne se compare pas, comme on nous l'affirme, à Rabelais, Dante et Shakespeare, mérite de l'étude. Pour le connaître, le petit volume d'essais que voici est un précieux manuel" (1929a, 234).

Although Roditi clearly saw *Finnegans Wake* as "Joyce's masterpiece" (Roditi 1990, 171), Salemson continued to affirm Joyce's talents but was troubled about the nature of the work. In his *Tambour* review, Salemson went on, "That the new undertaking Mr. Joyce has attempted is interesting, there is no doubt. Of its ultimate value, much is to be said. It is one of those things that people will never cease discussing unless, by some improbability, it should be forgotten. *Tales Told,* in most parts utterly incomprehensible, is beautifully presented. The volume of comment is provocatory" ("James Joyce" n.d., 75). The distinction that Salemson explored was between the aesthetic power of words and their ability to communicate. In his *Mercure* review of Black Sun's *Tales Told of Shem and Shaun,* he argues that Joyce "est aujourd'hui le phénomène le plus formidable qui soit dans la langue anglaise, cette langue dont il désespère justement au point d'avoir entrepris de la régénérer totalement. Rien ne sert (ou presque) de connaître l'anglais pour lire ces trois contes, d'ailleurs en grande partie incompréhensibles. Joyce a refondu toutes les langues vivantes et mortes pour en former une qu'il considère plus expressive," and he went on to recommend the *Modern Quarterly* debate over Joyce to interested readers ("Lettres Anglo-Américaines" 1929b, 746–47). Salemson was beginning to question whether literature could be both of enduring importance and incomprehensible at the same time, and he emphasized works like Gilbert's and *Our Exagmination* that helped foster understanding of formally challenging work.

Moreover, affirming his growing sense that modernist literature—though of great importance in revitalizing the language—had somehow become excessive, in the fourth issue of *Tambour* Salemson wrote that,

> All the American magazines of interest are devoted in part, these days, to those that Max Eastman calls the unintelligibles. *transition* publishes a *Manifesto* that may bring more unintelligibility but that has many good points and proclaims entire freedom for the artist. *Blues,* a magazine of the younger generation, would be the most important magazine appearing in English, if it did not devote itself *entirely* to these same unintelligibles between whom and us the breach is widening. *Blues* may wake up to find the gap too great, and they on the wrong side. ("The Unintelligibles" n.d., 76)[12]

Eastman's polemic, "The Cult of Unintelligibility," is an important volley in the ongoing cultural wars raging in America over Joyce that Segall traces. Although he had broken from the Communist Party and eschewed the Stalinist ideological condemnation of *Ulysses* on party lines, Eastman nevertheless had long since moved away from the modernism that he had printed in *The Masses* in earlier years. He critiqued Cummings, Eliot, Stein, Sitwell, and Joyce for moving into obscurity and ceasing to communicate with their audiences. Like Salemson, he asserts Joyce's linguistic genius, but argues that "The goal toward which he seems to be travelling with all this equipment of

---

12. I would like to emphasize that Salemson was not anti-modernist, as Eastman had become by this time, but rather wished to reform modernism from within. Charles Henri Ford, the editor of *Blues,* praised *Tambour* in a letter to Gertrude Stein, sending her a copy of an issue containing two of his poems. He informed her that Salemson contributed a Paris letter to the upcoming issue of *Blues* and had a poem in *Blues*'s "Expatriate Number" (TLS, Charles Henri Ford to Gertrude Stein, 19 Oct. 1929. Charles Henri Ford Collection. Harry Ransom Humanities Research Center. Univ. of Texas, Austin).

genius is the creation of a language of his own—a language which might be superior poetically, as Esperanto is practically, to any of the known tongues. It might be immortal—as immortal as the steel shelves of the libraries in which it would rest. But how little it would communicate, and to how few" (Eastman 1935, 65–66). He concludes, "Until we establish an international bureau for the decoding of our contemporary masterpieces, I think it will be safe to assert that Joyce's most original contribution to English literature has been to lock up one of its most brilliant geniuses inside of his own vest" (1935, 66).

While no one writing for *Tambour* would have gone as far as Eastman to suggest that *Work in Progress* was essentially solipsistic, *Tambour*—and in particular Salemson, Samuel Putnam, and Richard Thoma—always seemed to have an ambivalent relationship to *Work in Progress*. Gilbert and Salemson's praise for *Ulysses* was limitless, but Salemson contributed to the *Modern Quarterly* debate on the "New Word" a piece titled "James Joyce and the New Word," in which he began claiming that "Among the contemporary experiments in literature, that of James Joyce is undoubtedly one of the most outstanding. . . . The new book, *Work in Progress,* arrests our interest in a more profound manner. Never has any author attempted so systemically to disintegrate the word, to strip it of its standardized meaning and to reform it by uniting it with other words or by having these words affect it, in one way or another" (Salemson 1929c, 294). Yet the rest of the article criticizes *Our Examination* for its own inscrutability and excess, beginning with its title. And he complains that "Joyce's new language is not meant for current use" (1929c, 297) and that "Joyce has exaggerated the permissible liberties" (298). He goes on to offer a reading of "The Ondt and the Gracehoper" section of *Work in Progress,* but argues, finally, that the new direction needed "will be the Revolution of the Idea, the new point-of-view, an entirely renovated outlook, purely ideological, which may be correlated with but will be independent of both the Revolution of the Word and the Revolution of the Act. When we have gone up that road . . . we will meet the very few who were able to surmount that very high wall in the blind alley. Whether Joyce (the Joyce of *Work in Progress*) will be among those few, time alone will tell. It hardly seems so today" (Salemson 1929c, 310).

The culmination of *Tambour*'s polemic against *transition*'s "Revolution of the Word" came in late 1930 in another manifesto signed by Salemson,

Thoma, and Putnam, called "Direction." Putnam remembers that "There were a good many who felt that the much-advertised "revolution" was getting nowhere rapidly and that it would be a salutary thing to call some kind of halt, at least long enough for a calm and sane consideration of the question of language and modernism" (Putnam 1947, 226–27). Putnam describes the beginnings of the discussion "in Montparnasse around a café table," and he recalls that "There was a general feeling that a statement or a declaration of principles of some sort was called for; but when it came to the actual drawing up and signing of a manifesto, most of those who had participated in our discussions exhibited an inclination to keep in the background; for *transition*, I found, cast a spell even over those that did not approve of it, and these latter, not wishing to be branded as mere dull-witted conservatives, were accordingly none too keen about having their names appear" (Putnam 1947, 227). Thus "Direction" was signed only by Salemson, Putnam, and Thoma, all three of whom had contributed both to *transition* and to *Tambour*, and, as Putnam explains, was "printed in black letters on a large yellow sheet . . . [and] blossomed out one morning on the walls of all the Montparnasse cafés (the usual medium of publicity), and another battle was soon in progress, the Battle of the Left Bank" (Putnam 1947, 227).

Putnam asserts that "probably almost no Americans who did not happen to be in Paris at the time ever heard of 'Direction' " (1947, 229), but Salemson's surviving correspondence shows that he sent it around to influential writers and editors in America in an effort to bring it into the American debate. James T. Farrell advised him of some places to send it, and he sent a copy to Theodore Dreiser as well (TLS, Farrell to Salemson 1931; TLS, Salemson to Dreiser 1930b). Waldo Frank, a figure from Max Eastman's corner of the American Left, nevertheless cautioned against completely dismissing formal considerations: "Your manifesto is really quite splendid. But there is much to add to it: content, yes—by all all all means. The technique or method whereby this content may be reached, mined, transfigured—this must not be neglected" (TLS, Frank to Salemson 1931). H. L. Mencken hinted at the problem with most manifestos—they rarely produced distinguished work that lived up to their proclamations: "Your manifesto, I think, is excellent. You clear off a lot of nonsense, and probably come as close to the essential facts as anyone ever gets. But where is the writing to fit it? If any such writing exists I'll be glad to print it in The American Mercury" (TLS, Mencken to Salemson 1930). And Harriet Monroe, the editor of *Poetry* in Chicago who had more or less introduced modernist poetry into American drawing rooms with Pound and Alice Corbin Henderson's help in 1912, wrote "I hope *Direction* will down the Joyce imitators and the Stein babblers, and find the kind of content the *manifesto* longs for" (ALS Monroe to Salemson 1931).

But what had "Direction" said about Joyce himself? While the manifesto clearly dismissed Stein's work in no uncertain terms—"the infantile stammerings of Miss Stein"—Monroe was correct in perceiving that the polemic was aimed not specifically at Joyce but at his imitators. The American attacks from the Soviet-directed Communist Left had largely dismissed Joyce's work as bourgeois decadence, the New Humanist-inspired "Right" attacked Joyce for "romantic" repudiation of traditional forms and values, and Eastman had attacked Joyce for his failure to clearly communicate to broad audiences; but Salemson, Thoma, and Putnam, in fact, decided to bracket Joyce off from the crowd as a unique and inimitable figure who did not spring from the same fashionable modernity of the Parisian avant-garde and took him to task for *Finnegans Wake* spawning an unhealthy preoccupation with form:

> There is much young muddlement at the present time on the subject of form, and much of this muddlement is due to the mountainous figure, continent-like in its individual proportions, of James Joyce. We concede the mountain, but point to the RIDICULOUS MOUSE that the mountain spawns (in that part of Mr. Joyce's output which is primarily occupied with the future of form). We would, also, call attention to the fact that Mr. Joyce is in no sense of the word "modern." This, in spite of Bergson and the "stream of consciousness," in spite of Herr Freud and his patented "dream." He is directly out of the later fifteenth and early sixteenth century, a contemporary of Rabelais. He merely has wed native Irish blarney to the late-medieval *fatrasie*. He is a figure enormous and out-of-time. Admiration is in order, and inevitable; but that he should have influenced a writing generation is deplorable. (Salemson, Putnam, and Thoma 1930)

Picking up Eastman's dig at Stein as insane, they continued, "Whatever has been learned, from Joyce, Stein or any other, that may be of use to the *con-*

*temporary* artist in his task should be, and will be, utilized; but we shall not succumb to the illusion that either the *fatrasie* or a psychosis is in any way 'modern' " (1930).

Rhetorically positioning modernism as a post-war phenomenon—a move that ignores the pre-World War I origins of many of the modernist experiments they take to task, but allows a kind of explanation for modernism's predicament to emerge—the authors boldly proclaimed that "The War has set literature back one hundred years." They argued, in a way that should not seem entirely inconsistent with Eliot's, Pound's, and even Joyce's interest in a classical literary heritage, that many features of modernism were unknowingly imitative (a problem for writers who fetishized "the new" and "revolutions"): modernist "hardboiledness" had been around since Baudelaire, Byron was a forgotten precursor, the first modernist manifesto was Hugo's preface to *Cromwell* ("most of the others have been mere repetitions or painfully obvious and infantile expansions"), and even the desire to shock the bourgeoisie was a worn-out gesture ("Only a bourgeois would ever want to shock a bourgeois," they sniped). Moreover, "As for a much-ballyhooed 'Revolution of the Word,' it is all to be found in the *Ars Poetica* of Horace, the *De Oratore* of Cicero, the *Poetics* of Aristotle, the gruntings of the first caveman, and any highschool rhetoric, while our young friend gets it via Lautrémont, Rimbaud, Huysmans, Mallarmé, *et Cie*" (Salemson, Putnam, and Thoma 1930). Moving back even beyond the romantic heritage invoked in Byron (and its early modernist continuation in Baudelaire), Salemson, Thoma, and Putnam invoked a classical heritage, not to argue that nothing new can be done—the manifesto goes on to cry "IS THERE NOTHING NEW UNDER THE SUN?"—but rather to argue that what had come to seem empty and imitative formal preoccupations would not approach modernity in a way that would produce a new literature: "WE SEEK THE NEW. We seek a *new* that shall be not simply the *old in disguise*. In other words, we go forward rather than backward. We demand a true and vital contemporaneity of thought, feeling and expression. We are aware, however, that such a contemporaneity is not to be achieved by overstriving or by posturing, but only by a sincere, prolonged and patient search" (1930).

As with "Essential: 1930," this kind of manifesto rhetoric, of course, always begs the question of how such a new literature can be accomplished, of what precisely the signatories envisioned. "Direction" primarily aims its polemic at what we would now call intellectual fads—the kind of half-baked "knowledge" that is derived from a truly significant source but is little understood in its facile repetition: "We are fed up with 'Bergsonians' who cannot frame a syllogism, with 'Freudians' who do not know the technique of the simple laboratory experiment, with 'Einsteinians' who cannot solve a quadratic equation, with 'word-revolutionists' who have never *mastered* the word. Amen" (Salemson, Putnam, and Thoma 1930). Itself echoing (without acknowledging it) calls for attention to craft and the professional mastery of the medium in earlier modernist documents, such as Ford Madox Ford's preface to the 1914 *Collected Poems,* his 1908 and 1909 *English Review* editorials, and Pound's 1913 imagist manifestos in *Poetry* that had also turned to scientific metaphors to legitimate the profession of writing, the manifesto affirmed a kind of professionalization of knowledge. Bergson is a philosopher, but his disciples are incapable of logical exercise; Freud is a founder of a new school of psychology, not because he gushes about dreams, but because he is a trained medical researcher; Einstein changes the way we think about space and time not because he fetishizes the "new" but because he is a brilliant mathematician. The manifesto implicitly continues the sequence of professional responsibility to include literary writers, finding Joyce's *Work in Progress* and Stein's poetry lacking something crucial by having, the manifesto argues, focused entirely upon form and the aesthetic qualities of language itself. So who are the exemplary professional equivalents in literature to be understood and not simply imitated? The manifesto proclaims,

We take our stand with Cocteau and Valéry (different as they are) in France. . . . We believe that the object of art, if we may lift certain words of M. Valéry, is to "rendre la proie éternellement présente dans son attitude éternellement fuyante." We likewise take our stand (which does not necessarily commit us, man for man, to a theory of neo-Thomism) beside Thomas Aquinas and the thirteenth century, in behalf of a dominating, incisive and concise *intelligence.* We believe that "when reason goes to sleep, monsters are begot." Yet we would not, preposterously, restrain art to pure reason. We do not believe, needless to state, in "automatic writing,"—at least, not so long as we are sober. The brain has its inalienable rights and the brain should dominate even the subconscious. . . . We call, in other words, for a RETURN TO ORDER, the object of art as of existence being, in so far as we are able to determine either, *the creation of order* out *of chaos*. (Salemson, Putnam, and Thoma 1930)

One can imagine Joyce himself applauding much of this statement, including the choice of Valéry as an example of mastery and intellect in poetry (see Rabaté 1997, 95–96). Cocteau in film and Valéry in literature represent the kind of attention to craft, to conscious construction of phrase and image, that Joyce admired, and "Direction," of course, gets in its dig at surrealist automatic writing as an abdication of aesthetic responsibility. It would, of course, be possible to read this manifesto as an attack on modernism, like that by Irving Babbitt or Paul Elmer More, or even that of Max Eastman, and certainly such phrases as "Innovation in form is justified only in so far as it is demanded by content" were aimed at the "Revolution of the Word." But certainly the Anglo-American strain of modernism embodied in Pound and Eliot would have had some sympathy for the sentiments expressed in "Direction," and such statements as "We condemn aberration for the sake of aberration—pure 'experimentation.' . . . *Had Pasteur carried his experiments further, he might have poisoned, instead of purifying, his milk, M. Tristan Tzara, please copy*" suggest that we should read this moment in the Parisian reception of Joyce not as an anti-modernist move as was so often the case in America, but as essentially a reining in of the more experimental formal impulses of the avant-garde. In fact, Salemson, Thoma, and Putnam had, in allying their manifesto with Valéry and Cocteau over Tzara and Breton, affirmed the critical project of such established Parisian revues as the *Mercure de France, La Nouvelle Revue Française,* and even the conservative *Revue des Deux Mondes,* which had also accepted Joyce's writing with increasing alacrity at the turn of the decade. All of these revues, including *Tambour,* aimed at making modernism more accessible to broader reading audiences (much more so than the famous *transition*)—and recognized the modern "new word" in literature and in film.

*Tambour* provides an unusual window on the reception of *Finnegans Wake* and allows us to understand better its key role in this refiguring of modernism by modernists themselves. While it would be foolish to argue, after the last decade of work on modernism and Joyce's political interests, that modernism was apolitical or entirely preoccupied with form for its own sake, by the end of the liveliest phase of Parisian modernism in 1930, it seemed to the contributors to *Tambour* that modernism needed to be reconnected to the social and political landscape of 1930. *Tambour* is a testament to that hope, and its exaltation of film and desire for a less solipsistic and formalist vision of modernism than *transition* had put forward drew a wide variety of readers to the ranks of *Tambour*'s subscribers—including writers and artists like Cocteau, Cendrars, T. S. Eliot, and Sherwood Anderson; intellectuals like Julien Benda and Henri Bergson; and filmmakers at MGM, Fox-Film, and Garrison Films; but also two such seemingly antithetical figures as Max Eastman—and James Joyce.

# 13

## Eternest cittas, heil!
### A Genetic Approach

JEAN-MICHEL RABATÉ

Amtsadam, sir, to you! Eternest cittas, heil! Here we are again! I am bubub brought up under a camel act of dynasties long out of print, the first of Shitric Shikanbeard (or is it Owllaugh MacAuscullpth the Thord?), but, in pontofact massimust, I am known throughout the world wherever my good Allenglisches Angleslachsen is spoken" (*FW* 532.6–11). Here is my point of departure, a point that is also a point of return in the cycles of repetition that endow the *Wake* with its peculiar rhythm of "again and again." The "Haveth Childers Everywhere" episode in book III, chapter three, has often been studied by Joyceans precisely because in this case the composition method appears clear[1] while the author's intentions have been diversely appreciated. In the few lines quoted, we already recognize typical references, from Amsterdam, overloaded with Adam's "office" (Amt) and Lenehan's palindrome ("Madam, I'm Adam") to Dublin and the battle of Clontarf, with Sitric Silkenbeard, chief of the Danes, and Ansculph Mac Torcall, the Irish king at the time of the Anglo-Irish wars in the twelfth century. But since the foundation of Dublin sends us back to Genesis, less to Adam than to Cain—killer, sinner, and builder—we may wonder at the presence of the Nazi salute:

1. See the important appendix in Danis Rose and John O'Hanlon, *Understanding "Finnegans Wake"* (1982), 331–40.

Heil! Joyce added this German phrase in 1929, anticipating with curious prescience on a political context that extends beyond Irish limits. Whether it is identified with Rome or New Amsterdam, the "eternal city" can embody all cities only if it carries its onus of guilt, betrayal, and totalitarianism. The question I wish to address is whether Joyce intends to denounce the fascism seen to be lurking behind any foundational act or whether he glibly condones it in the name of a mythical creativity. My hope is that a closer look at the history of the episode will shed some light on this complex issue; a genesis of urban *Genesis* should thus not only be possible but entirely necessary.

As David Hayman has shown, this episode provides a good example of Joyce's "revise and complete" method (Hayman 1990). Each time he revised, Joyce would rewrite the whole draft and add marginal insertions. The division of the episode into two parts as in the final version appears thus only as a secondary product of the incredibly rapid accretion of levels. The proliferating and disseminating theme of cities functions here as an equivalent of the way "rivers" made the A.L.P. episode a watery passage. In the context of "Haveth Childers Everywhere," we have the useful insights into Joyce's creative process provided by Stuart Gilbert's *Paris Journal*. Gilbert notes on January 31, 1931, that Joyce is again at work on the *Wake*, making extensive use of the *Encyclopedia Britannica:*

> At last J.J. has recommenced work on *Work in Progress*. The *de luxe edition* by? soon to come out—about the old lady A.L.P. I think. Another about the city (H.C.E. building Dublin). Five volumes of the *Encyclopedia Britannica* on his sofa. He has made a list of 30 towns, New York, Vienna, Budapest, and Mrs. [Helen] Fleischmann has read out the articles on some of these. I "finish" Vienna and read Christiania and Bucharest. Whenever I come to a name (of a street, suburb, park, etc.) I pause. Joyce thinks. If he can Anglicize the word, i.e. make a pun on it, Mrs. F. records the name or its deformation in the notebook. Thus "Slotspark" (I think) at Christiana becomes Sluts' park. He collects all queer names in this way and will soon have a notebook full of them. (Gilbert, *Reflections on James Joyce* 1993, 20–21)

This scene will be familiar to any student of Joyce's notebooks, who will immediately recognize Joyce's city notes culled in notebooks VI.B.24 and

VI.B.29. Gilbert's particular example poses a problem, though, since the word "Slotspark" is indeed to be found in the notebooks (VI.B.24–227) and generates "Slutsgartern" in the *Wake* ("in Kissilov's Slutsgartern or Gigglotte's Hill when I would touch her dot" [*FW* 532.22–23]), which adds to "slut" its sly "garters." And "in Slutsgartern" was inserted to MS 4748b–356, a typescript for *transition* number 15 in a passage dated July-August 1929 by the editors of the James Joyce Archive. The riddle will no doubt have to be solved by a change in the Archive chronology. Let us briefly survey the text's history, going back to its inception. In 1925 Joyce drafted and rewrote the first version of the Yawn inquest with which book III, chapter three, begins. This version, more or less what we find in David Hayman's *First Draft Version,* does not engage with the theme of cities, and the only city evoked is Dublin. The section beginning with a dash followed by: "Sir, to You! Here we are again. I am bubub brought up" (MS 47484a–114) remains without major changes in the first proofs of *transition* 15, dated April 18, 1928. Then we can see how the typescript for the same proofs (dated December 1928 to January 1929) shows the handwritten insertion of city names (47484a–234). Here "Amsterdam" is the first, followed by "Mannequins Passe" (Brussels), and "Lambeyth and Dolekey" (London coupled with a Dublin suburb) on the following page. The second proofs for the same issue of *transition* add more cities to the list, including in January 1929 "Eternest Cittas, heil!" (47484b–351).

In August 1929, or perhaps later, at least if we follow the chronology provided by Gilbert's *Paris Journal,* the draft is typewritten, which allows Joyce and other amanuenses (Paul Léon, Padraic Colum, Stuart Gilbert, and Helen Joyce) the opportunity to add various interlinear words. Among them one can distinguish "in Kissilov's Slutsgarten" written in Joyce's own hand, immediately changed into "Slutsgartern" by the addition of an extra "r" (47484b–356). The passage is then typed again as such some time early in 1930 when Joyce prepares the typescript for *Haveth Childers Everywhere* that was to be published in June 1930. There, one can read together the beginning "Amtsadam, Sir, to you! Eternest cittas, heil!" (in which periods have been replaced by handwritten exclamation marks) and on the same page the reference to "Kissilov's Slutsgartern or Giglotte's Hill" (47484b–426). This is of course H.C.E.'s defensive speech, by which he awkwardly tries to exculpate himself of various sins (here, just "malfeasance trespass against parson with the person of a youthful gigirl") while accusing himself all the more damningly in his stammering half-confession. Other cities than Dublin seem merely to provide a backdrop of universal gossip, facing which Earwicker's reputation seems to have suffered: "<baad>bahad, nieceless to say, to my reputation on Babbyl <m>Malket for daughter-in-trade being lightly clad" (47484b–426).

What is then the significance of the systematic addition of echoes taken from at least forty (if not more—I have counted in fact forty-two) cities of the world chosen from entries in the *Encyclopedia Britannica*? Let us return to Joyce's composition as described by Stuart Gilbert. In this case, his associative and collective method implies enlisting the help of many other people and induces a mechanical linguistic process. Three persons at least are needed in order to constitute this Atlas of puns, this Baedeker of spoonerisms. Gilbert remains highly critical of a method he finds both too simple and too complicated:

> The system seems bad for (1) there is little hope of the reader knowing all these names—most seem new even to Joyce himself, and certainly are to me. And supposing the reader, knowing the fragment dealt with *towns,* took the trouble to look up the Encyclopedia, would he hit on the 30 Joyce has selected. (2) The insertion of these puns is bound to lead the reader away from the basic text, to create divagations and the work is hard enough anyhow! The good method would be to write out a page of plain English and then rejuvenate dull words by injection of new (and appropriate) meanings. What he is doing is too easy to do and too hard to understand. (Gilbert 1993, 21)

There is indeed something maddeningly simplistic in this writing method (Joyce always insisted that his ideas were simple and basic). The notebooks bear evidence of endless word lists, cryptic allusions, half-elaborated portmanteau words—seemingly the weird pastimes of a demented lexicographer who would have, on top of that, thrown overboard all philological probity! However, there is something perverse in imagining that Joyce requires that his readers should be looking around for encyclopedias and travel guides while they grapple in vain after thousands of local names only to find the key to a few dubious puns.

This methodological flippancy triggers scorn from Gilbert, who describes Joyce "curled on his sofa, while I struggle with Danish or Rumanian names, pondering puns. With foreign words it's too easy. The provincial Dubliner. Foreign equals funny" (Gilbert 1993, 21). The severity evinced by such a close and often nasty "anticollaborator" relies on a belief in a different textuality. Why not write in "plain English" first and then only add polyglot and intertextual allusions?: "The good method would be to write out a page of plain English and then rejuvenate dull words by injection of new (and appropriate) meaning. . . . I think I shall try my hand at the simple method myself" (21). This explains why Gilbert never became a novelist, in spite of real literary gifts (evinced, for instance, in his translation of Dujardin's novel, *Les Lauriers sont coupés*). Gilbert's position corresponds to that of the reductive reader who imagines that a "First-draft version" of *Finnegans Wake* written in almost "normal" English, providing a paraphraseable "basic text," would produce a continuous narrative that could be summarized as a "plot" or "skeleton-key." Or it suggests conversely the kind of reductive source hunting Danis Rose and others have offered as a model. These reductive models seem to be the contrary of Joyce's method, a method which is not just perversely too easy and too difficult, because it supposes an "ideal reader." Joyce's first ideal reader was thus not Stuart Gilbert but Miss Weaver—not only was her very name a pun, but she was also Joyce's patron, who was asked to "prime the pump" by ordering specific bits of writing. Miss Weaver distinguished herself from Gilbert above all because she never tried to understand his methods without first playing along with them, without reducing them to a preconceived notion of "meaning." Finally, she was rewarded by the gift of Joyce's manuscripts; thus she not only rendered the writing of the book possible but also provided the paradigm for the "ideal genetic reader" intended by Joyce. Could it be that this ideal reader should be, first and foremost, a "Quaker reader"?

However, my focus will be less another application of the concept of "ideal reader" than a meditation on the meaning of Joyce's curiously collective compositional practice in order to build the "city words" that loom larger and larger at the end of book III, chapter three. The questions I would like to pose stem directly from Gilbert's reservations. Is Joyce's method sound or is it a little crazy? Is there a link, or rather can one establish a structural homology, between this allegedly mechanistic and collective way of writing and the "content" or theme—sketched more or less by the idea of building cities—or should we simply condemn Joyce's absorption in linguistically complicated but fundamentally simple language games? Is it true that Joyce simply "anglicizes" the words he culls from the encyclopedia in a way that betrays his provincial chauvinism?

If we take the counter-example of words that are already in English, as when Joyce (or rather an amanuensis in this case) takes notes on New York, we can see that the technique in this case is identical with the other more exotic cities. His aim is always to create puns that are less gratuitous than the Slutspark example might indicate. Some are obvious, as when he transforms "Bronx" (VI.B.24–205) into "bronxitic" (*FW* 536.13) or when "Gramercy Park" is reintroduced as "by gramercy of justness" (*FW* 534.13). Others imply the constitution of a dense network that keeps on adding layers to itself; for instance, the notes: "(Red) Fifth Avenue / (Red) Avenulceen!" (VI.B.24–206) generates "avenyue" (549.20) with a rich reinscription of the N.Y. while "(Red) Tombs (city prison)" (VI.B.24–206) is spliced with Dublin in the final version: "through toombs and deempeys" (*FW* 532.28) that link the acronym for Dublin Metropolitan Police and the famous New York prison. Joyce's tendency is thus to shake the drifting signifiers until they are caught in a new *clinamen* that creates new couplings and compounds while allowing the reader to make out elements from the original map. For instance, two discrete items that have also been crossed in red, "Mulberry Bend Park" and "Coney Island" both found in the same "New York Continued" page of VI.B.24, are chiasmically inverted so as to cross their properties: "and I did spread before my Livvy, where Lord street lolls and ladies linger and Cammomile Pass cuts Primrose Rise and Coney Bend bounds Mulbreys Island" (*FW* 553.4–6). Not only do London (with Camomile Street and Primrose Street) and New York overlap, but the very signifiers all allegorize "coupling." On the one hand, geography is not inanimate but is caught up in a spiral of love and carnal desire: we never forget that H.C.E uses the recitation of cities so as to praise his wife and sing their love. On the other hand, the puns carefully collected from the enormous repertoire provided by the dense entries in the eleventh edition of the *Encyclopedia Britannica* function as so many "passages," to take up Walter Benjamin's concept. What Benjamin attempted to

allegorize with Paris as the "capital of the nineteenth century" in his voluminous and unfinished *Passagenwerk* (1983) becomes for Joyce the dream landscape of a Dublin multiplied by all the cities in the world. Because Joyce and
Benjamin are aware that they cannot literally reproduce an encyclopedia of the
city, the question becomes how to enact it in a dynamic language.[2]

If we look at the notes collected under "Warsaw" in VI.B.24 223–24, the
picture becomes even clearer. Interestingly, one can notice that the name of
the city first occurs in VI.B.24–190 in a Dublin context, already transformed
into "Warshow." Most notes have been left uncrossed, and it is clear that
Joyce was not extremely stimulated by the reading of this entry. The notes are
in his hand, and it looks as if he was more inclined to capture the sounds than
to be accurate. Hence potential puns are produced, stressing negative elements, as with "Muckatucksy Parade" that distorts "Mokotowski parade
ground" or "Przedndmessy," from the "Przedmiescie Street" said by the *Encyclopedia* to be the finest in Warsaw. The notes begin with a few signposts, like
"Sliwicki," "Luzyenky" for "Lazienki gardens," and Sasky Ogrot" for "Saski
Ogrod" (the saxon garden), but Joyce gets tired after a short while and stops
when he is halfway through the description of the Old Town and then moves
on to Madrid on the same page (VI.B.24–224). The uncrossed entries
"Wolla" (for the suburb of Wola) and "stare miast" for "Stare Miasto" (the
old town) later blend with Prague's own "staremesto" (old town) in the
rather poetic coining of "under starrymisty" (*FW* 539.21).

The Madrid notes are in another hand, probably Helen Fleischman's, and
they quickly spill over to Vienna; after two barred entries ("Puerta del Sol"
and "Buen Retiro") one reads "Plaza," followed by "Amiens" and "Rastro"
in uppercase letters, and then "Kaiserlane" and "Kaisersstadt." The top of the
following page (VI.B.24–225) also mixes up hints to Madrid (with "Prado")
and a list of terms taken from Vienna, all in uppercase letters and crossed out:
"Ringstress" opens the list, a distortion of "Ringstrasse" that finds its way into
the final version as "ringstrsse" (*FW* 547.32); followed by an illegible entry
and then by "Schottenhof," "Freiung," "Rathouse," "Graben," and "Stock
im Eisen." They are all kept more or less intact in the final version, with

---

2. In *Benjamin, Philosophy, Aesthetics, History* (1989), edited by Gary Smith. The original
is to be found in Walter Benjamin, *Das Passagenwerk* (Frankfurt: Suhrkamp, 1983).

"Schottenhof" (*FW* 538.32), "freiung" (*FW* 538.27), "ratshause" (*FW* 535.17), "graben" (*FW* 545.34), and "my dart to throw" (*FW* 547.21) developed by "a tritan stock" (*FW* 547.24) to call up the Viennese grove marked by a stump of a tree with a piece of iron in it. "Alserfound" is after a false start (one can read "A," then "Alse," both crossed out) transformed in the notebook into "Elserground"—found in 546.11 as "elsergound." It looks as if the relative literality was due to the amanuensis, who did his or her best to copy the exact spelling of the encyclopedia entry, while Joyce himself was taking more liberties. On the whole, most of the entries are not substantially modified once they have generated a pun (or even without a pun) in the notebook. All of this tends to confirm that the description given by Gilbert is faithful: Joyce does work in a team, he does not really know the meanings or references of the names he works from, but he is interested in a decorative overlay applied in an almost mechanistic manner.

If this process shows that the notebooks belong entirely to the creative process of the *Wake,* Gilbert is mistaken when he believes that they contain all the plot and substance of the text. When he suggested, as we saw, that a better "method would be to write out a page of plain English and then rejuvenate dull words by injection of new (and appropriate) meanings" (Gilbert 1993, 21), he either forgot or did not know that Joyce had in fact another text from which he was working, in this case Yawn's dreamy "polylogue" in which, almost at the end, Yawn's disembodied voice returns as the voice of H.C.E. praising his wife and defending himself from calumny. The new "word-machine" invented by Joyce in the winter of 1930, after a period when he had lost interest in his own "work in progress," was designed to radically alter a previous text. The number of layers piled up on the "first draft version" is staggering: the building materials used to transform the interaction between H.C.E. and A.L.P. into a hymn to all the cities of the world are complex but easily distinguishable. We find, first of all, a rich layer focusing on Dublin, documenting its history and present situation, with notes taken from books such as A. Peter's *Dublin Fragments: Social and Historic,* Dillon Cosgrave's *North Dublin—City and Environs,* D. A. Chart's *The Story of Dublin,* and a few others. Then we reach the forty or so cities taken from the *Encyclopedia Britannica:* Amsterdam, Athens, Belfast, Belgrade, Berlin, Bern, Brussels, Bucharest, Budapest, Buenos Aires, Cairo, Christiana, Constantinople,

Copenhagen, Delhi, Edinburgh, Kabul, Lisbon, London, Madrid, Mecca, Melbourne, Mexico City, New York, Oslo, Ottawa, Paris, Peking, Philadelphia, Prague, Rangoon, Rio de Janeiro, Saint Petersburg, Sofia, Stockholm, Teheran, Tokyo, Vienna, Warsaw, Washington, Wellington. (I have added Philadelphia at least for one entry, "Liberty Bell" on VI.B.29–41.)

Another layer is provided by a series of direct quotations carefully copied in the notebooks: the infamous charter by which Henry II granted Dublin to the inhabitants of Bristol; Holinshed's often-quoted description of the beauties of Dublin in his *Chronicles;* long passages taken more or less literally from Rowntree's book on poverty, well studied by James Atherton in *The Books at the Wake* (1960); all of Ibsen's plays and characters, quoted with a curious equanimity; the list of all the Lord-Mayors of Dublin, all bringing something to H.C.E.; the eight main statues of Dublin that one encounters going down from Parnell Square to College Green; the list of the fourteen main architects of Dublin—Cassels, Redmond, Gandon, Deane, Shepperd, Smyth, Neville, Heaton, Stoney, Foley, Farrell, Van Nost, Thorneycrofdt, and Hogan—all neatly copied in longhand and added to MS 47484b–455 (except for poor John Van Nost, whose name was first distorted as "Zmot" and then became just Vnost—as he still survives in the final text on 552.12). One is tempted to shout in despair "Enouch!," as the text has it on 535.22, in a wry allusion to the city built by Cain after his murder and flight "East of Eden."

The main issue is therefore the fact, lamented by Gilbert, that the reader will never know all the names and if she or he looks up the *Encyclopedia Britannica* would never recognize those selected by Joyce. Or, in another key, this leads to the contention put forward by Danis Rose in his 1978 *Index Manuscript* and then taken up with John O'Hanlon in their *Understanding "Finnegans Wake"* (1982) that all the words in the *Wake* are easily derivable from some written source mediated by the notebooks. Only when all the sources are provided can the text's meaning be revealed. It seems to me that a category mistake is performed here, or that we are laboring under the illusion that genesis is explication. I would call this the genetic fallacy, and I believe that "Haveth Childers Everywhere" is a good passage to work from in order to try to dispel this fallacy. Because in this case we have retrieved almost all the sources from which the text is constructed, can we say that the meaning of the text is clear? Does Joyce want to depict Dublin as a universal and eternal city?

Probably. But where does he stand facing the disturbing insertion of "heil!" in 532.6? After all, he did not delete the term, introduced at a time when it may have sounded innocuous, but that in 1939 would have quite a different ring. Is he poking fun at H.C.E.'s sexual hubris ("Since I perpetually kept my ouija ouija wicket up" [FW 532.17–18]) and its link with the imperialism of the English language ("in pontofact massimust, I am known throughout the world wherever my good Allenglisches Angleslachsen is spoken" [FW 532.9–11]) or is he condoning it in the name of some mythical reunification of all and sundry?

In other words, is this picture of a Dublin containing all the other cities in the world a political one? Or are we to allow Joyce to perform the "eternizing" metaphor of essentialist or Jungian mythmaking? One of the keys to these questions seems to lie in the composition, indeed, but at the level of the interaction between the "first draft" and its overlays. Or, to narrow the focus, the issue is what took place between January 1929, when Joyce was revising the proofs for *transition* 15 (published in February 1929), and May 1930, when Joyce had finished revising the sixty-four pages of *Haveth Childers Everywhere*. The final version of "Haveth Childers Everywhere" found in *Finnegans Wake* (FW 532.6–554.10) does not significantly differ from the book publication of 1930. The flurry of activity recorded by Gilbert in the early months of 1930 can be explained by the relatively short time Joyce disposed of to alter the meaning of his piece.

A reading of the typescript used for the last pages of book III, chapter three, in *transition* 15 (FW 231–38) will find all-too-familiar features; Earwicker betrays himself, as we have seen, through slips, double entendres, and stutterings while he reminisces on his marriage, the foundation of his family, and the expansion of his commercial endeavors. His love for a fluvial A.L.P. is embodied in the typical geography of Dublin:

> But I was firm with her: and I did take the hand of my delights, my jealousy, and did raft her riverworthily and did lead her overland the pace whimpering by Kevin's port and Hurdlesford and Gardener's mall to Ringsend ferry and there on wavebrink did I uplift my magicianer's puntpole and I bade those polyfizzyboisterous seas to retire with himselves from us (rookwards, thou seasea stammerer!) and I abridged with domfire Norsemanship her maiden

race, my baresark bride, and knew her fleshly when with all my bawdy did I her worhsip, min bryllupswipe. (Princeton–43)

The *transition* pages already insist on the prototype of a male dominator who remains in control of his wife ("and I did encompass her about, my vermin-celly vinegarette, with all loving kindness as far as in man's might it lay and en-franchised her to liberties of fringes" [Princeton–43]), but there is no other voice that could offer a discordant commentary or take a critical distance.

When we reach the same passage in the 1930 version, it is less the inser-tion of allusions to some cities we can recognize ("whimpering by Kevin's creek and Hurdlesford and Gardener's Mall, long Riverside Drive" [47484b–486 v] "and to ringstresse I thumbed her with iern of Erin" [47484b–487]) that creates a different atmosphere than the sheer excess of references. Earwicker's jealousy leads him to chain A.L.P. to a chastity belt ("I chained her chastemate to grippe fiuming snugglers, her chambrett I bestank so to spunish furiosos" (47484b–487v) and the very presents he offers sound so dismissive that become truly ridiculous: "and I gave until my lilienyounger turkeythighs soft goods and hardware (catalogue, passim) and ladderproof hosiery lines . . . trancepearances such as women cattle bare" (47484b–488). H.C.E.'s unbearable paternalism and vainglorious praise of his prowesses ap-pear clearly as the equivalent not only of British imperialism but also of the ex-pansion of commerce identified with capitalism.

Let me quote a passage from *Haveth Childers Everywhere* that clearly indi-cates a much more critical mode of writing:

Like as my palmer's past policy I have had my best master's lessons as the public he knows, and do you know, homesters, I honestly think if I have failed lamentably by accident benefits through shintoed, spitefired, per-plagued and cramkrieged, I am doing my dids bits and have made of my pru-dentials good. I have been told I own stolenmines or something of that sorth in the sooth of Spainien. Hohohoho! Have I said ogso how I abhor myself vastly (truth to tell) and do repent to my netherheart of <sundry>suntry clothing? The amusin part is I will say, hotelmen, that since I, over the deep drowner athacleeath to seck again Irrlanding, shamed in mind, with three plunges of my ruddertail, yet not a bottlenim, <poisted>vaneed imperial standard by weaponright and platzed mine residenze, taking bourd and burgage under starrimisty and ran and operated my brixtol selection here. (47484b–474v)

Here we are closer to an open confession of guilt, denouncing all the "absurd bargains" (*FW* 538.19) that have made Dublin what it is, not excluding Henry II's charter giving away Dublin to Bristol. This is why it is not a coincidence to see Joyce insert the text of the charter itself: the typed text ("Wherfor I will and firmly command that they do inhabit it and hold it for me and my heirs firmly and quietly, amply and honestly, and with all the liberties and free customs which the men of Tolbris have at Tolbis, and through whole my land") ends here in the addition, and one can see Joyce's hand adding the more pointed words: "fee for farm, enwreak us wrecks" (4748b–374). They echo the nursery rhyme Stephen sings to himself in "Proteus"—"Feefawfum. I zmells de bloodz olds an Iridzman" (*U* 3:293)—and suggest that the "freedom" implied by the charter spells out slavery for the natives of the island. Read in the final version (*FW* 454.14–23) the effect is devastating.

The words come as the climax of a long paragraph stretching over six pages and beginning with a recapitulation of the changes wrought on the city by history. The paragraph is announced by the voice of a guide inviting visitors to discover *"Drumcollogher-la-Belle"* and then takes stock of legal, financial, and political changes: "Things are not as they are. Let me briefly survey. . . . The end of aldest mosest ist the beginning of all thisorder so that the mast of their <benbailiffs>hansbailis shall the first in our sheriffsby" (4748b–476). The Dublin motto ("Obeyance from the townsmen spills felixity by the toun" (4748b–477–476v and 540.25–26) is followed by a series of platitudes that debunk their own optimism: "Our bourse and politico-ecomedy are in safe with good Jock Shepherd, our lives are on sure in sorting with Jonathans wild and great. Been so free! Thanks you besters! Hattentats have mindered" (4748b–476v and 540.26–28). The mention of the two famous English criminals both hanged for their crimes could leave one skeptical about the future of the Dublin *"Bourse"* (both Stock exchange and purse). But this does not seem to embarrass the speaker, because these are precisely the methods he extols:

"By fineounce and imposts I got and grew and by grossscruple gat I grown ontreachesly: murage and lestage were my mains for Ouerlord's tithing and my drains for render and prender the doles and the tribute" (4748b–477–477v and 541.7–10). This paean to financial exploitation is not of course limited to Dublin ("Bulafest onvied me, Corkcuttas graatched" [4748b–477v and 541.16–17]) but applies to all the new imperialist empires, including the United States: "In the humanity of my heart I sent out heywey-women to refresh the ballwearied and then, doubling megalopolitan poleet-ness, my great great greatest of these charities, devaleurised the base fellows for the curtailment of their lower man: with a slog to square leg I sent my boundary to Botany Bay and I ran up a score and four of mes while the Yanks were huckling the Empire" (4748b–480 and 542.35–543.6). Once more, the Dublin Metropolitan Police is taken to task and metamorphosed into a megalopolitan expansion that keeps "doubling" all the time while severely punishing the inferiors. The law and economy go hand in hand in this exploitative process, since one hears the name of De Valera in "devaleurised" meaning that base money has been devalued, which calls up Swift's campaign against the devaluation of the pence in Ireland. The cricket terms calling up some foul play and the allusions to Huck Finn suggest that the business of empire building is indeed dirty while the assertion that there are twenty-four cities named Dublin in the United States merely sets off the fact that the speaker seems satisfied with a world limited to the quadrangle in Trinity College (Botany Bay).[3]

Then a mention of all those who should be grateful to the display of these good deeds ("in homage all and felony" [*FW* 543.21]) ushers in the long insertion of the jumbled notes taken from B. S. Rowntree's *Poverty: A Study of Town Life*. These notes, culled from the book in notebook VI.B.29, 139–53 and 164–65, are not all in Joyce's hand and some have been dictated, probably by Joyce himself. The litany of "respectable" (three times, 139), "fairly respectable" (twice, 140) and then "as respectable as respectable can be" (143) is relatively restrained in the notebook entries, while the term "respectable" and its cognates is repeated twenty-one times as early as the long typed insertion in 47484b–459–60 more or less identical with the final text (*FW*

---

3. See MacHugh's *Annotations to "Finnegans Wake"* (1991), 543. McHugh refers to Dillon Cosgrave's book *North Dublin—City and Environs* (1909) for this piece of information.

543.22–545.14). The litany climaxes with "and respected and respectable, as respectable as respectable can respectably be" (*FW* 545.11–12), creating what Atherton calls a "sardonic refrain"[4] that undermines the bland matter-of-factness of these staccato notations on urban poverty in the North of England. It is a Swiftian Joyce who appears here to denounce not only destitution but also wooden language of state bureaucracy that sees, indeed, children as vermin: "children treacly and verminous have to be separated" (a note in Joyce's hand in VI.B.29 144–45).

This often-hilarious prose simply splices and accelerates a few pages from Rowntree. The text reaches surrealist peaks at times, as when we hear about someone who is "mentally strained from reading work on German physics" or about a "decoration from Uganda chief in locked ivory casket"—but reality is stranger than fiction, for all the details are indeed provided by Rowntree's text. Or to go back to the analogy with Walter Benjamin "Passagenwerk," it looks as if, when confronted with the stark reality of urban decay, Joyce and Benjamin prefer to "remain silent," act like *bricoleurs* who simply salvage trivia. In the theoretical section of his magnum opus, Benjamin writes, "Method of this project: literary montage. I need say nothing. Only exhibit. I won't filch anything of value or appropriate any ingenious turns of phrase. Only the trivia, the trash—which I don't want to inventory, but simply allow it to come into its own in the only way possible: by putting it to use."[5] Joyce suggests that the history of Dublin, like that of any "capital" city, confirms that its formation must indeed have been "dirty." Facing such a mixture of concrete accomplishments (as Lacan would say, civilization begins with sewers) and the underside showing the exploitation of the majority, progress appears indissociable from abjection and subjection, and the mere act of quoting suffices. Its bittersweet irony exposes how Stephen's "nightmare of history" has left traces in monuments, in its own refuse, and above all in language.

One could strongly oppose this new rhetoric of multilayered denunciation with Bloom's messianic projections in the Circe episode. The delirious

4. James Atherton, *The Books at the Wake* (1960), 76.

5. Walter Benjamin, "N. Re The Theory of Knowledge, Theory of Progress," translated by Leigh Hafrey and Richard Sieburth, in *Benjamin, Philosophy, Aesthetics, History* (1989), 47. The original is found in Benjamin, *Das Passagenwerk* (1983), 574.

socialism of Bloom is often undercut by parody, and he sees the new Bloomusalem of the future in the shape of a gigantic kidney. In "Haveth Childers Everywhere," the dominant tense is not the future but is the present perfect of a recapitulation ("Lo, I have looked upon my pumpadears in their easancies and my drummers have tattled tall tales of me in the land" [*FW* 545.26–25]) in the name of a strong "I" who is glorified or himself glorifies his accomplishments. As the evolution of the text has shown, the Dublin that originally embodied the love and eternal desire linking H.C.E. and A.L.P. then generates a more fragmented "drama parapolylogic" (*FW* 474.5) that stresses contradiction. The community of anonymous sufferers offers a poignant counterpoint to the shrill and inflated egotism of H.C.E.

Joyce nevertheless needs the single voice of one speaker (with a few inter-polations from the four [*FW* 534, 535, 540, 546, 547, 550, and 552]) as a rhythmical basis that will now and then modulate toward other inflections un-dercut its steady surge forward and upward. A relatively clear passage reflects on this cumulative function occupied by the speaker:

> Idle were it, repassing from elserground to the elder disposition, to inquire whether I, draggedasunder, be the forced generation of group mariage, holy-cryptogram, of my essenes, or carried of cloud from land of locust, in ouzel galley borne, I, huddled til summone be the massproduct of teamwork, three surtouts wripped up in itchother's, two twin pritticoaxes lived as one, trou-bled in trine or dublidin too, for abram nude be I or roberoyed with the faineans, of Freejeean grafter ape on merfish, surrounded by obscurity, by my virtus of creation and by boon of promise, by my natural born freeman's journeymanright and my otherchurch's inher light, in so and such a manner as me it so besitteth, most surely I pretend and reclam to opt for simultane-ous. Till daybowbreak and showshadows flee. (*FW* 546.11–23)

Earwicker admits here that he sums up in himself if not all of humanity at least his own family. The three soldiers and two tempting girls in the park are known are the main sigla of the Doodles family. Freedom is asserted in such a way that it can connote the Freeman's Journal, Fijian mermaids, Sin Féinn in-verted, or even "les rois fainéants" (the last merovingian kings). In this context, creativity is confirmed not by the number of children or of satellite plantations but by the simultaneity of a group structure.

Joyce's composite portrait of a man who embodies a city belongs to an unanimistic technique—one can think of Jules Romains or Dos Passos—but here it is more an "Arcimboldo city" that is depicted, one made up of all the cities in the world summed up by a few basic names. The link between quotation of the city has never been stronger, as one can still see it in French (cité— citation). Quotation implies montage—without losing the idea of a general architectonics—and the limit set by the morning and waking up from obscurity. Benjamin uses Proust to define the general outline of his *Passagenwerk* in a paragraph that might be taken as a description of *Finnegans Wake:* "Just as Proust begins his life story with the moment of awakening, so every historical presentation must begin with awakening and, in fact, should deal with nothing else. This one deals with awakening from the nineteenth century." [6]

Because we are kept waiting for this impossible moment when we wake up from the dream conjured by the book we are even now reading, the effect is a dynamic portrayal of the universal city. The city in book III, chapter three, is not the stable site that can be reconstructed or confirmed with the help of street maps and directories. It is rather an expanding linguistic site that never bypasses real history (for instance, the name Ouzel Galley calls up a Dublin ship thought to have disappeared and returned miraculously in 1700) but that "re-pairs" it by a system of grafts, duplications, and additions. Dublin is always compared and paired with other cities; cities tend to be coupled, thus New York goes with Kyoto (*FW* 534.2), Budapest with Belfast, Cork with Calcutta (*FW* 541.16), Bucharest with Berlin (*FW* 540.21), London with Buenos Aires (*FW* 540.34–35), and so on. Less than a theme, the city becomes a way of reading the world, a series of dynamic intertranslations. Naming acquires a tremendous weight, and in fact even if no reader could remember all the streets and squares culled from the *Encyclopedia Britannica* entries, it is surprising to see that many names are familiar to, say, a well-traveled tourist.

The last point I would like to make is linked with my first: the issue of lan-

6. Benjamin, "N. Re The Theory of Knowledge, Theory of Progress" (1989), 52 (modified) and Benjamin, *Das Passagenwerk* (1983), 580.

guage is crucial, and here it is clear that English provides the basic structure. It is therefore true that Joyce "anglicizes" the foreign names, but with his tongue in cheek, and also without being duped by the implicit imperialism this can conceal. We have seen how much the issue of an international language or of a bilingual Ireland preoccupied him. As Mallarmé wrote in his *Mots Anglais,*[7] English is properly speaking the "language of angels," but in Joyce's celestial and terrestrial cities, angels do laugh; "wherever my good AllEnglishes Angles *lachsen* is spoken" (*FW* 532.10–11) also suggests the German "lachen" meaning laugh, while "Eternest cittas" (*FW* 532.6) contains the opposite idea of "ernst" (ernest, serious). A "citizen" for Joyce is also someone who can laugh at (and in) his own city.

---

7. Stéphane Mallarmé wrote, "Who were the saxons? Angles: Angles, just as they called themselves." "Les Mots Anglais" in *Ouevres Complètes,* edited by Mondor (Paris: Gallimard, 1961), 905.

Works Cited

Index

# Works Cited

Abel, Richard. 1988. *French Film Theory and Criticism*. Princeton: Princeton Univ. Press.

Atherton, James. 1960. *The Books at the Wake*. New York: Viking.

Barta, Peter I. 1996. *Bely, Joyce, and Döblin: Peripatetics in the City Novel*. Gainesville: Univ. Press of Florida.

Begnal, Michael H. 1988. *Dreamscheme: Narrative and Voice in "Finnegans Wake."* Syracuse, N.Y.: Syracuse Univ. Press.

———. 1999. "Stephen, Simon, and Eileen Vance: Autoeroticism in *A Portrait*." In *Joyce Through the Ages: A Nonlinear View*, edited by Michael Patrick Gillespie, 107–16. Gainesville: Univ. Press of Florida.

Benjamin, Walter. 1989. *Benjamin, Philosophy, Aesthetics, History*. Edited by Gary Smith. Chicago: Univ. of Chicago Press.

———. 1999. *The Arcades Project*. Cambridge, Mass.: Belknap Press.

Benstock, Bernard. 1982. *The Seventh of Joyce*. Bloomington: Indiana Univ. Press.

———, ed. 1988. *James Joyce: The Augmented Ninth*. Syracuse, N.Y.: Syracuse Univ. Press.

Benstock, Shari. 1988. "City Spaces and Women's Places in Joyce's Dublin." In Bernard Benstock, *James Joyce: The Augmented Ninth*, 293–307. Syracuse, N.Y.: Syracuse Univ. Press.

———. 1989. "Apostrophizing the Feminine in *Finnegans Wake*." *Modern Fiction Studies* 35, 587–614.

Bersani, Leo. 1990. *The Culture of Redemption*. Cambridge, Mass.: Harvard Univ. Press.

Black, Martha Fodaski. 1995. *Shaw and Joyce*. Gainesville: Univ. Press of Florida.

"Body in the Bog, The." 2000. *Galway Advertiser.* Feb. 24: 2, 18.

Boone, Joseph A. 1998. *Libidinal Currents: Sexuality and the Shaping of Modernism.* Chicago: Univ. of Chicago Press.

Brown, Frederick. 1968. *An Impersonation of Angels: A Biography of Jean Cocteau.* New York: Viking.

Brown, Richard. 1990. "Shifting Sexual Centres: Joyce and Flaubert." In *Scribble 2, Joyce and Flaubert,* 28–58. Paris: Menard.

Brown, Terence. 1996. "Yeats, Joyce, and the Irish Critical Debate." In *Yeats's Political Identities,* edited by Jonathan Allison, 279–91. Ann Arbor: Univ. of Michigan Press.

Brunsdale, Mitzi. 1993. *James Joyce: A Study of the Short Fiction.* New York: Twayne.

Budgen, Frank. 1960. *James Joyce and the Making of "Ulysses."* Bloomington: Indiana Univ. Press.

Bullock, Marcus, and Michael W. Jennings, eds. 1996. *Selected Writings.* By Walter Benjamin. Cambridge, Mass.: Belknap Press.

Charpentier, John. 1930. "Figures: Jean Cocteau." *Mercure de France* (Apr. 30): 116–18.

Charters, Ann, ed. 1987. "On the Elaboration of Style and Form in Joyce's 'The Dead,' " by Frank O'Connor. In *The Story and Its Writer: An Introduction to Short Fiction,* 27–51. New York: Saint Martin's.

Cheng, Vincent. 1991. *"Finnegans Wake:* All the World's a Stage." In *James Joyce's "Finnegans Wake": A Casebook,* edited by John Harty, 69–84. New York: Garland Publishing.

———. 1995. *Joyce, Race, and Empire.* Cambridge: Cambridge Univ. Press.

Clements, Robert J., and Joseph Gibaldi. 1977. *Anatomy of the Novella.* New York: New York Univ. Press.

Colum, Mary, and Padraic Colum. 1958. *Our Friend James Joyce.* Garden City, N.J.: Doubleday.

Cope, Jackson I. 1981. *Joyce's Cities: Archaeologies of the Soul.* Baltimore, Md.: Johns Hopkins Univ. Press.

Cosgrove, Dillon. 1909. *North Dublin—City and Environs.* Dublin: Catholic Truth Society.

Costanzo, William V. 1984. "Joyce and Eisenstein: Literary Reflections of the Reel World." *Journal of Modern Literature,* 175–80.

Crisp, Colin. 1993. *The Classic French Cinema 1930–1960.* Bloomington: Indiana Univ. Press.

Daiches, David. 1939. *The Novel and the Modern World*. Chicago: Univ. of Chicago Press.

Dames, Michael. 1992. *Mythic Ireland*. New York: Thames and Hudson.

Deane, Seamus. 1990. *Nationalism, Colonialism, Literature*. Minneapolis: Univ. of Minnesota Press.

De Certeau, Michel. 1984. *The Practice of Everyday Life*. Berkeley: Univ. of California Press.

Deleuze, Gilles, and Felix Guattari. 1987. *A Thousand Plateaus*. Minneapolis: Univ. of Minnesota Press.

Deming, Robert H., ed. 1970. *James Joyce: The Critical Heritage*. 2 vols. London: Routledge.

Devlin, Kimberley. 1994. "Pretending in 'Penelope': Masquerade, Mimicry, and Molly Bloom." In *Molly Blooms: A Polylogue on "Penelope" and Cultural Studies*, edited by Richard Pearce, 80–102. Madison: Univ. of Wisconsin Press.

DiYanni, Robert, ed. 1998. *Literature: Reading Fiction, Poetry, Drama, and the Essay*. Boston: McGraw-Hill.

Duffy, Enda. 1994. *The Subaltern Ulysses*. Minneapolis: Univ. of Minnesota Press.

Eagleton, Terry. 1991. *Ideology: An Introduction*. London: Verso.

Eastman, Max. 1935. "The Cult of Unintelligibility." *The Literary Mind: Its Place in an Age of Science*. New York: Scribner.

Eliot, T. S. 1970. *Collected Poems 1909–1962*. New York: Harcourt.

Ellmann, Richard. 1982. *James Joyce*. New York: Oxford Univ. Press.

Fargnoli, A. Nicholas, and Michael Patrick Gillespie, eds. 1995. *James Joyce A to Z*. New York: Facts on File.

Farrell, James. 1931. TLS to Harold J. Salemson (Mar. 26). In possession of Steve Salemson.

Ferguson, Frances. 1977. *Wordsworth: Language as Counter-Spirit*. New Haven, Conn.: Yale Univ. Press.

Fetterley, Judith. 1997. "Introduction: On the Politics of Literature." In *Feminisms: An Anthology of Literary Theory and Criticism*, edited by Robyn Warhol and Diane Herndl, 564–73. New Brunswick, N.J.: Rutgers Univ. Press.

Fitch, Noel Riley. 1983. *Sylvia Beach and the Lost Generation*. New York: Norton.

Ford, Charles Henri. 1929. TLS to Gertrude Stein (Oct. 19). Charles Henri Ford Collection. Harry Ransom Humanities Research Center. Univ. of Texas, Austin.

Frank, Waldo. 1931. TLS to Harold J. Salemson (Mar. 5). In possession of Steve Salemson.

Freud, Sigmund. 1963. *Sexuality and the Psychology of Love*. Edited by Philip Rieff. New York: Collier Books.

Froula, Christine. 1996. *Modernism's Body: Sex, Culture, and Joyce*. New York: Columbia Univ. Press.

Garvey, Johanna. 1995. "City Limits: Reading Gender and Urban Spaces in *Ulysses*." *Twentieth Century Literature*, 108–23.

Gilbert, Stuart. 1952. *James Joyce's "Ulysses."* New York: Vintage.

———. 1990. "Selections from the Paris Diary of Stuart Gilbert." Edited by Thomas F. Staley and Randolph Lewis. *Joyce Studies Annual*, 3–25.

———. 1993. *Reflections on James Joyce*. Edited by Thomas F. Staley and Randolph Lewis. Austin: Univ. of Texas Press.

———. n.d. "Marching On." *Tambour* 5: 46.

Glasheen, Adaline. 1963. *A Second Census of "Finnegans Wake."* Evanston: Northwestern Univ. Press.

———. 1977. *A Third Census of "Finnegans Wake."* Berkeley: Univ. of California Press.

Gordon, John. 1986. *"Finnegans Wake": A Plot Summary*. Syracuse, N.Y.: Syracuse Univ. Press.

Gorman, Herbert. 1929. "Experimentalism—And Experimentalists." *Modern Quarterly* (fall): 292–93.

Hayman, David. 1990. *The Wake in Transit*. Ithaca, N.Y.: Cornell Univ. Press.

Heaney, Seamus. 1980. *Preoccupations: Selected Prose 1968–1978*. New York: Farrar.

———. 1990. *Selected Poems 1966–1987*. New York: Noonday Press.

———. 1995. "Crediting Poetry." *New Republic* (Dec. 25): 27–34.

———. 1995. *The Redress of Poetry*. New York: Farrar.

———. 1996. *The Spirit Level*. New York: Farrar.

Henke, Suzette. 1989. "Anna the 'Allmaziful': Toward the Evolution of a Feminine Discourse." In *James Joyce and his Contemporaries*, edited by Diana Ben-Merre and Maureen Murphy, 37–47. New York: Greenwood Press.

Herr, Cheryl. 1994. " 'Penelope' as Period Piece." In *Molly Blooms: A Polylogue on "Penelope" and Cultural Studies*, edited by Richard Pearce, 63–79. Madison: Univ. of Wisconsin Press.

Herring, Phillip. 1982. "Structure and Meaning in Joyce's 'The Sisters.' " In *The Seventh of Joyce*, edited by Bernard Benstock, 119–47. Bloomington: Indiana Univ. Press.

Hirsch, Edward. 1991. "The Imaginary Irish Peasant." *PMLA*, 1116–33.

Hodgart, Matthew. 1978. *James Joyce*. London: Routledge.

Hutcheon, Linda. 1989. *The Politics of Postmodernism.* New York: Routledge.

Irigaray, Luce. 1985. *This Sex Which Is Not One.* Ithaca, N.Y.: Cornell Univ. Press.

Johnston, Dillon. 1997. *Irish Poetry After Joyce.* Syracuse, N.Y.: Syracuse Univ. Press.

Joyce, James. 1993. *A Portrait of the Artist as a Young Man.* Edited by Hans Walter Gabler with Walter Hettche. New York: Garland.

Kelleher, John. 1965. "Irish History and Mythology in James Joyce's 'The Dead.' " *Review of Politics,* 414–33.

Kiberd, Declan. 1996. "The Center and the Periphery." *South Atlantic Quarterly* 95, 7.

Lacan, Jacques. 1987. *Joyce avec Lacan.* Paris: Navarin.

Lawrence, Karen. 1990. "Joyce and Feminism." In *A Cambridge Companion to James Joyce,* edited by Derek Attridge, 237–58. Cambridge: Cambridge Univ. Press.

———, ed. 1998. *Transcultural Joyce.* Cambridge: Cambridge Univ. Press.

Lee, A. Robert. 1989. *The Modern American Novella.* London: Vision.

Lefebvre, Henri. 1991. *The Production of Space.* London: Blackwell.

Lehan, Richard. 1998. 1982. "Joyce's City." In *The Seventh of Joyce,* edited by Bernard Benstock, 247–61. Bloomington: Indiana Univ. Press.

———. 1998. *The City in Literature: An Intellectual and Cultural History.* Berkeley: Univ. of California Press.

Leonard, Garry. 1993. *Reading "Dubliners" Again.* Syracuse, N.Y.: Syracuse Univ. Press.

———. 1998. *Advertising and Commodity Culture in Joyce.* Gainesville: Univ. Press of Florida.

Levin, Harry. 1960. *James Joyce: A Critical Introduction.* New York: New Directions.

Levitt, Annette S. 1979. "Joyce and Surrealism." In *Joyce & Paris 1902 . . . 1920–1940,* edited by Jacques Aubert and Maria Jolas, 38–64. Paris: Editions du C.N.R.S.

Liu, Alan. 1989. *Wordsworth: The Sense of History.* Stanford, Ca.: Stanford Univ. Press.

Lloyd, David. 1993. *Anomalous States: Irish Writing and the Post-Colonial Moment.* Durham, N.C.: Duke Univ. Press.

Lobner, Corrina. 1989. *James Joyce's Italian Connection.* Iowa City: Univ. of Iowa Press.

Loe, Thomas. 1991. " 'The Dead' as Novella." *James Joyce Quarterly* 28, 485–97.

Lyon, Janet. 1992. "Militant Discourse, Strange Bedfellows: Suffragettes and Vorticists Before the War." *Differences* 4, 100–33.

Mabbott, Thomas O., ed. 1978. *Collected Works of Edgar Allan Poe.* 3 vols. Cambridge, Mass.: Belknap Press.

MacCabe, Colin. 1979. *James Joyce and the Revolution of the Word.* New York: Harper.

Maddox, Brenda. 1988. *Nora: The Real Life of Molly Bloom.* Boston: Houghton Mifflin.

Magalaner, Marvin, and Richard Kain. 1956. *Joyce: The Man, the Work, the Reputation.* New York: New York Univ. Press.

Mahaffey, Vicki. 1998. *Reauthorizing Joyce.* Gainesville: Univ. Press of Florida.

Maley, Willy. 1996. "Specters of Joyce: Memory and Mourning in 'The Dead.' " In *Memory, History, and Critique,* edited by Frank Brinkhuis, 11–18. Cambridge: MIT Press.

Mallarmé, Stéphane. 1961. *Ouevres Completes.* Paris: Gallimard.

Manganiello, Dominic. 1980. *Joyce's Politics.* London: Routledge.

Matthews, J. H. 1971. *Surrealism and Film.* Ann Arbor: Univ. of Michigan Press.

McCole, John. 1993. *Walter Benjamin and the Antimonies of Tradition.* Ithaca, N.Y.: Cornell Univ. Press.

McGee, Patrick. 1988. *Paperspace: Style as Ideology in Joyce's "Ulysses."* Lincoln: Univ. of Nebraska Press.

McHugh, Roland. 1991. *Annotations to "Finnegans Wake."* Baltimore, Md.: Johns Hopkins Univ. Press.

Mencken, H. L. 1930. TLS to Harold J. Salemson (Dec. 23). In possession of Steve Salemson.

Monaco, Paul. 1976. *Cinema & Society: France and Germany during the Twenties.* New York: Elsevier.

Monroe, Harriet. 1931. ALS to Harold J. Salemson (Feb. 16). In possession of Steve Salemson.

Morrisson, Mark. 1996. "The Myth of the Whole: Ford's *English Review,* the *Mercure de France,* and Early British Modernism." *ELH* 63(summer): 513–33.

Muldoon, Paul. 1994. *The Annals of Chile.* New York: Farrar.

Mumford, Lewis. 1961. *The City in History: Its Origins, Its Transformations, and Its Prospects.* New York: Harcourt, Brace.

Murillo, L. A. 1968. *The Cyclical Night: Irony in James Joyce and Jorge Luis Borges.* Cambridge, Mass.: Harvard Univ. Press.

Murphy, Michael. 1997. "Parable and Politics." *Irish Studies Review* 5, 31–34.

Murphy, Sean P. 1995. "Passing Boldly into That Other World of (W)Holes: Narrativity and Subjectivity in James Joyce's 'The Dead.' " *Studies in Short Fiction* 34, 463–74.

Nemerov, Howard. 1985. "Composition and Fate in the Short Novel." In *New and Selected Essays,* 59–73. Carbondale: Southern Illinois Univ. Press.

Norris, Margot. 1992. *Joyce's Web: The Social Unraveling of Modernism.* Austin: Univ. of Texas Press.

O'Laoi, Padraig. 1982. *Nora Barnacle Joyce: A Portrait.* Galway: Kennys Bookshops.

———. 1994. Fr. Griffin: 1892–1920. *Galway: The Connacht Tribune Ltd.*

Orr, Leonard. 1991. *Yeats and Postmodernism.* Syracuse, N.Y.: Syracuse Univ. Press.

Palmer, R. Barton. 1985. "Eisensteinian Montage and Joyce's *Ulysses*: The Analogy Reconsidered." *Mosaic* 18, 73–85.

Pearce, Richard, ed. 1994. *Molly Blooms: A Polylogue on "Penelope" and Cultural Studies.* Madison: Univ. of Wisconsin Press.

———. 1994. "How Does Molly Bloom Look Through the Male Gaze?" In *Molly Blooms: A Polylogue on "Penelope" and Cultural Studies,* edited by Richard Pearce, 40–60. Madison: Univ. of Wisconsin Press.

Pecora, Vincent P. 1986. " 'The Dead' and the Generosity of the Word." *PMLA,* 233–45.

Potts, Willard, ed. 1979. *Portraits of the Artist in Exile.* Seattle: Univ. of Washington Press.

Power, Arthur. 1974. *Conversations with James Joyce.* Edited by Clive Hart. Chicago: Univ. of Chicago Press.

Putnam, Samuel. 1947. *Paris Was Our Mistress.* New York: Viking.

Rabaté, Jean-Michel. 1993. *James Joyce.* Paris: Hachette.

———. 1997. "Joyce the Parisian." In *Cambridge Companion to James Joyce,* edited by Derek Attridge, 83–102. New York: Cambridge Univ. Press.

Rabinowitz, Peter. 1987. *Before Reading.* Ithaca, N.Y.: Cornell Univ. Press.

———. 1994. " 'A Symbol of Something': Interpretive Vertigo in 'The Dead.' " In *The Dead,* edited by Daniel Schwarz, 137–49. Boston: Saint Martin's.

Restuccia, Frances L. 1985. "Molly in Furs: Deleuzean/Masochian Masochism in the Writing of James Joyce." *Novel* 6, 101–16.

Reynolds, Mary. 1981. *Joyce and Dante.* Princeton, N.J.: Princeton Univ. Press.

Roditi, Edouard. 1990. "A Paris Memoir." *James Joyce Quarterly* 27, 169–78.

Rose, Danis, and John O'Hanlon. 1982. *Understanding "Finnegans Wake."* New York: Garland.

Sadoul, Georges. 1972. *French Film.* New York: Arno Press.

Salemson, Harold J. 1929a. "Lettres Anglo-Américaines." *Mercure de France* (Aug. 15): 230–36.

———. 1929b. "Lettres Anglo-Américaines." *Mercure de France* (Nov. 1): 739–47.

———. 1929c. "James Joyce and the New Word." *Modern Quarterly* (fall): 294–312.

———. 1930a. "Essential: 1930." *Tambour* 7 (May): 1–7.

————. 1930b. TLS to Theodore Dreiser (Dec. 16). Theodore Dreiser Papers, Univ. of Pennsylvania.

————. n.d. "Cinéma-Théâtre." *Tambour* 6: 73.

————. n.d. "From Magazines." *Tambour* 2: 57.

————. n.d. "James Joyce." *Tambour* 4: 75.

————. n.d. "Professional Background," resume. In possession of Steve Salemson.

————. n.d. "The Unintelligibles." *Tambour* 4: 76.

Sandelescu, C. George. 1987. *The Language of the Devil*. Gerrards Cross: Colin Smythe.

Schwarz, Daniel, ed. 1994. *The Dead*. Boston: Saint Martin's.

Segall, Jeffrey. 1993. *Joyce in America*. Berkeley: Univ. of California Press.

Shaw, George Bernard. 1931. *The Complete Plays*. London: Constable.

————. 1987. *Back to Methuselah*. London: Penguin.

Smyth, Gerry. 2001. *Space and the Irish Cultural Imagination*. London: Palgrave.

Sontag, Susan. 1967. *Against Interpretation*. New York: Farrar.

Springer, Mary Doyle. 1975. *Forms of the Modern Novella*. Chicago: Univ. of Chicago Press.

"Strange Case of Patrick Joyce, The." 1998. *Galway Advertiser*. July 16: 2.

Theall, Donald. 1995. *Beyond the Word: Reconstructing Sense in the Joyce Era of Technology, Culture, and Communication*. Toronto: Univ. of Toronto Press.

————. 1997. *James Joyce's Techno-Poetics*. Toronto: Univ. of Toronto Press.

Ussher, Arland. 1952. *Three Great Irishmen: Shaw, Yeats, and Joyce*. London: Gollancz.

Wagner, C. Roland. 1995. "A Birth Announcement in 'The Dead.' " *Studies in Short Fiction* 34, 447–62.

Walz, Robin. 1996. "Serial Killings: Fantomas, Feuillade, and the Mass-Culture Genealogy of Surrealism." *The Velvet Trap* 37, 51–57.

Walzl, Florence. 1973. "Joyce's 'The Sisters': A Development." *James Joyce Quarterly* 10, 375–421.

Werner, Gosta. 1990. "James Joyce and Sergei Eisenstein." *James Joyce Quarterly* 27, 491–507.

Wheeler, Michael. 1990. *Death and the Future Life in Victorian Literature and Theology*. Cambridge: Cambridge Univ. Press.

Wordsworth, William. 1949. *Poetical Works*. Edited by Ernest de Selincourt and Helen Darbishire. 5 vols. Oxford: Oxford Univ. Press.

————. 1974. *Prose Works*. Edited by W. J. B. Owen and Jane W. Smyser. 3 vols. Oxford: Oxford Univ. Press.

Wright, David G. 1995. "Interactive Stories in *Dubliners*." *Studies in Short Fiction* 34, 285–93.

# Index